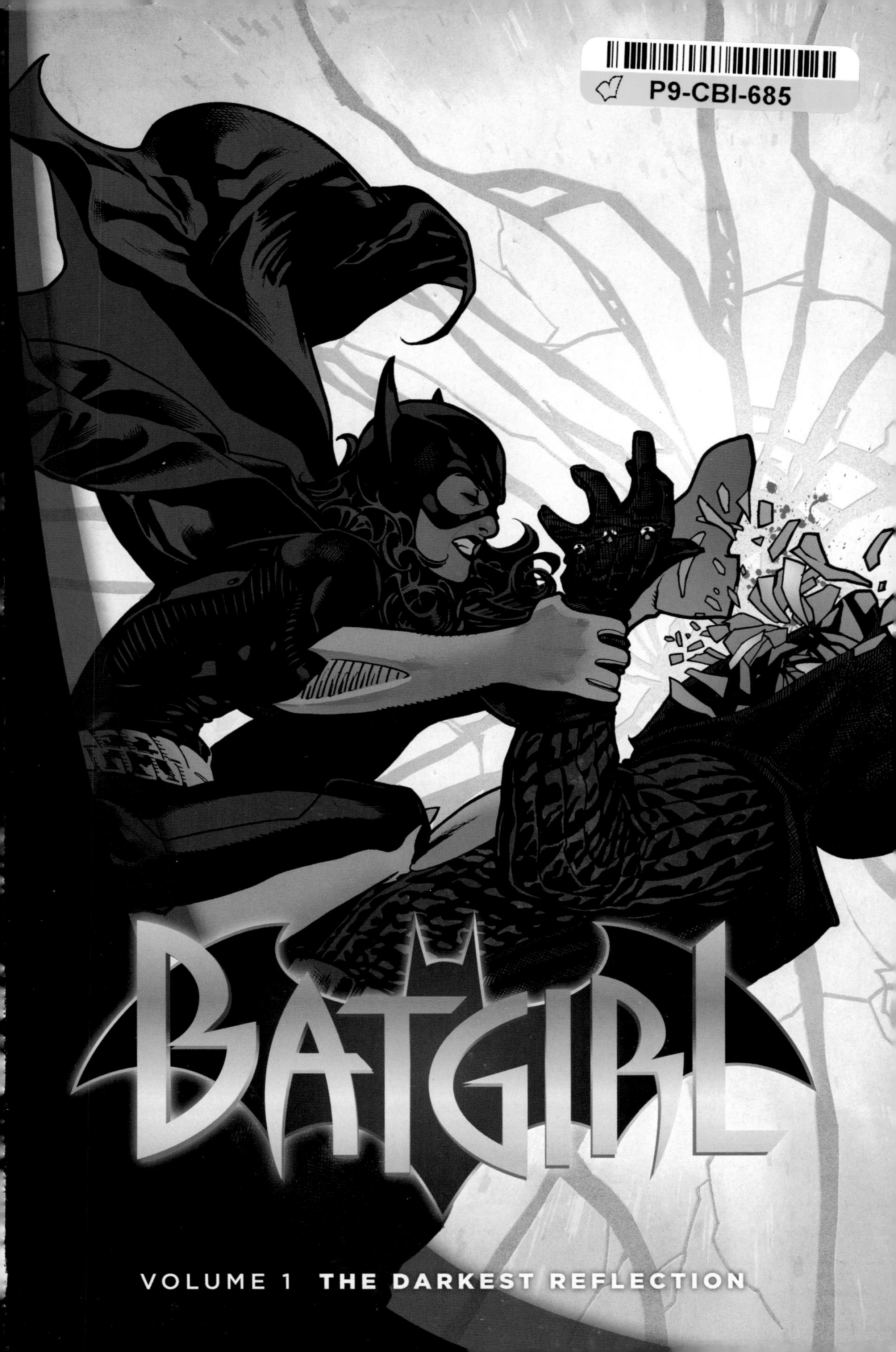
BATGIRL
VOLUME 1 THE DARKEST REFLECTION

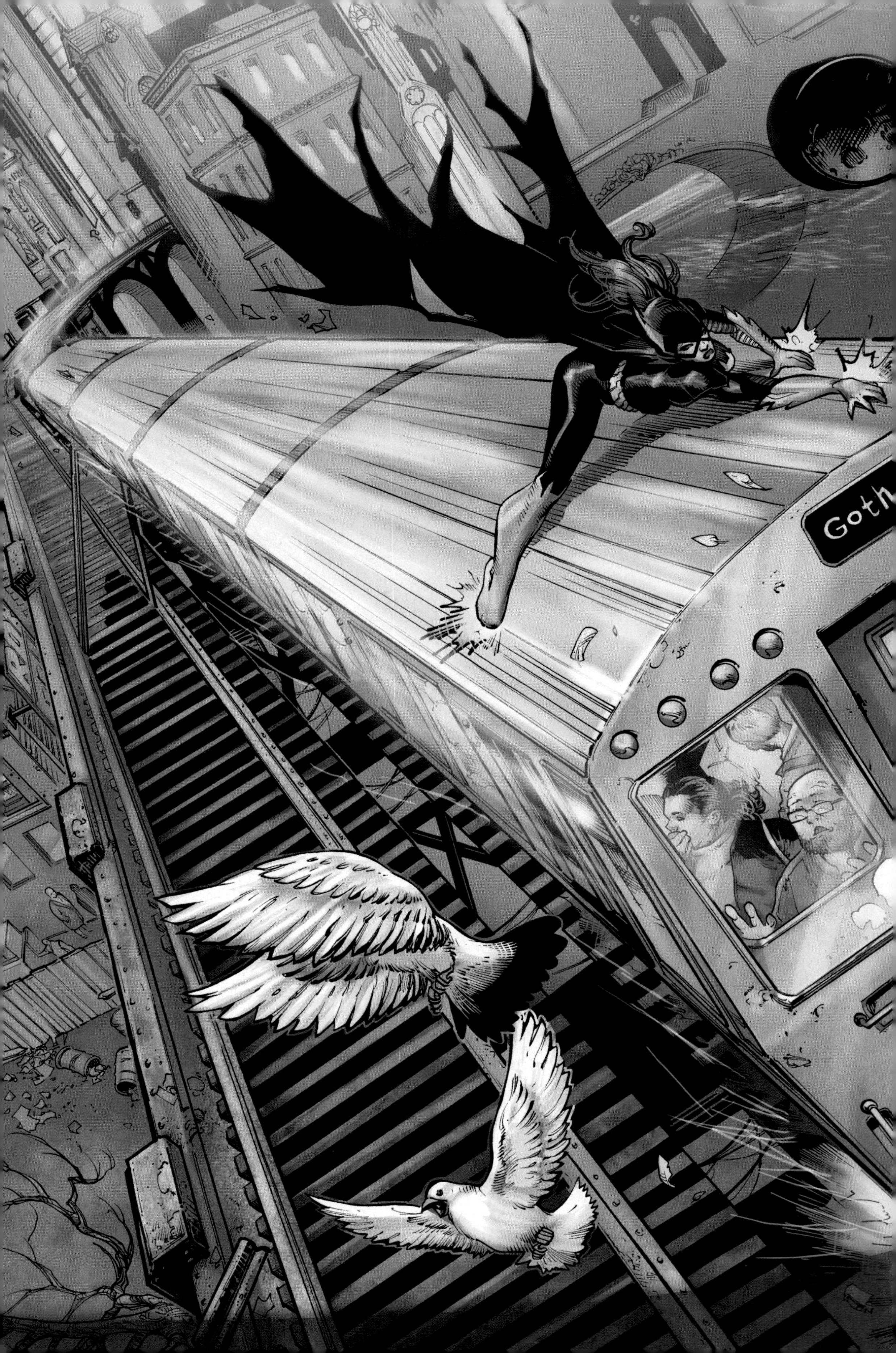
Goth

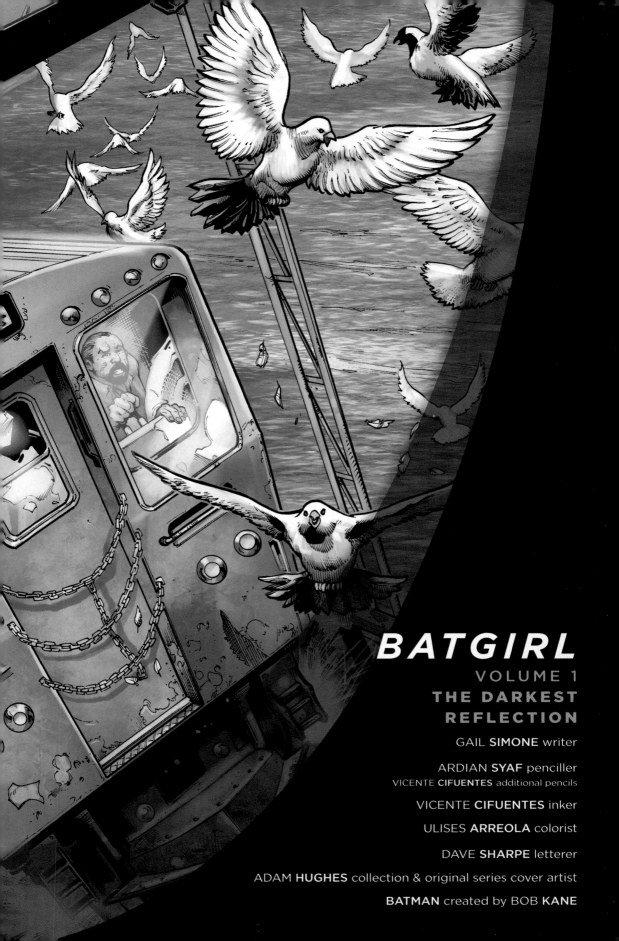

BATGIRL

VOLUME 1
THE DARKEST REFLECTION

GAIL **SIMONE** writer

ARDIAN **SYAF** penciller
VICENTE **CIFUENTES** additional pencils

VICENTE **CIFUENTES** inker

ULISES **ARREOLA** colorist

DAVE **SHARPE** letterer

ADAM **HUGHES** collection & original series cover artist

BATMAN created by BOB **KANE**

BOBBIE CHASE Editor – Original Series KATIE KUBERT Assistant Editor – Original Series PETER HAMBOUSSI Editor
ROBBIN BROSTERMAN Design Director – Books ROBBIE BIEDERMAN Publication Design

BOB HARRAS Senior VP – Editor-in-Chief, DC Comics

DIANE NELSON President DAN DIDIO and JIM LEE Co-Publishers
GEOFF JOHNS Chief Creative Officer
JOHN ROOD Executive VP – Sales, Marketing & Business Development
AMY GENKINS Senior VP – Business & Legal Affairs NAIRI GARDINER Senior VP – Finance
JEFF BOISON VP – Publishing Planning MARK CHIARELLO VP – Art Direction & Design
JOHN CUNNINGHAM VP – Marketing TERRI CUNNINGHAM VP – Editorial Administration
ALISON GILL Senior VP – Manufacturing & Operations HANK KANALZ Senior VP – Vertigo & Integrated Publishing
JAY KOGAN VP – Business & Legal Affairs, Publishing JACK MAHAN VP – Business Affairs, Talent
NICK NAPOLITANO VP – Manufacturing Administration SUE POHJA VP – Book Sales
COURTNEY SIMMONS Senior VP – Publicity BOB WAYNE Senior VP – Sales

DC Comics, 1700 Broadway, New York, NY 10019
A Warner Bros. Entertainment Company
Printed by RR Donnelley, Salem, VA. 6/14/13. Second Printing.
ISBN: 978-1-4012-3814-8

Library of Congress Cataloging-in-Publication Data

Simone, Gail.
Batgirl. Volume 1, The darkest reflection / Gail Simone, Ardian Syaf, Vicente Cifuentes.
p. cm.
"Originally published in single magazine form in BATGIRL 1-6" _ T.p. verso.
ISBN 978-1-4012-3475-1
1. Graphic novels. I. Syaf, Ardian. II. Cifuentes, Vicente. III. Title. IV. Title: Darkest reflection.
PN6728.B358S56 2012
741.5'973 — dc23
2012010303

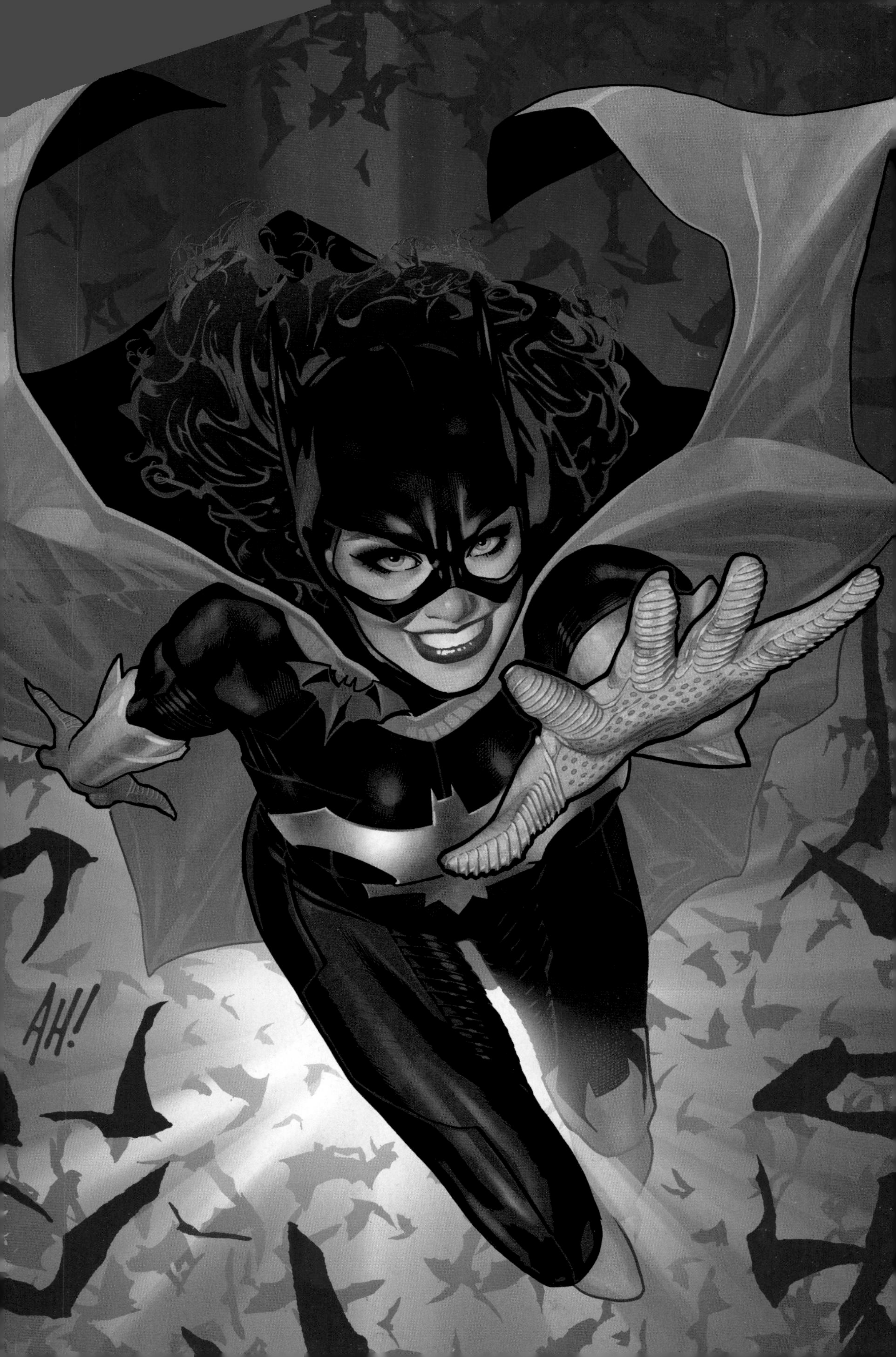
AH!

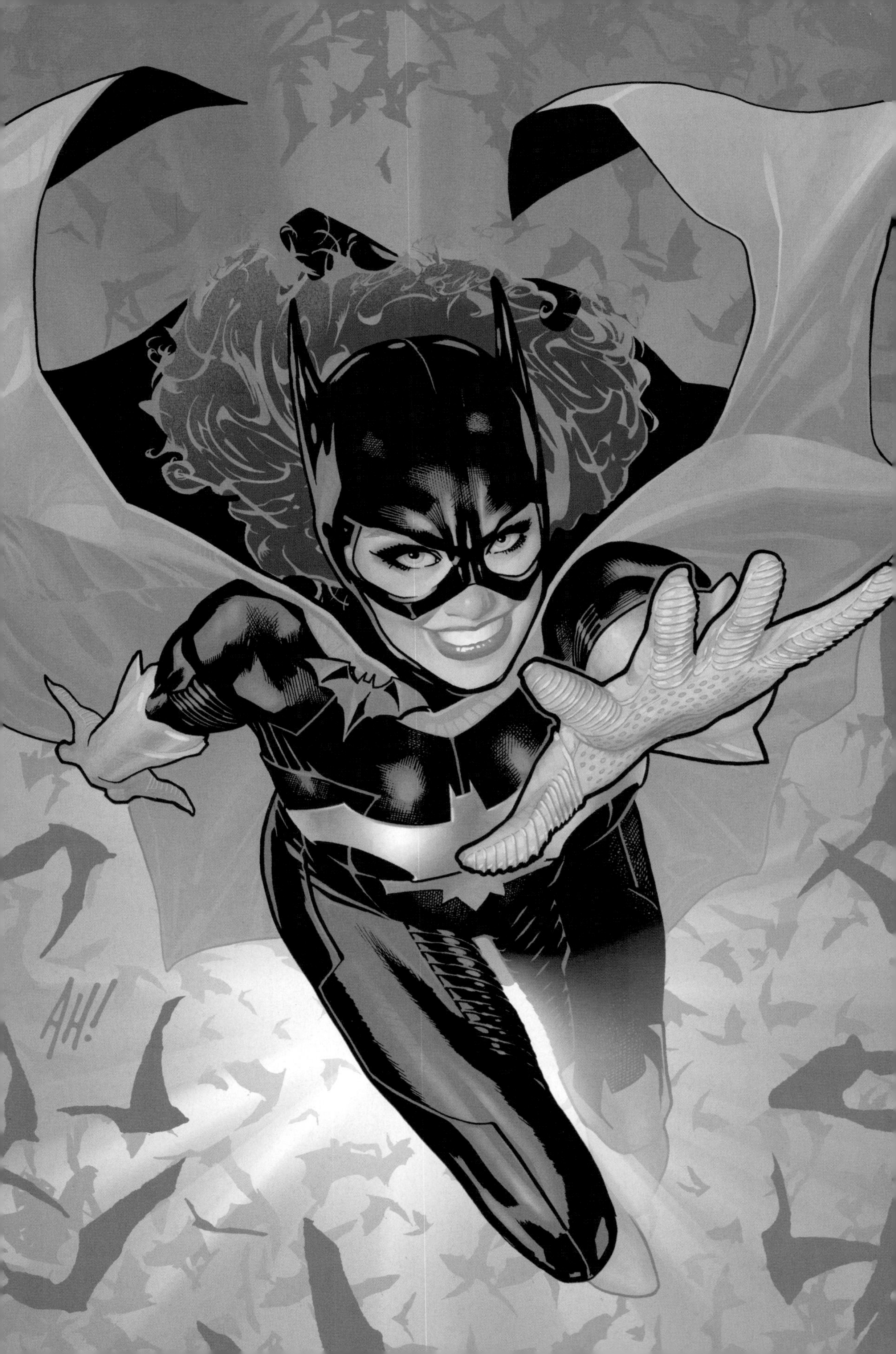
AH!

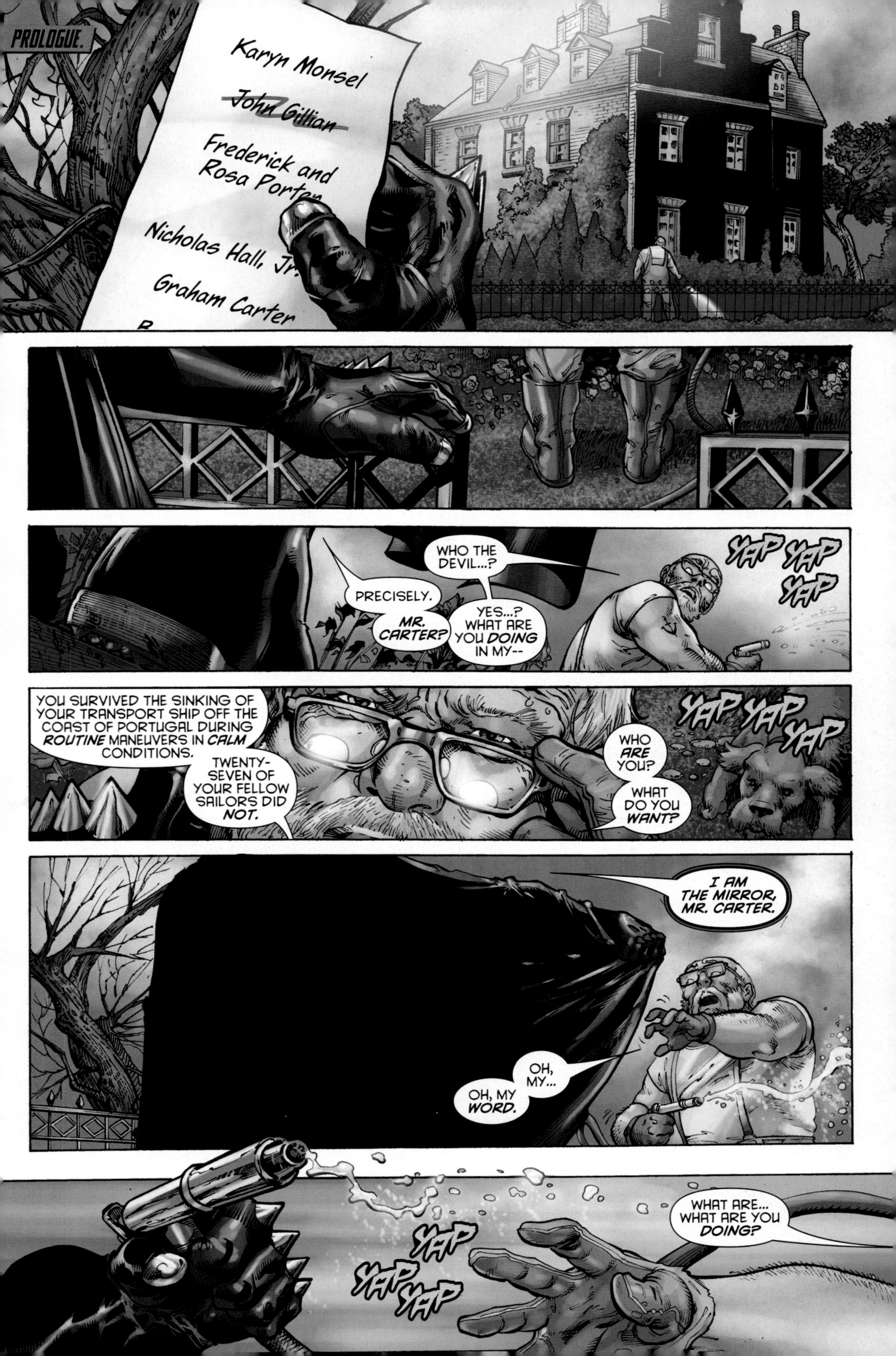
PROLOGUE.
Karyn Monsel
John Gillian
Frederick and Rosa Porter
Nicholas Hall, Jr.
Graham Carter
WHO THE DEVIL...?
PRECISELY.
MR. CARTER?
YES...? WHAT ARE YOU DOING IN MY--
YAP YAP YAP
YOU SURVIVED THE SINKING OF YOUR TRANSPORT SHIP OFF THE COAST OF PORTUGAL DURING ROUTINE MANEUVERS IN CALM CONDITIONS.
TWENTY-SEVEN OF YOUR FELLOW SAILORS DID NOT.
WHO ARE YOU?
WHAT DO YOU WANT?
YAP YAP YAP
I AM THE MIRROR, MR. CARTER.
OH, MY...
OH, MY WORD.
WHAT ARE... WHAT ARE YOU DOING?
YAP YAP YAP

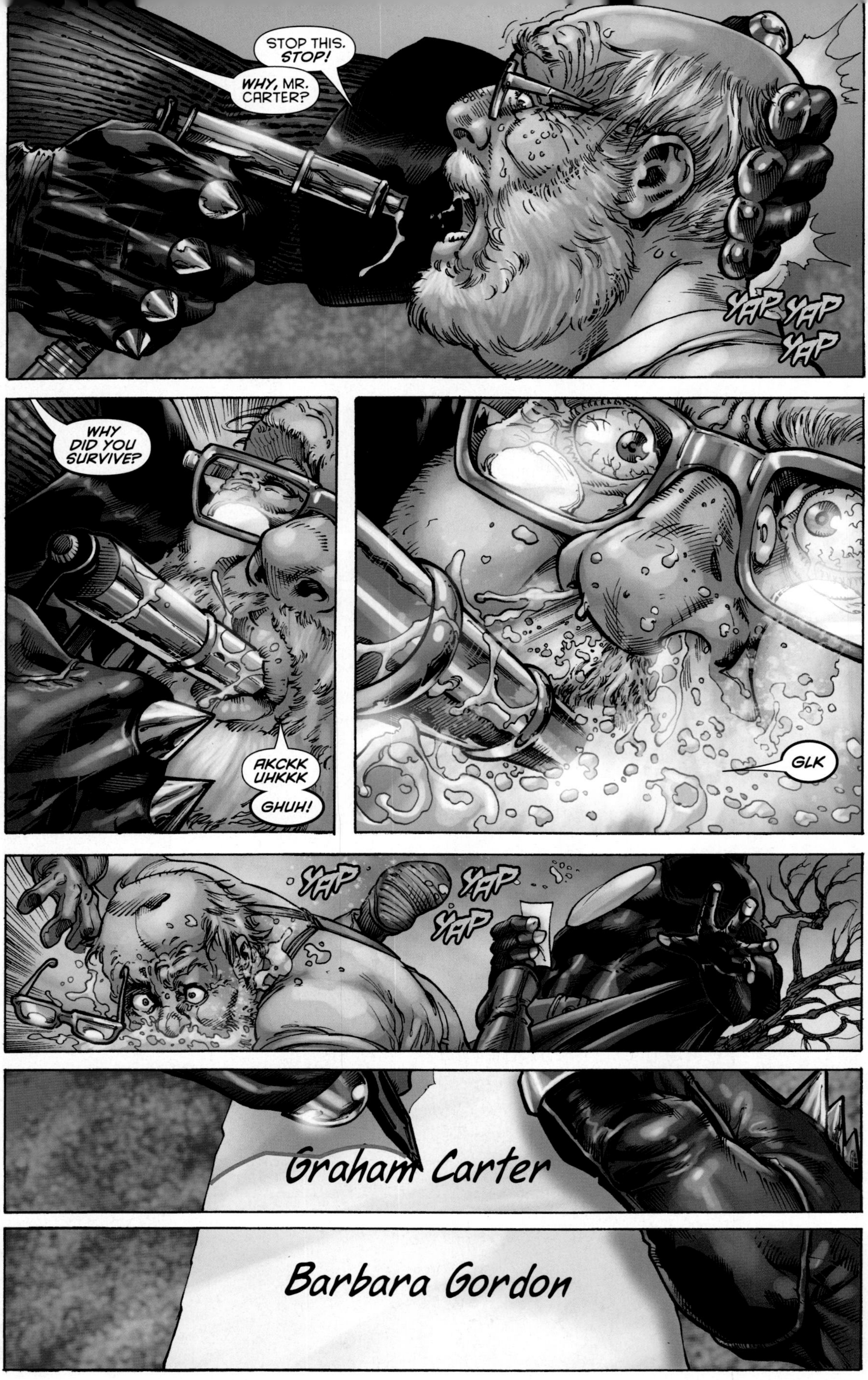
STOP THIS. STOP!
WHY, MR. CARTER?
YAP YAP YAP
WHY DID YOU SURVIVE?
AKCKK UHKKK
GHUH!
GLK
YAP YAP YAP
Graham Carter
Barbara Gordon

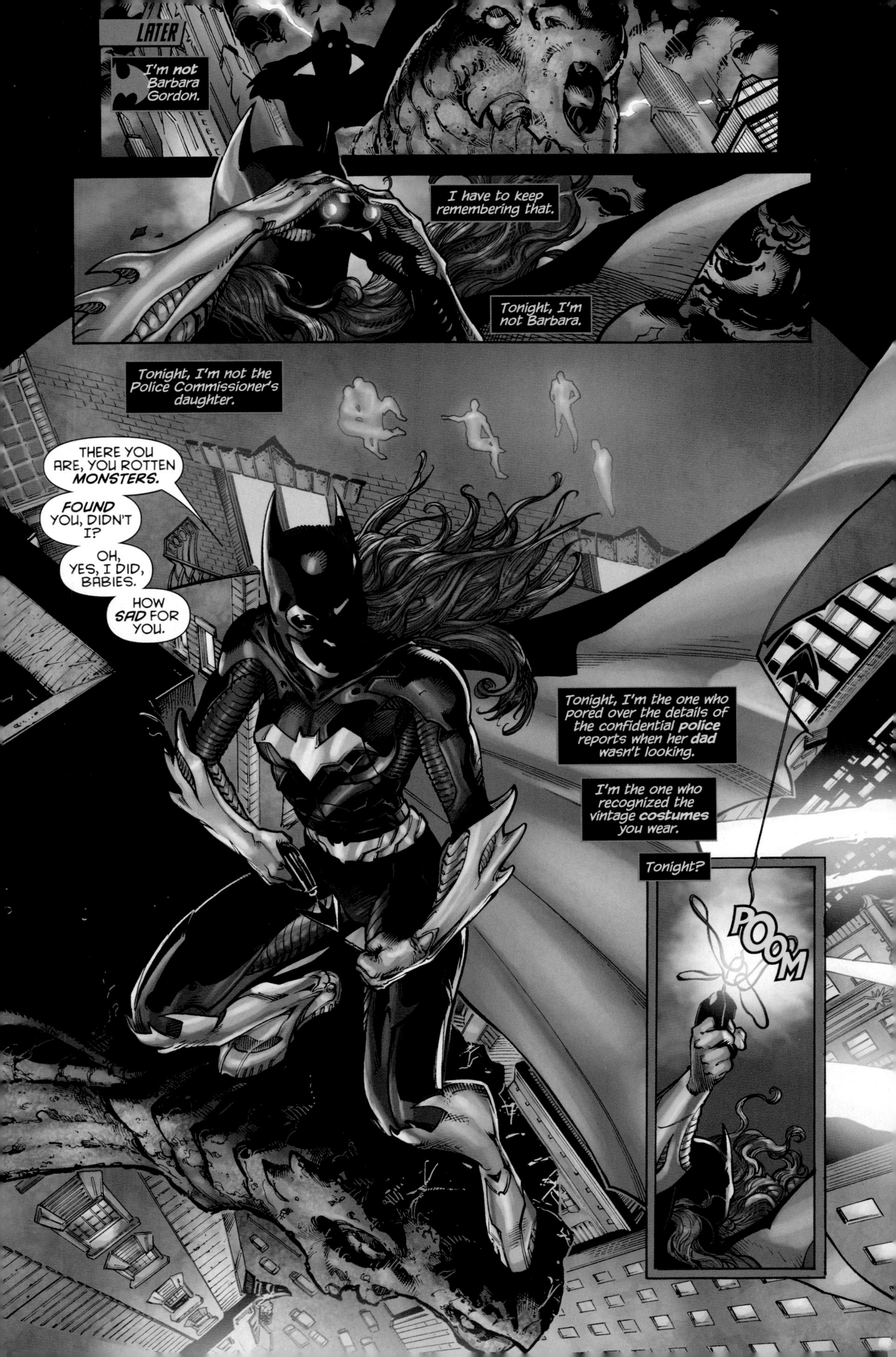
LATER
I'm not Barbara Gordon.
I have to keep remembering that.
Tonight, I'm not Barbara.
Tonight, I'm not the Police Commissioner's daughter.
THERE YOU ARE, YOU ROTTEN MONSTERS.
FOUND YOU, DIDN'T I?
OH, YES, I DID, BABIES.
HOW SAD FOR YOU.
Tonight, I'm the one who pored over the details of the confidential police reports when her dad wasn't looking.
I'm the one who recognized the vintage costumes you wear.
Tonight?
POOOM

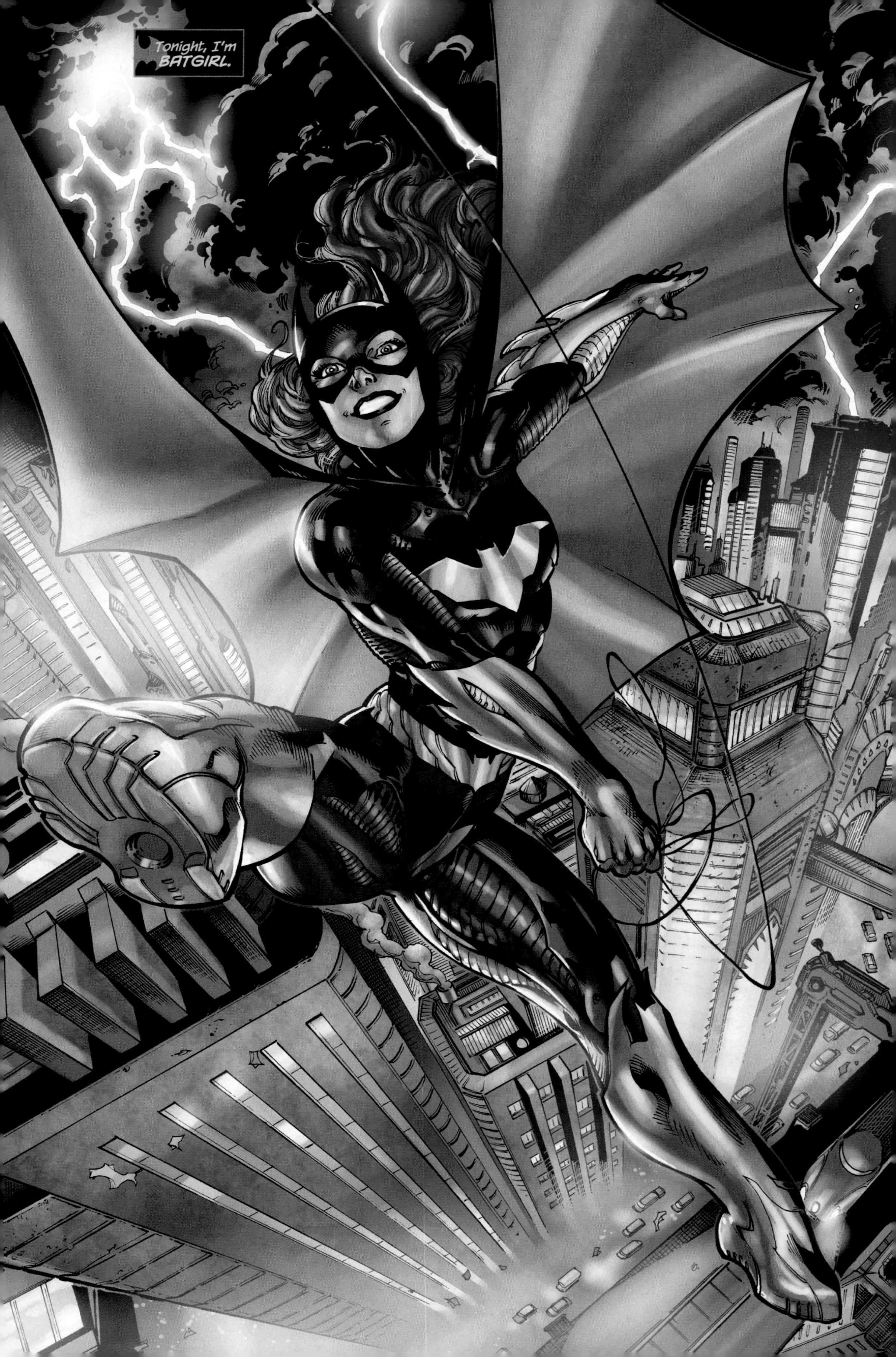
Tonight, I'm BATGIRL.

"HAVE YOU EVER WANTED SOMETHING SO BADLY THAT IT WAS ALL YOU THOUGHT ABOUT, DAY AND NIGHT?"

"TO BE FREE, I MEAN. UNFETTERED. WITHOUT THE CHAINS THAT HOLD US DOWN."

YOU CAN'T CALL IT A DREAM, EVEN. IT'S A NEED. A *NECESSITY*.

SO DEEP, IT'S IN THE BLOOD. IT'S IN THE *BONES*.

THAT'S HOW I FEEL ABOUT *HOME INVASION* AND *MURDER*.

SPOOKY

PLEASE. PLEASE, JUST *LEAVE*. WE WON'T...WE WON'T...

WHO *ARE* YOU?

OH. WHERE ARE MY MANNERS?

I'M SORRY, I THOUGHT YOU KNEW.

DANNY, GIVE THE ORTEGAS THE SCRAPBOOK, WOULD YOU?

WE'RE *THE BRISBY KILLERS*.

FAMILY MASSACRE IN GOTHAM SUBURB
Jack Ryder
World Associated Press and Times

Only Surviving Daughter Returns to Gruesome Scene

Tonight, the peaceful Gotham suburb of Brisby is quiet for the most tragic reason possible. Brisby is the retirement community of choice for former members of the Gotham City Police Force, and is known as an area local criminals stay well clear of. Yet, tragedy managed to find one family even in this quiet, ...t in what witnesses say ...d shocking

"BRISBY KILLERS" LIKELY PERPETRATORS IN SECOND BLOODBATH

Breaking News, Central News Desk
In a horrifying scene that alarmed even the most hardened of state troopers, a second family was found killed in the Brisby area outside of Gotham City lines early Thursday morning when neighbors were alerted by the terrified barking of the family's beloved pet dog. The bodies were posed in a grotesque mockery of
(CONT. PAGE TWO)

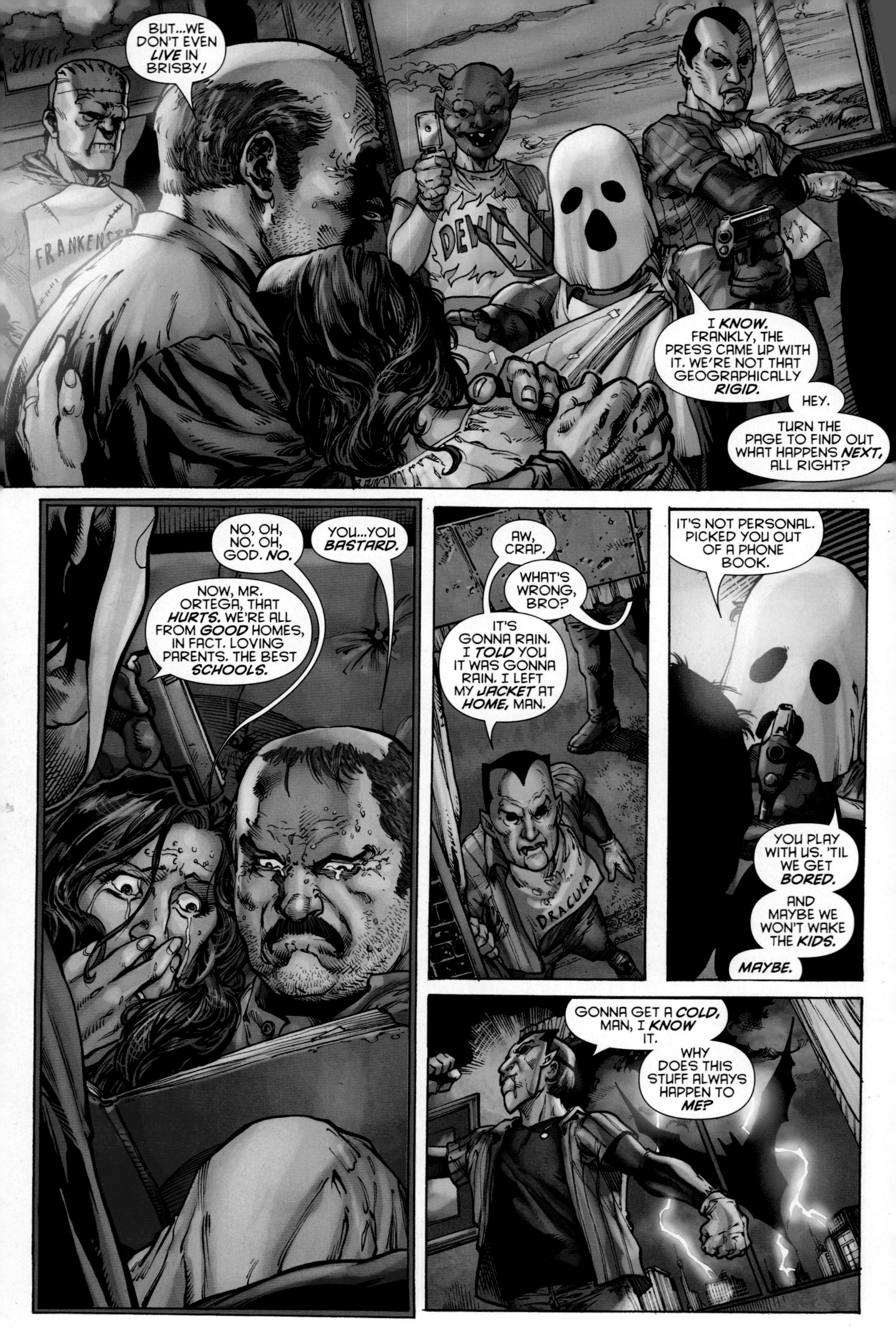
BUT...WE DON'T EVEN LIVE IN BRISBY!
FRANKENST
DEVIL
I KNOW. FRANKLY, THE PRESS CAME UP WITH IT. WE'RE NOT THAT GEOGRAPHICALLY RIGID.
HEY.
TURN THE PAGE TO FIND OUT WHAT HAPPENS NEXT, ALL RIGHT?
NO, OH, NO. OH, GOD. NO.
YOU...YOU BASTARD.
NOW, MR. ORTEGA, THAT HURTS. WE'RE ALL FROM GOOD HOMES, IN FACT. LOVING PARENTS. THE BEST SCHOOLS.
AW, CRAP.
WHAT'S WRONG, BRO?
IT'S GONNA RAIN. I TOLD YOU IT WAS GONNA RAIN. I LEFT MY JACKET AT HOME, MAN.
DRACULA
IT'S NOT PERSONAL. PICKED YOU OUT OF A PHONE BOOK.
YOU PLAY WITH US. 'TIL WE GET BORED.
AND MAYBE WE WON'T WAKE THE KIDS.
MAYBE.
GONNA GET A COLD, MAN, I KNOW IT.
WHY DOES THIS STUFF ALWAYS HAPPEN TO ME?

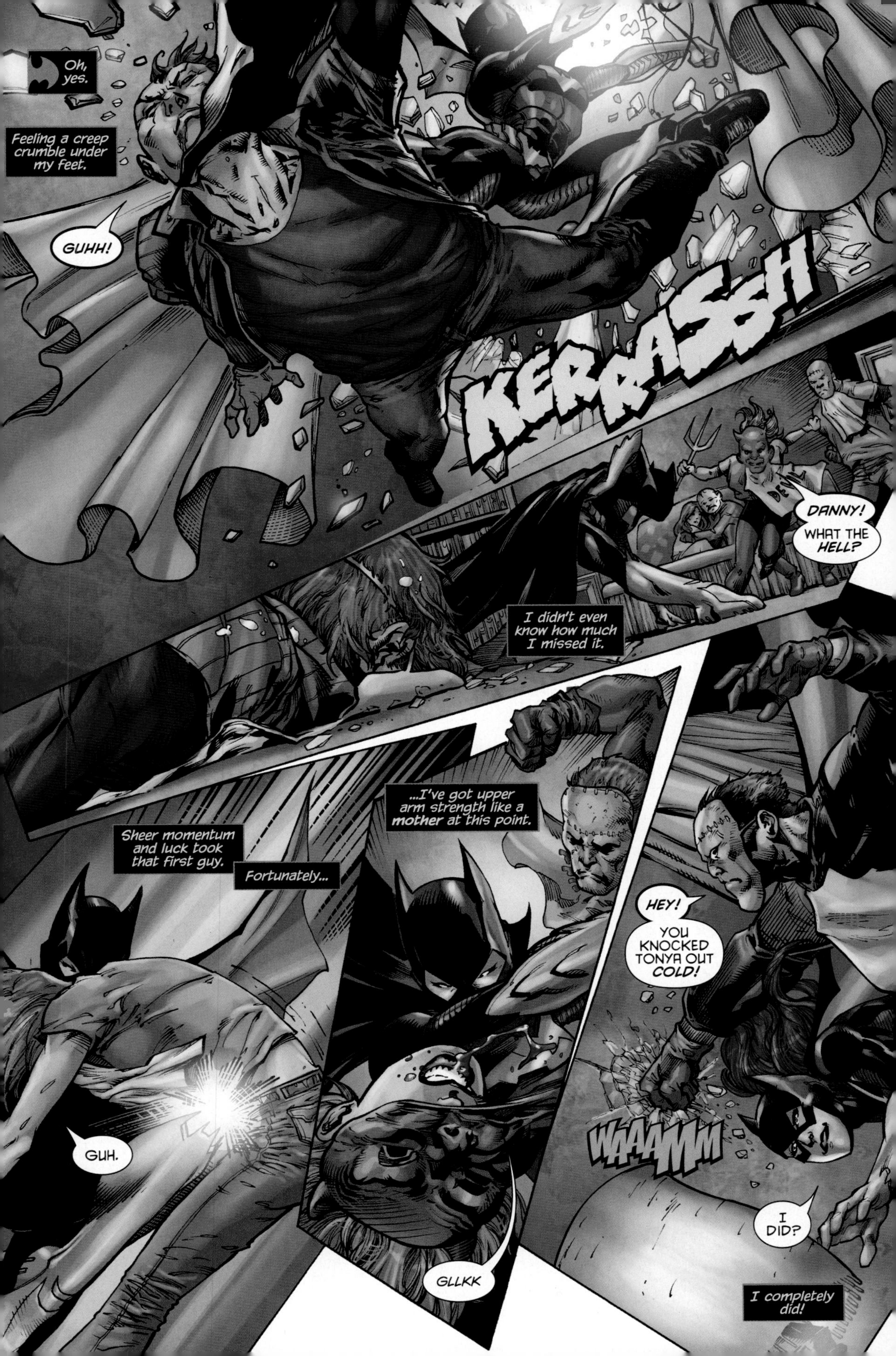
Oh, yes.
Feeling a creep crumble under my feet.
GUHH!
KERRASSH
DANNY! WHAT THE HELL?
I didn't even know how much I missed it.
Sheer momentum and luck took that first guy.
Fortunately...
...I've got upper arm strength like a mother at this point.
GUH.
GLLKK
HEY! YOU KNOCKED TONYA OUT COLD!
WAAAMM
I DID?
I completely did!

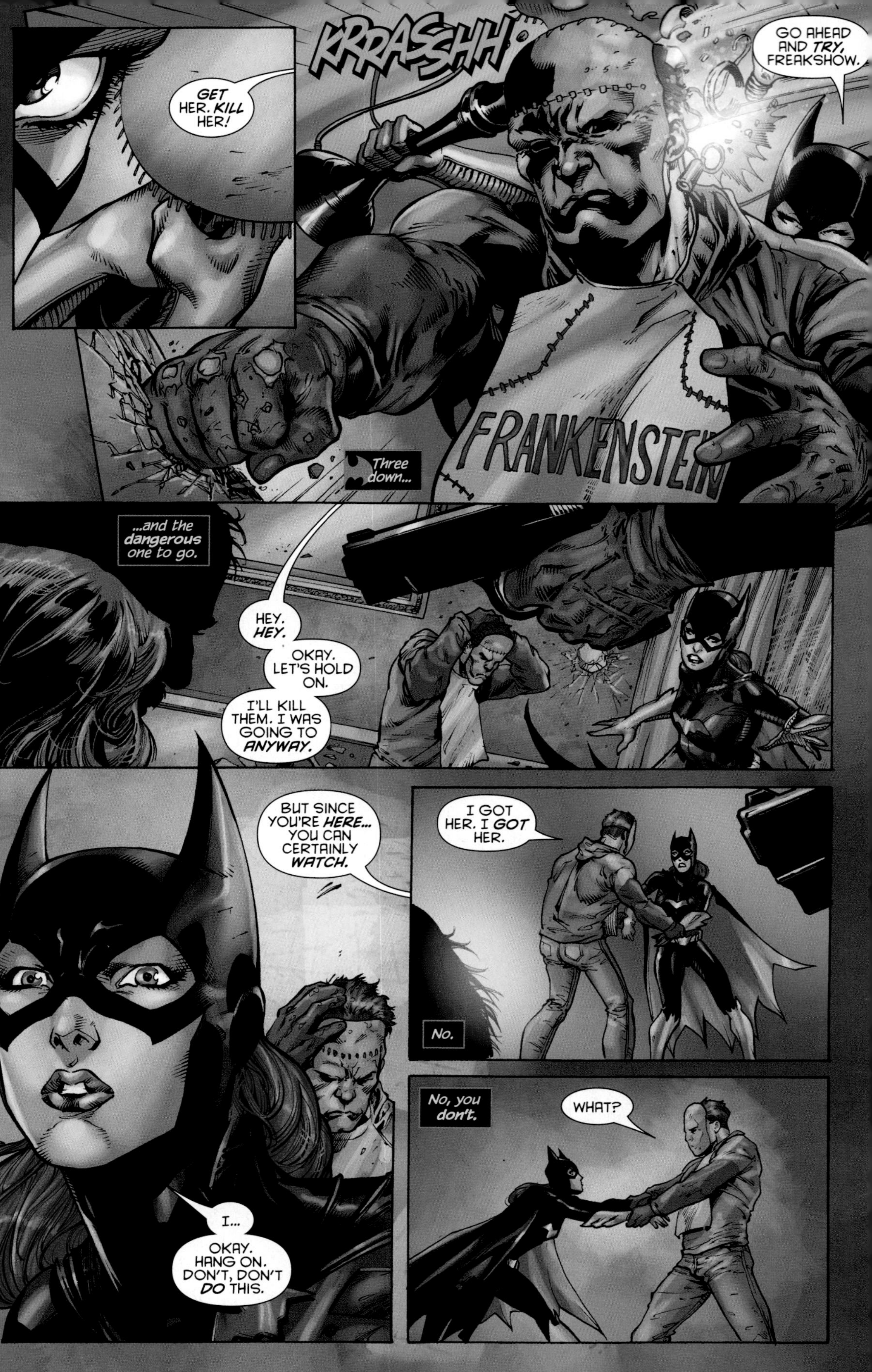

KRRASSHH
GET HER. KILL HER!
GO AHEAD AND TRY, FREAKSHOW.
FRANKENSTEIN
Three down...
...and the dangerous one to go.
HEY. HEY.
OKAY. LET'S HOLD ON.
I'LL KILL THEM. I WAS GOING TO ANYWAY.
BUT SINCE YOU'RE HERE... YOU CAN CERTAINLY WATCH.
I...
OKAY. HANG ON. DON'T, DON'T DO THIS.
I GOT HER. I GOT HER.
No.
No, you don't.
WHAT?

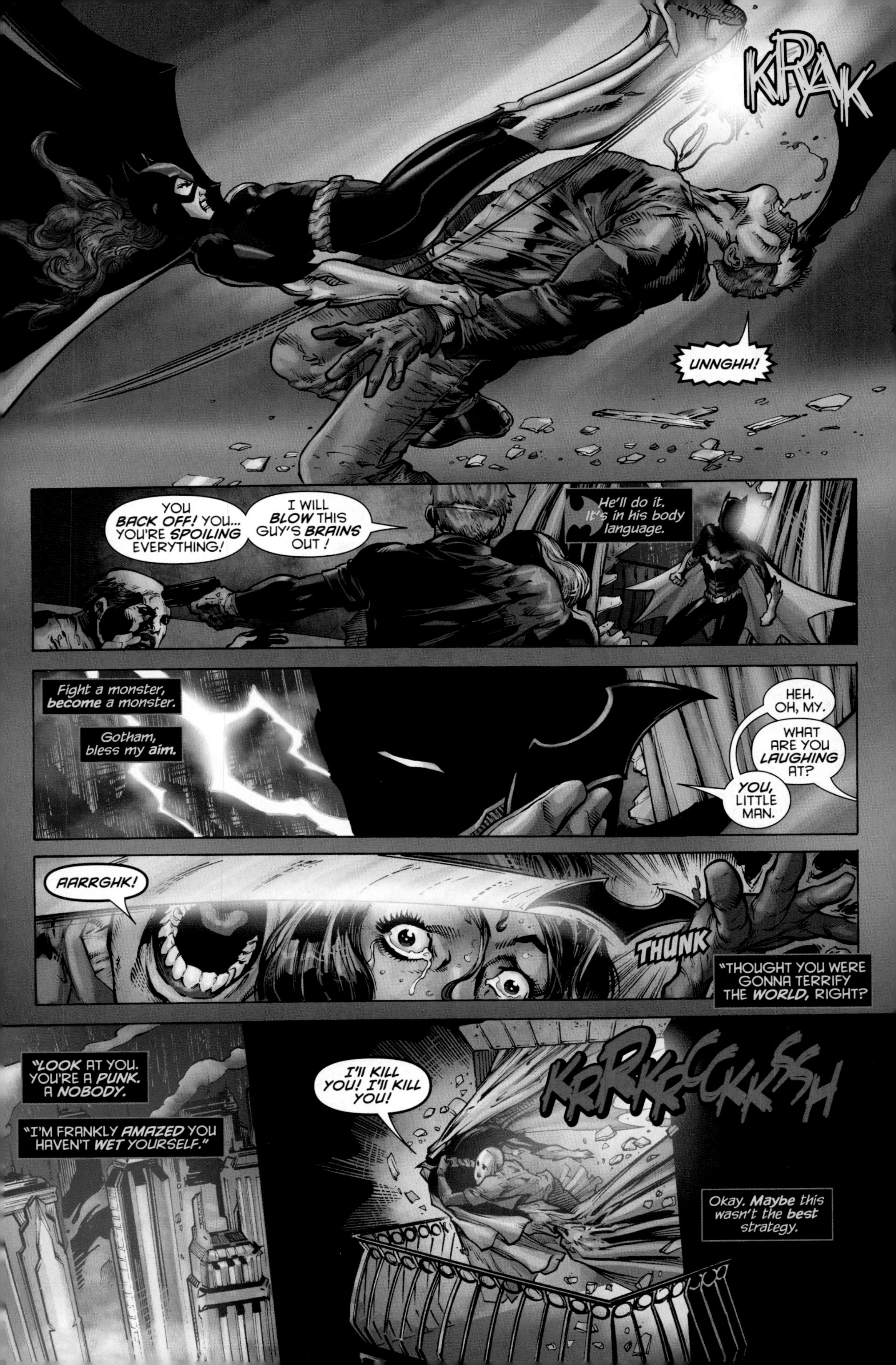

KRAK
UNNGHH!
YOU BACK OFF! YOU... YOU'RE SPOILING EVERYTHING!
I WILL BLOW THIS GUY'S BRAINS OUT!
He'll do it. It's in his body language.
Fight a monster, become a monster.
Gotham, bless my aim.
HEH. OH, MY.
WHAT ARE YOU LAUGHING AT?
YOU, LITTLE MAN.
AARRGHK!
THUNK
"THOUGHT YOU WERE GONNA TERRIFY THE WORLD, RIGHT?
"LOOK AT YOU. YOU'RE A PUNK. A NOBODY.
"I'M FRANKLY AMAZED YOU HAVEN'T WET YOURSELF."
I'LL KILL YOU! I'LL KILL YOU!
KRRKKCCKKSSH
Okay. Maybe this wasn't the best strategy.

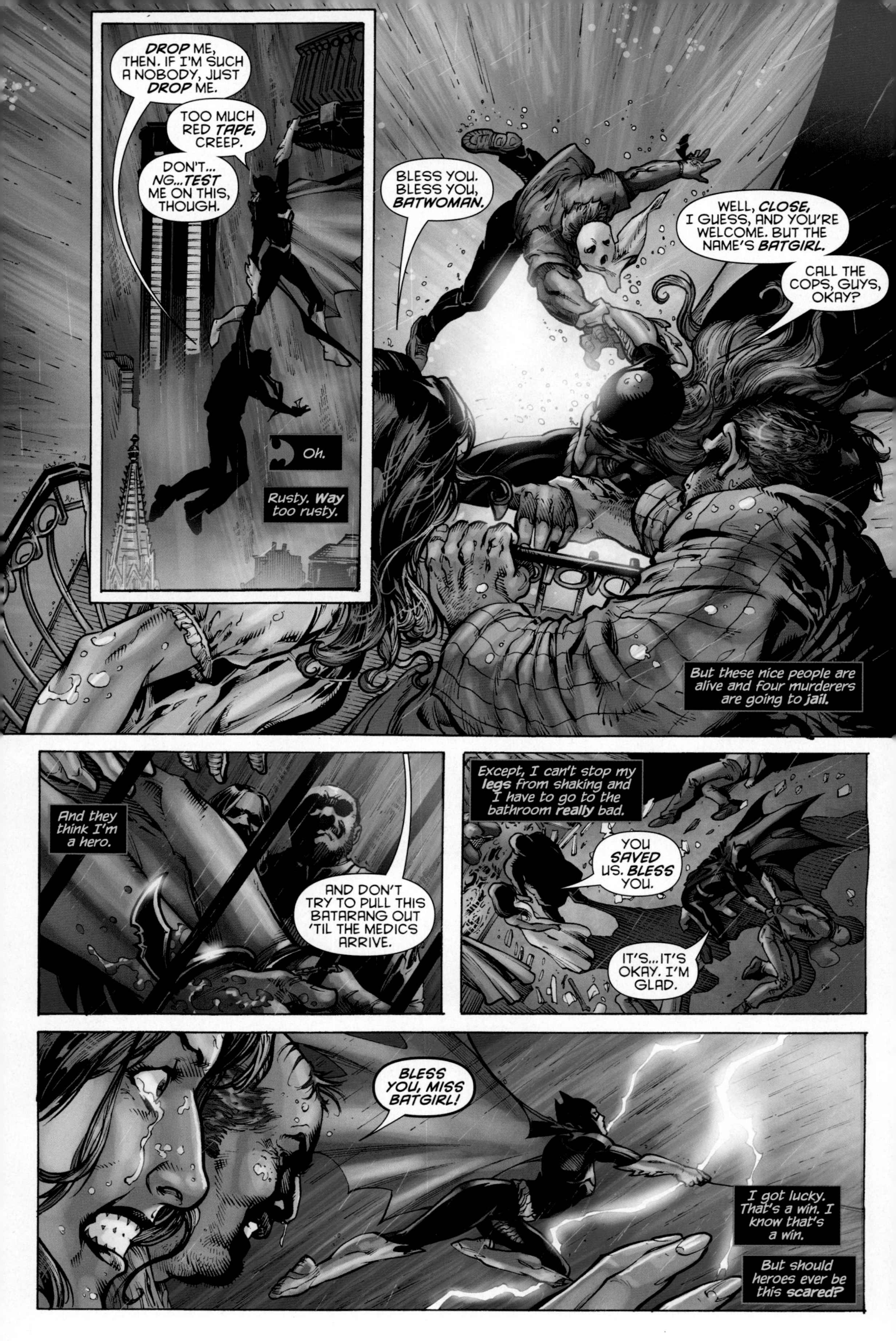

DROP ME, THEN. IF I'M SUCH A NOBODY, JUST DROP ME.
TOO MUCH RED TAPE, CREEP.
DON'T... NG...TEST ME ON THIS, THOUGH.
Oh.
Rusty. Way too rusty.
BLESS YOU. BLESS YOU, BATWOMAN.
WELL, CLOSE, I GUESS, AND YOU'RE WELCOME. BUT THE NAME'S BATGIRL.
CALL THE COPS, GUYS, OKAY?
But these nice people are alive and four murderers are going to jail.
And they think I'm a hero.
AND DON'T TRY TO PULL THIS BATARANG OUT 'TIL THE MEDICS ARRIVE.
Except, I can't stop my legs from shaking and I have to go to the bathroom really bad.
YOU SAVED US. BLESS YOU.
IT'S...IT'S OKAY. I'M GLAD.
BLESS YOU, MISS BATGIRL!
I got lucky. That's a win. I know that's a win.
But should heroes ever be this scared?

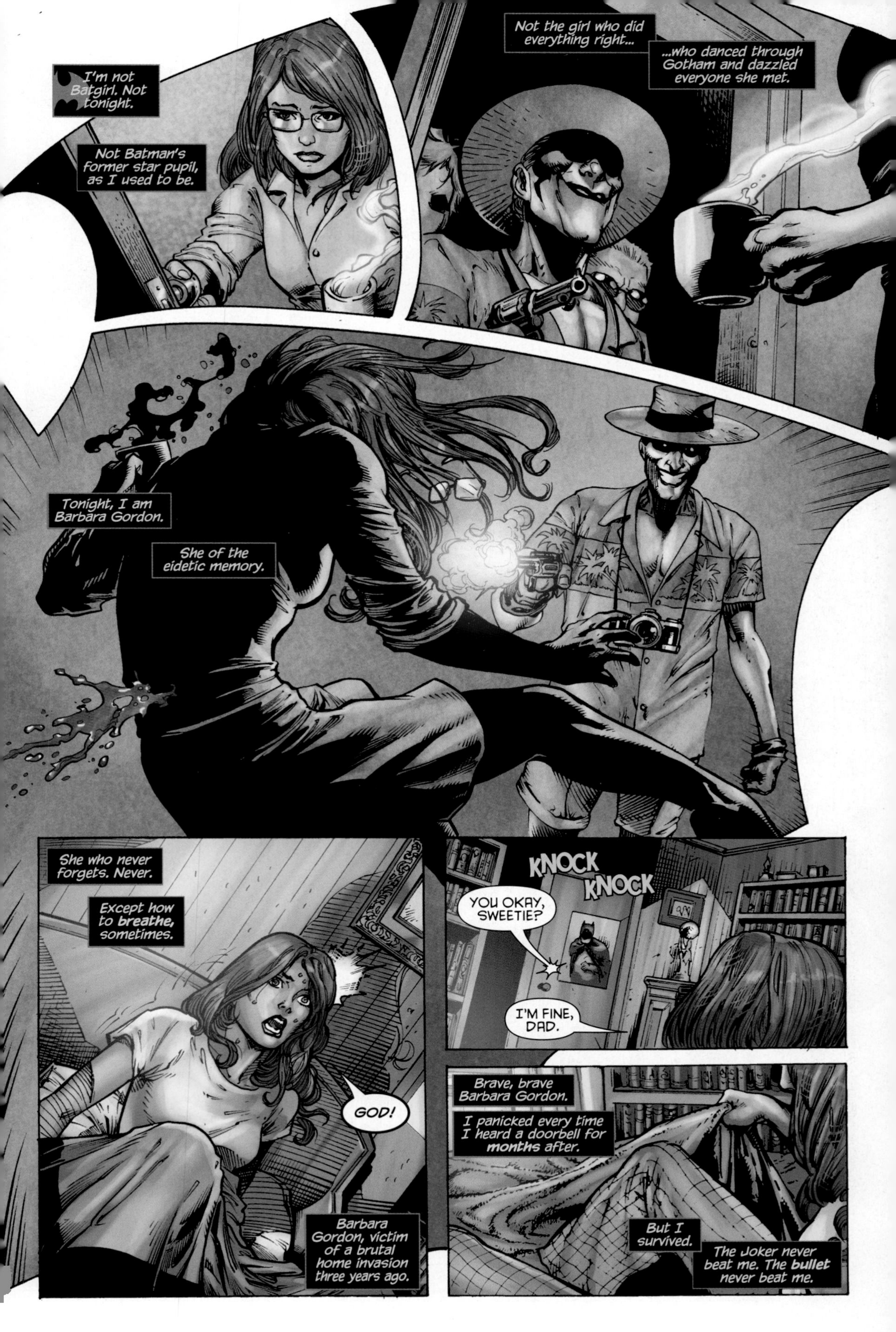

I'm not Batgirl. Not tonight.
Not Batman's former star pupil, as I used to be.
Not the girl who did everything right...
...who danced through Gotham and dazzled everyone she met.
Tonight, I am Barbara Gordon.
She of the eidetic memory.
She who never forgets. Never.
Except how to breathe, sometimes.
GOD!
Barbara Gordon, victim of a brutal home invasion three years ago.
KNOCK
KNOCK
YOU OKAY, SWEETIE?
I'M FINE, DAD.
Brave, brave Barbara Gordon.
I panicked every time I heard a doorbell for months after.
But I survived.
The Joker never beat me. The bullet never beat me.

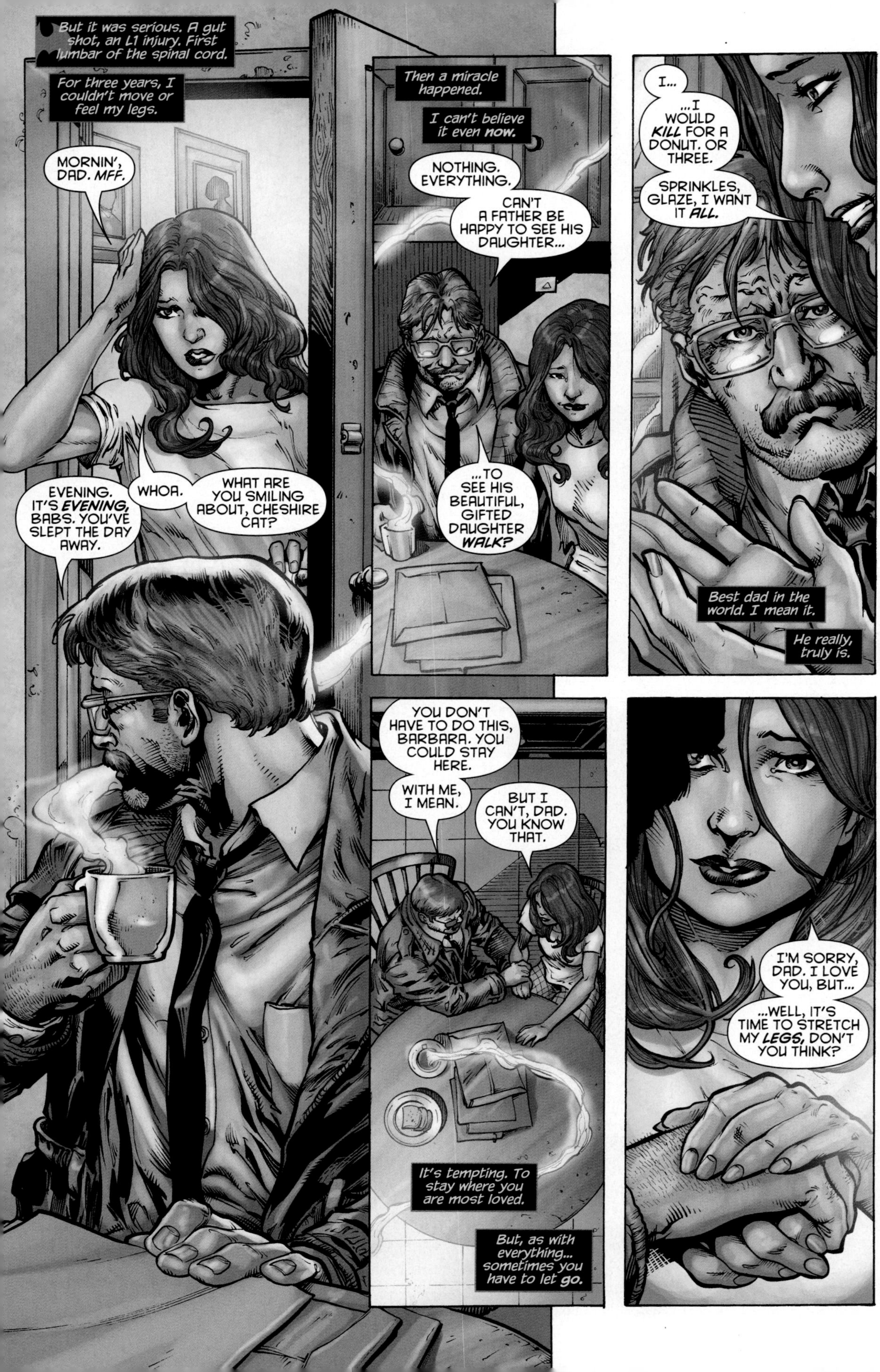

But it was serious. A gut shot, an L1 injury. First lumbar of the spinal cord.
For three years, I couldn't move or feel my legs.
MORNIN', DAD. MFF.
EVENING. IT'S EVENING, BABS. YOU'VE SLEPT THE DAY AWAY.
WHOA.
WHAT ARE YOU SMILING ABOUT, CHESHIRE CAT?
Then a miracle happened.
I can't believe it even now.
NOTHING. EVERYTHING.
CAN'T A FATHER BE HAPPY TO SEE HIS DAUGHTER...
...TO SEE HIS BEAUTIFUL, GIFTED DAUGHTER WALK?
I...
...I WOULD KILL FOR A DONUT. OR THREE.
SPRINKLES, GLAZE, I WANT IT ALL.
Best dad in the world. I mean it.
He really, truly is.
YOU DON'T HAVE TO DO THIS, BARBARA. YOU COULD STAY HERE.
WITH ME, I MEAN.
BUT I CAN'T, DAD. YOU KNOW THAT.
It's tempting. To stay where you are most loved.
But, as with everything... sometimes you have to let go.
I'M SORRY, DAD. I LOVE YOU, BUT...
...WELL, IT'S TIME TO STRETCH MY LEGS, DON'T YOU THINK?

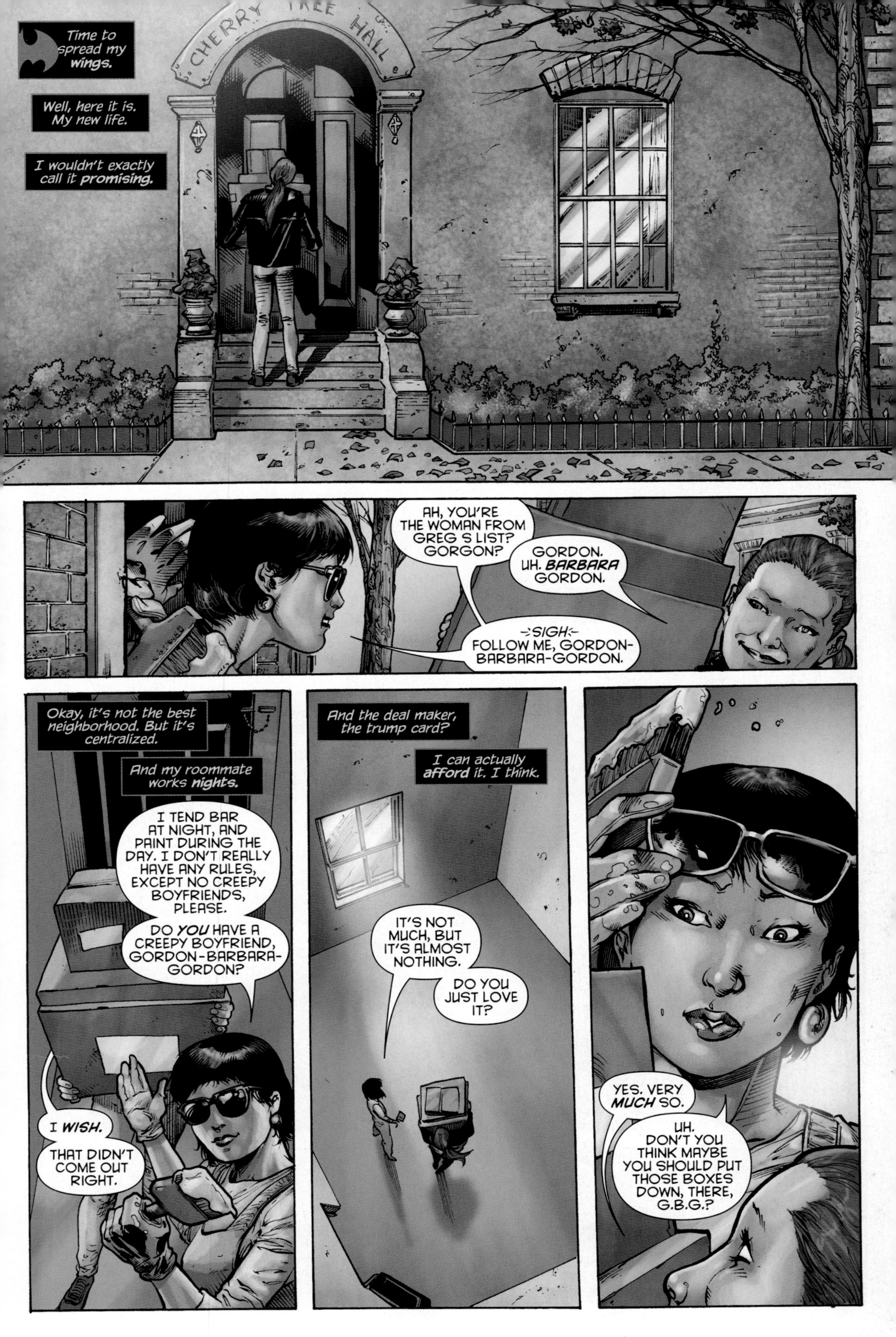

Time to spread my wings.
Well, here it is. My new life.
I wouldn't exactly call it promising.
CHERRY TREE HALL
AH, YOU'RE THE WOMAN FROM GREG S LIST? GORGON?
GORDON. UH. BARBARA GORDON.
-SIGH- FOLLOW ME, GORDON-BARBARA-GORDON.
Okay, it's not the best neighborhood. But it's centralized.
And my roommate works nights.
I TEND BAR AT NIGHT, AND PAINT DURING THE DAY. I DON'T REALLY HAVE ANY RULES, EXCEPT NO CREEPY BOYFRIENDS, PLEASE.
DO YOU HAVE A CREEPY BOYFRIEND, GORDON-BARBARA-GORDON?
I WISH.
THAT DIDN'T COME OUT RIGHT.
And the deal maker, the trump card?
I can actually afford it. I think.
IT'S NOT MUCH, BUT IT'S ALMOST NOTHING.
DO YOU JUST LOVE IT?
YES. VERY MUCH SO.
UH. DON'T YOU THINK MAYBE YOU SHOULD PUT THOSE BOXES DOWN, THERE, G.B.G.?

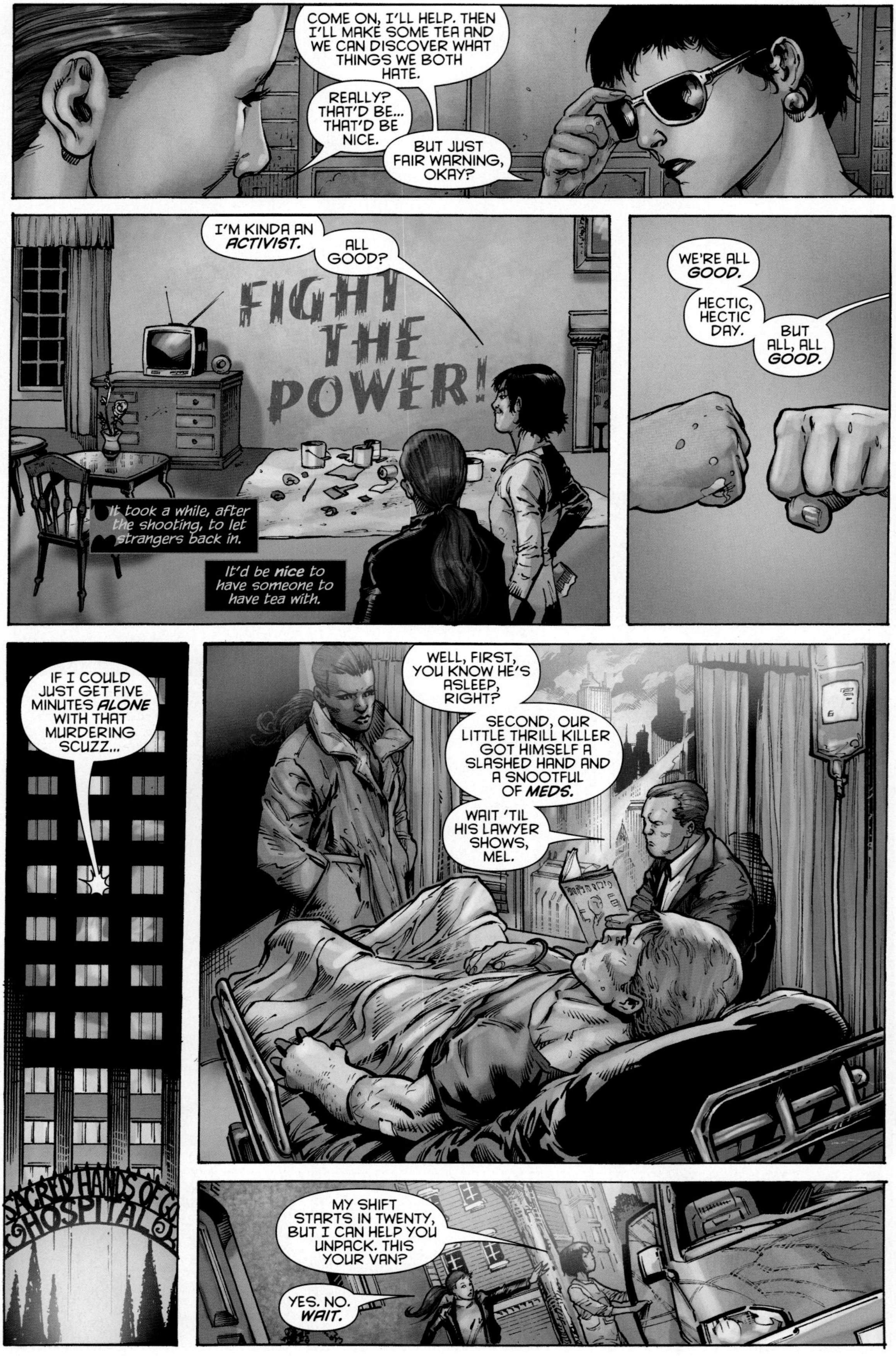

COME ON, I'LL HELP. THEN I'LL MAKE SOME TEA AND WE CAN DISCOVER WHAT THINGS WE BOTH HATE.
REALLY? THAT'D BE... THAT'D BE NICE.
BUT JUST FAIR WARNING, OKAY?
I'M KINDA AN ACTIVIST.
ALL GOOD?
FIGHT THE POWER!
It took a while, after the shooting, to let strangers back in.
It'd be nice to have someone to have tea with.
WE'RE ALL GOOD.
HECTIC, HECTIC DAY.
BUT ALL, ALL GOOD.
IF I COULD JUST GET FIVE MINUTES ALONE WITH THAT MURDERING SCUZZ...
SACRED HANDS OF GOD HOSPITAL
WELL, FIRST, YOU KNOW HE'S ASLEEP, RIGHT?
SECOND, OUR LITTLE THRILL KILLER GOT HIMSELF A SLASHED HAND AND A SNOOTFUL OF MEDS.
WAIT 'TIL HIS LAWYER SHOWS, MEL.
MY SHIFT STARTS IN TWENTY, BUT I CAN HELP YOU UNPACK. THIS YOUR VAN?
YES. NO. WAIT.

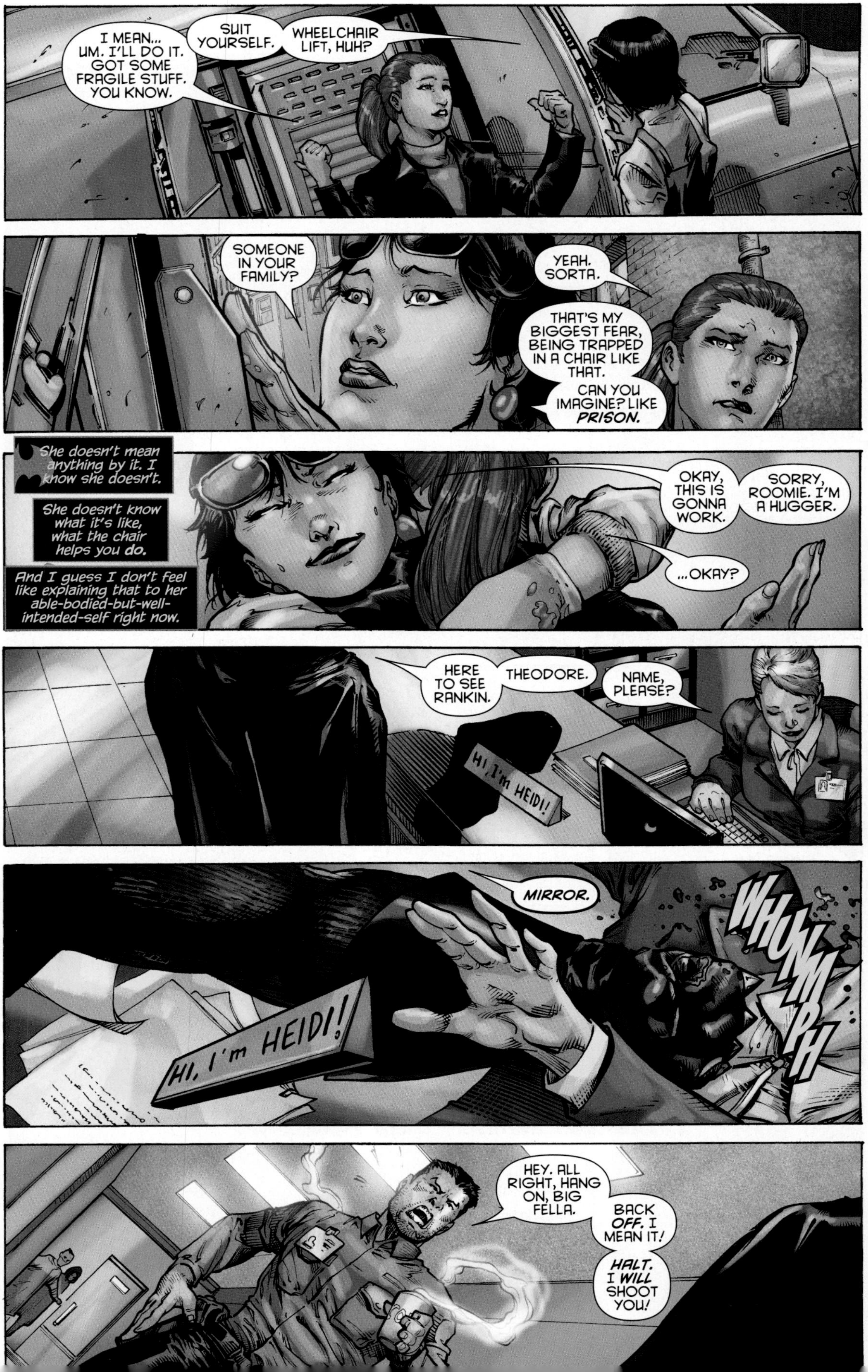
WHEELCHAIR LIFT, HUH?
SUIT YOURSELF.
I MEAN... UM. I'LL DO IT. GOT SOME FRAGILE STUFF. YOU KNOW.
SOMEONE IN YOUR FAMILY?
YEAH. SORTA.
THAT'S MY BIGGEST FEAR, BEING TRAPPED IN A CHAIR LIKE THAT.
CAN YOU IMAGINE? LIKE PRISON.
She doesn't mean anything by it. I know she doesn't.
She doesn't know what it's like, what the chair helps you do.
And I guess I don't feel like explaining that to her able-bodied-but-well-intended-self right now.
SORRY, ROOMIE. I'M A HUGGER.
OKAY, THIS IS GONNA WORK.
...OKAY?
NAME, PLEASE?
THEODORE.
HERE TO SEE RANKIN.
HI, I'm HEIDI!
MIRROR.
WHUMMPH
HI, I'm HEIDI!
HEY. ALL RIGHT, HANG ON, BIG FELLA.
BACK OFF. I MEAN IT!
HALT. I WILL SHOOT YOU!

I BELIEVE YOU.

BWOOMFF

SHOTS FIRED! WHAT THE *HELL* IS GOING ON?

CALL IT *IN*. CALL IT *IN*!

PRECINCT SIXTY-THREE, WE HAVE AN *EMERGENCY* HERE, REPEAT, WE HAVE...

Okay, so, yeah, I secretly routed it so I get my dad's text alerts.

Don't judge me, I don't have a Bat-signal to call my own.

Yet.

UH...ALYSIA? I HAVE TO GO NOW. SORRY!

WHAT... ALREADY?

BZZT BZZT

COME TO *MOMMA*, SWEETHEART!

Okay. I may not have a Batmobile.

But I still can arrive in *style*.

SHOTS ARE GETTING CLOSER... WE HAVE TO *INVESTIGATE*.

AND WALK INTO A POSSIBLE *TERRORIST* ATTACK?

WE WAIT FOR *BACKUP*, DETECTIVE, AS THE MANUAL *STATES*. THAT'S AN *ORDER*.

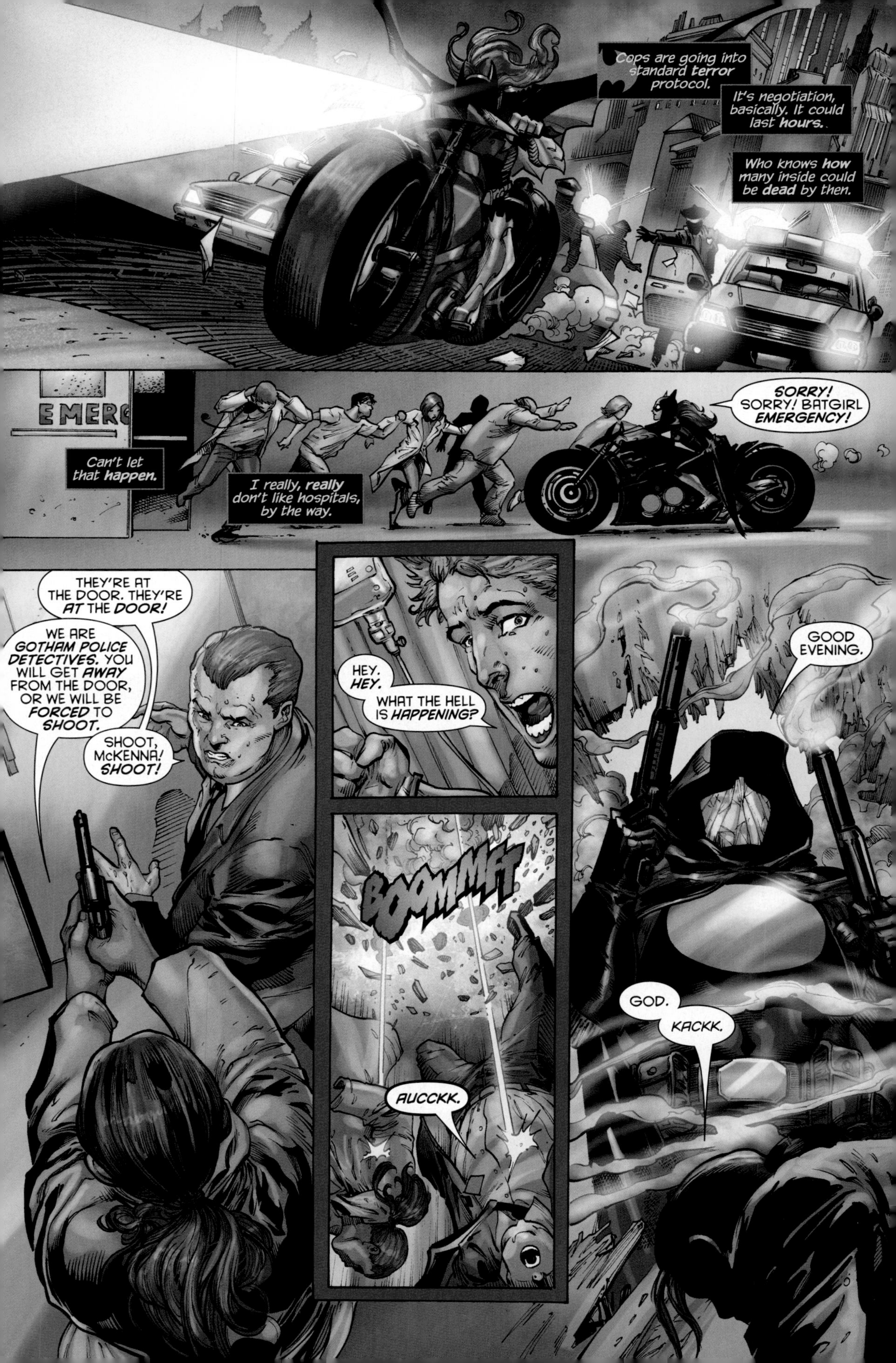
Cops are going into standard terror protocol.
It's negotiation, basically. It could last hours.
Who knows how many inside could be dead by then.
EMERG
SORRY! SORRY! BATGIRL EMERGENCY!
Can't let that happen.
I really, really don't like hospitals, by the way.
THEY'RE AT THE DOOR. THEY'RE AT THE DOOR!
WE ARE GOTHAM POLICE DETECTIVES. YOU WILL GET AWAY FROM THE DOOR, OR WE WILL BE FORCED TO SHOOT.
SHOOT, McKENNA! SHOOT!
HEY. HEY.
WHAT THE HELL IS HAPPENING?
BOOMMFT
AUCCKK.
GOOD EVENING.
GOD.
KACKK.

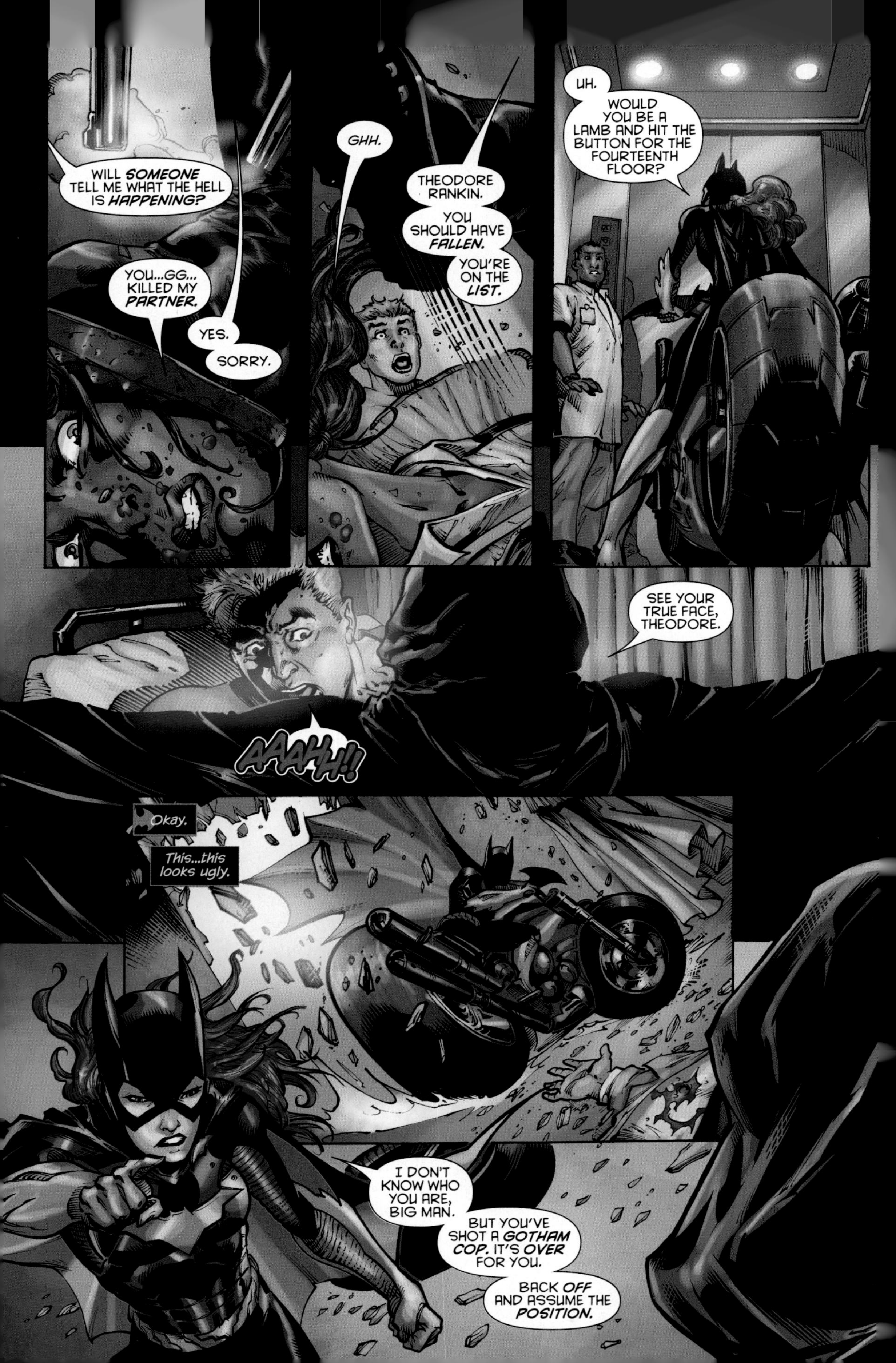
WILL SOMEONE TELL ME WHAT THE HELL IS HAPPENING?
YOU...GG... KILLED MY PARTNER.
YES.
SORRY.
GHH.
THEODORE RANKIN.
YOU SHOULD HAVE FALLEN.
YOU'RE ON THE LIST.
UH.
WOULD YOU BE A LAMB AND HIT THE BUTTON FOR THE FOURTEENTH FLOOR?
SEE YOUR TRUE FACE, THEODORE.
AAAHH!!
Okay.
This...this looks ugly.
I DON'T KNOW WHO YOU ARE, BIG MAN.
BUT YOU'VE SHOT A GOTHAM COP. IT'S OVER FOR YOU.
BACK OFF AND ASSUME THE POSITION.

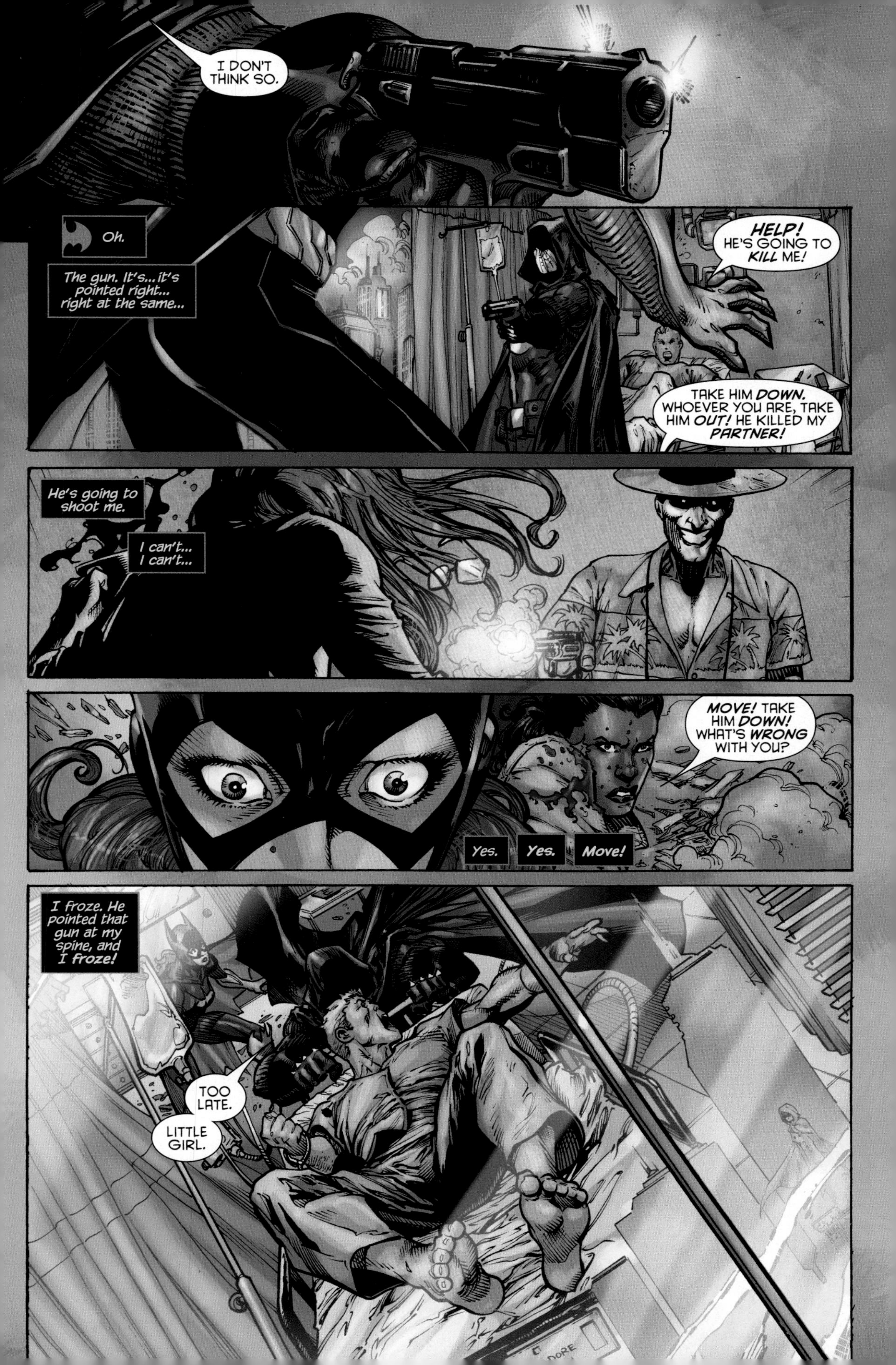

I DON'T THINK SO.
Oh.
The gun. It's... it's pointed right... right at the same...
HELP! HE'S GOING TO KILL ME!
TAKE HIM DOWN. WHOEVER YOU ARE, TAKE HIM OUT! HE KILLED MY PARTNER!
He's going to shoot me.
I can't... I can't...
MOVE! TAKE HIM DOWN! WHAT'S WRONG WITH YOU?
Yes.
Yes.
Move!
I froze. He pointed that gun at my spine, and I froze!
TOO LATE.
LITTLE GIRL.

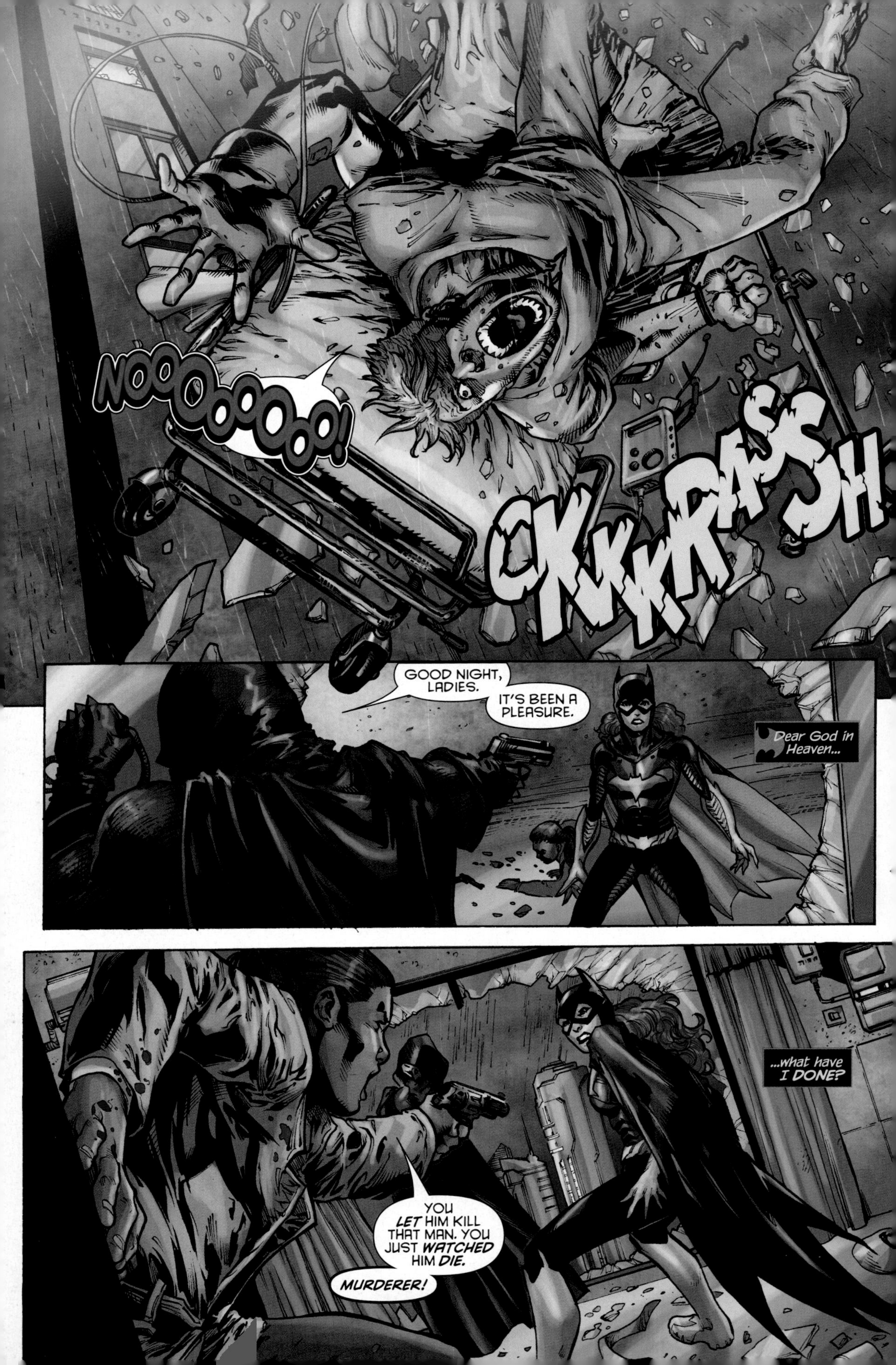
NOOOOOOOOO!
CKKKRASH
GOOD NIGHT, LADIES.
IT'S BEEN A PLEASURE.
Dear God in Heaven...
...what have I DONE?
YOU LET HIM KILL THAT MAN. YOU JUST WATCHED HIM DIE.
MURDERER!

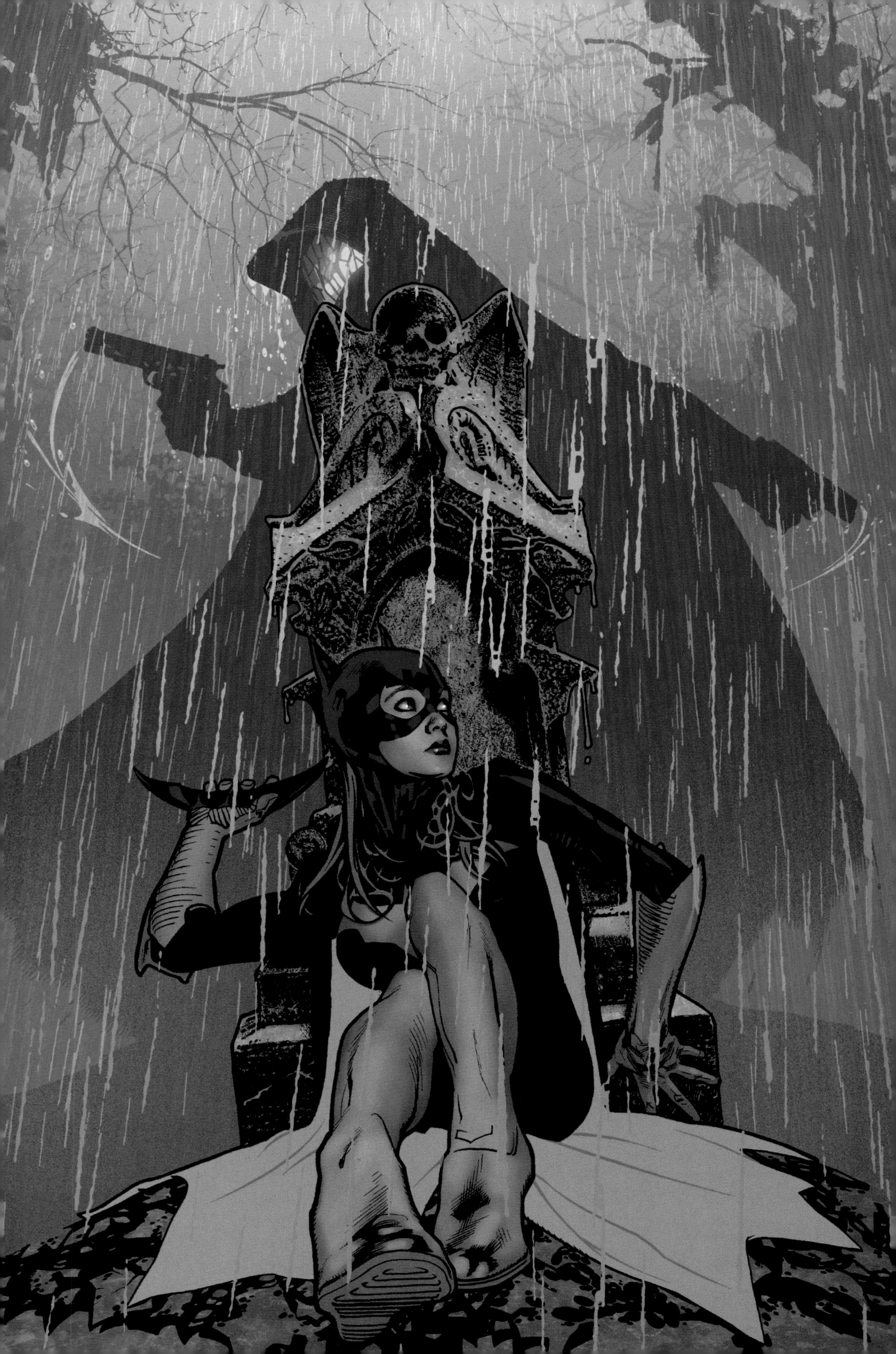

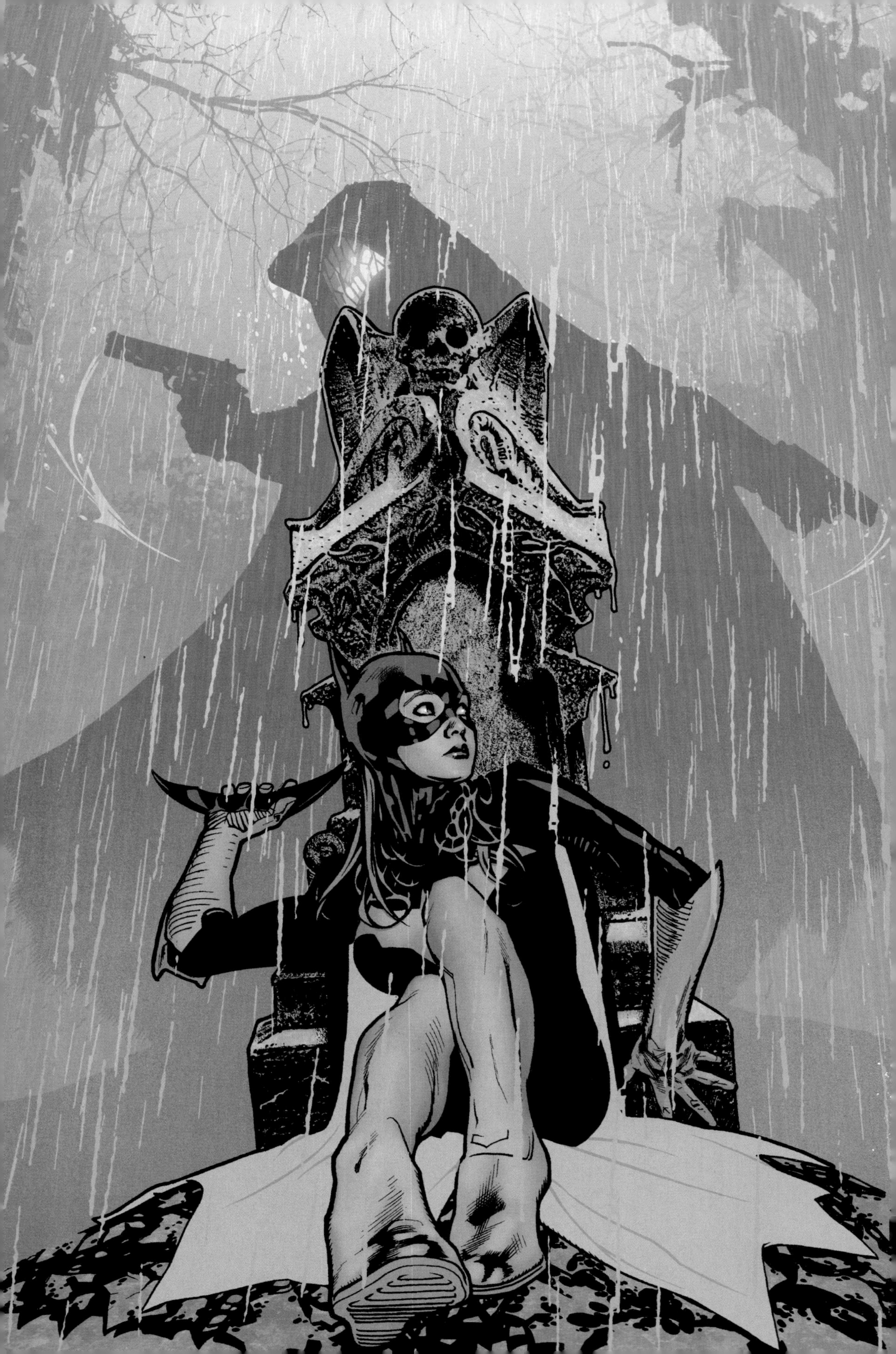

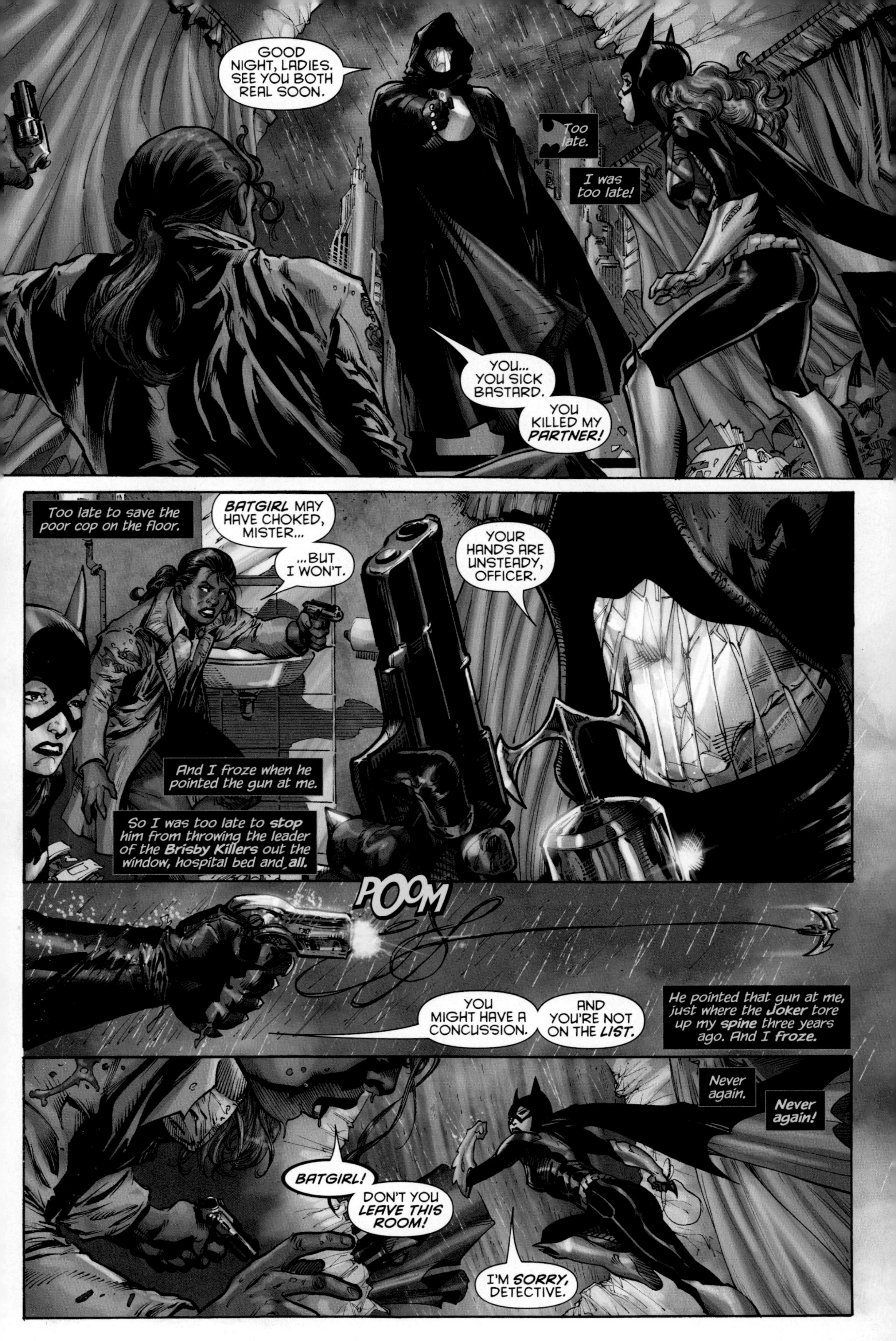

GOOD NIGHT, LADIES. SEE YOU BOTH REAL SOON.
Too late.
I was too late!
YOU... YOU SICK BASTARD.
YOU KILLED MY PARTNER!
Too late to save the poor cop on the floor.
BATGIRL MAY HAVE CHOKED, MISTER...
...BUT I WON'T.
YOUR HANDS ARE UNSTEADY, OFFICER.
And I froze when he pointed the gun at me.
So I was too late to stop him from throwing the leader of the Brisby Killers out the window, hospital bed and all.
POOM
YOU MIGHT HAVE A CONCUSSION.
AND YOU'RE NOT ON THE LIST.
He pointed that gun at me, just where the Joker tore up my spine three years ago. And I froze.
Never again.
Never again!
BATGIRL!
DON'T YOU LEAVE THIS ROOM!
I'M SORRY, DETECTIVE.

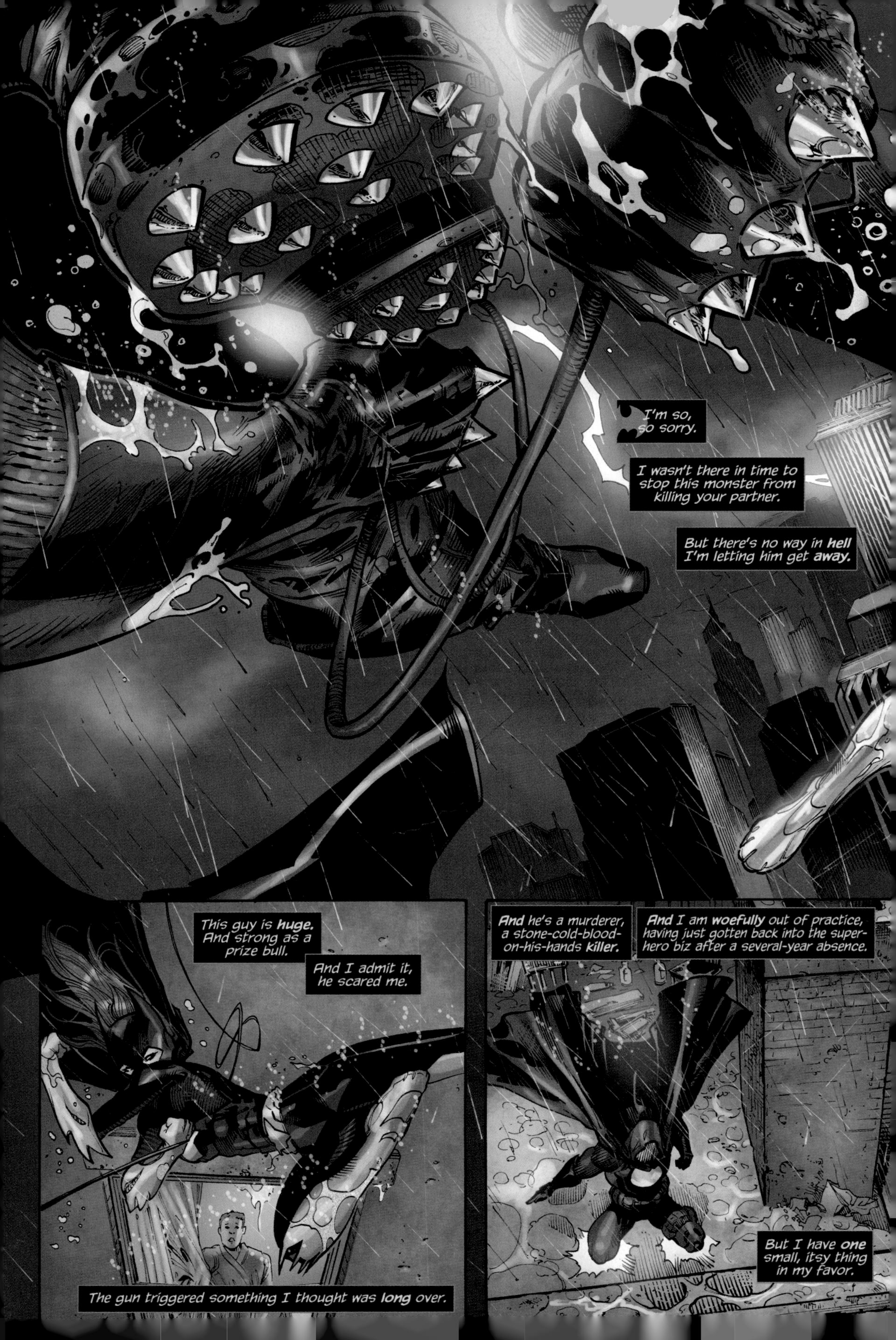
I'm so, so sorry.
I wasn't there in time to stop this monster from killing your partner.
But there's no way in **hell** I'm letting him get **away.**
This guy is **huge.** And strong as a prize bull.
And I admit it, he scared me.
The gun triggered something I thought was **long** over.
And he's a murderer, a stone-cold-blood-on-his-hands **killer.**
And I am **woefully** out of practice, having just gotten back into the super-hero biz after a several-year absence.
But I have **one** small, itsy thing in my favor.

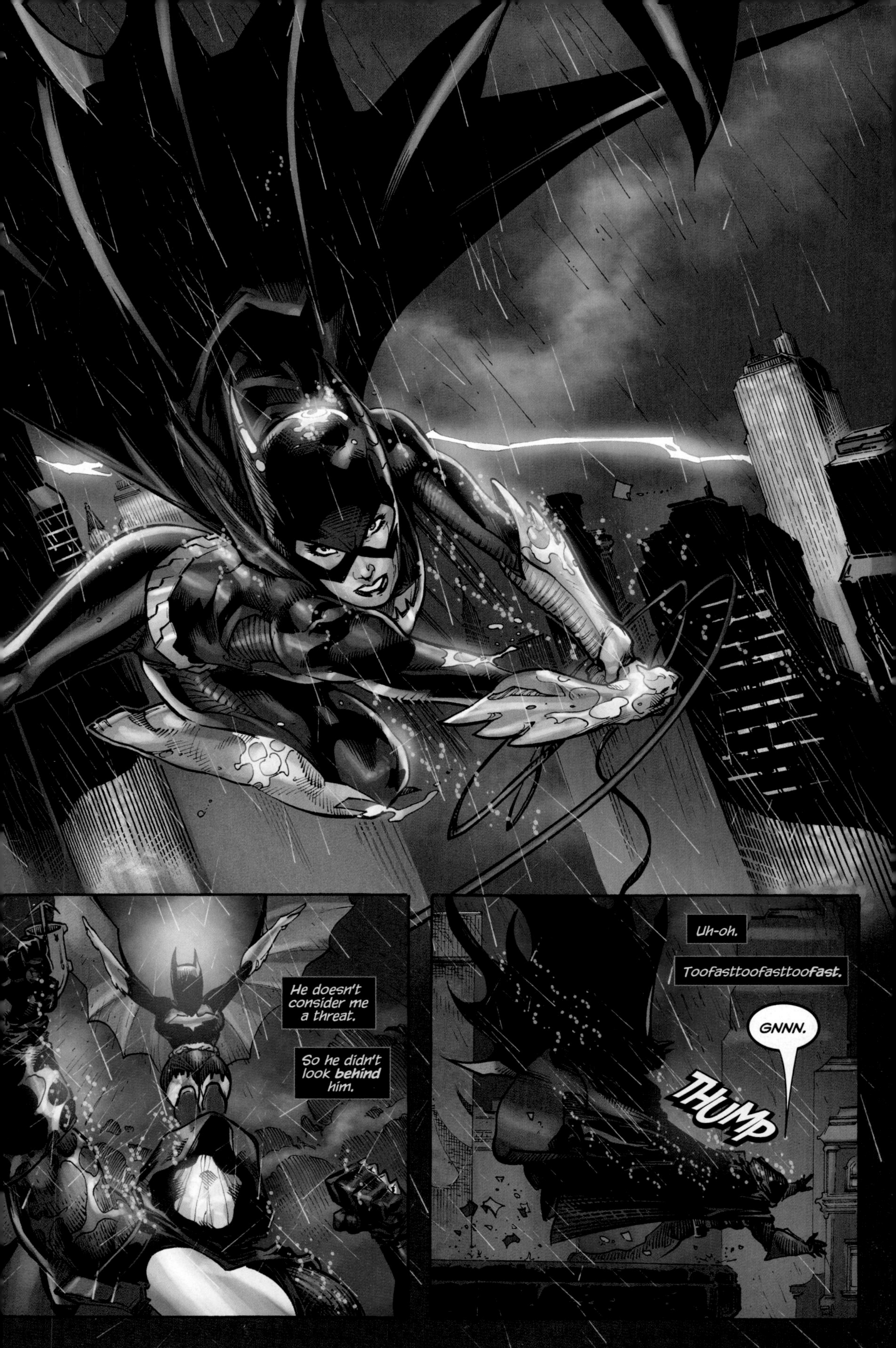
He doesn't consider me a threat.
So he didn't look behind him.
Uh-oh.
Toofasttoofasttoofast.
GNNN.
THUMP

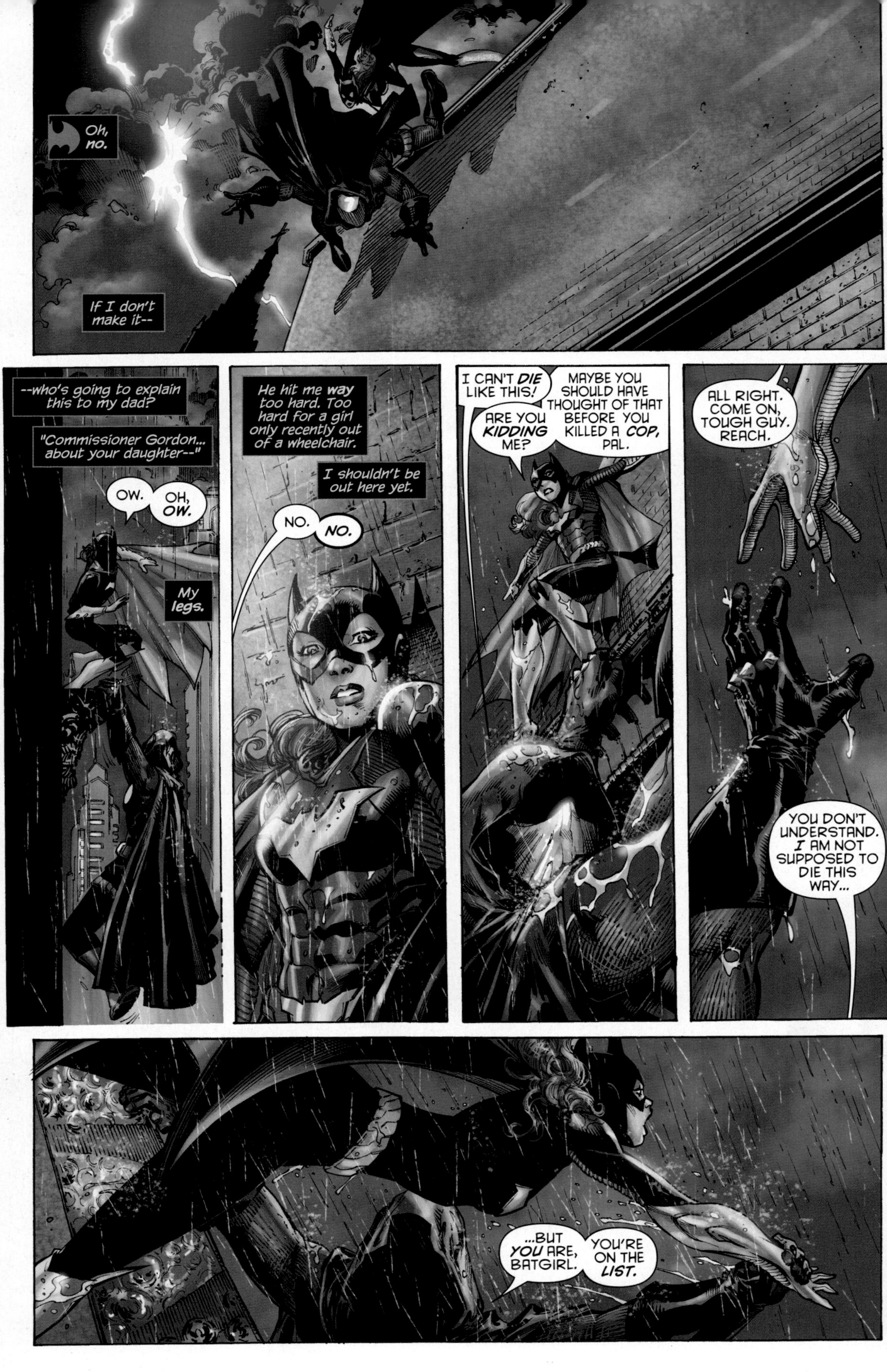
Oh, no.
If I don't make it--
--who's going to explain this to my dad?
"Commissioner Gordon... about your daughter--"
OW.
OH, OW.
My legs.
He hit me way too hard. Too hard for a girl only recently out of a wheelchair.
I shouldn't be out here yet.
NO.
NO.
I CAN'T DIE LIKE THIS!
ARE YOU KIDDING ME?
MAYBE YOU SHOULD HAVE THOUGHT OF THAT BEFORE YOU KILLED A COP, PAL.
ALL RIGHT. COME ON, TOUGH GUY. REACH.
YOU DON'T UNDERSTAND. I AM NOT SUPPOSED TO DIE THIS WAY...
...BUT YOU ARE, BATGIRL.
YOU'RE ON THE LIST.

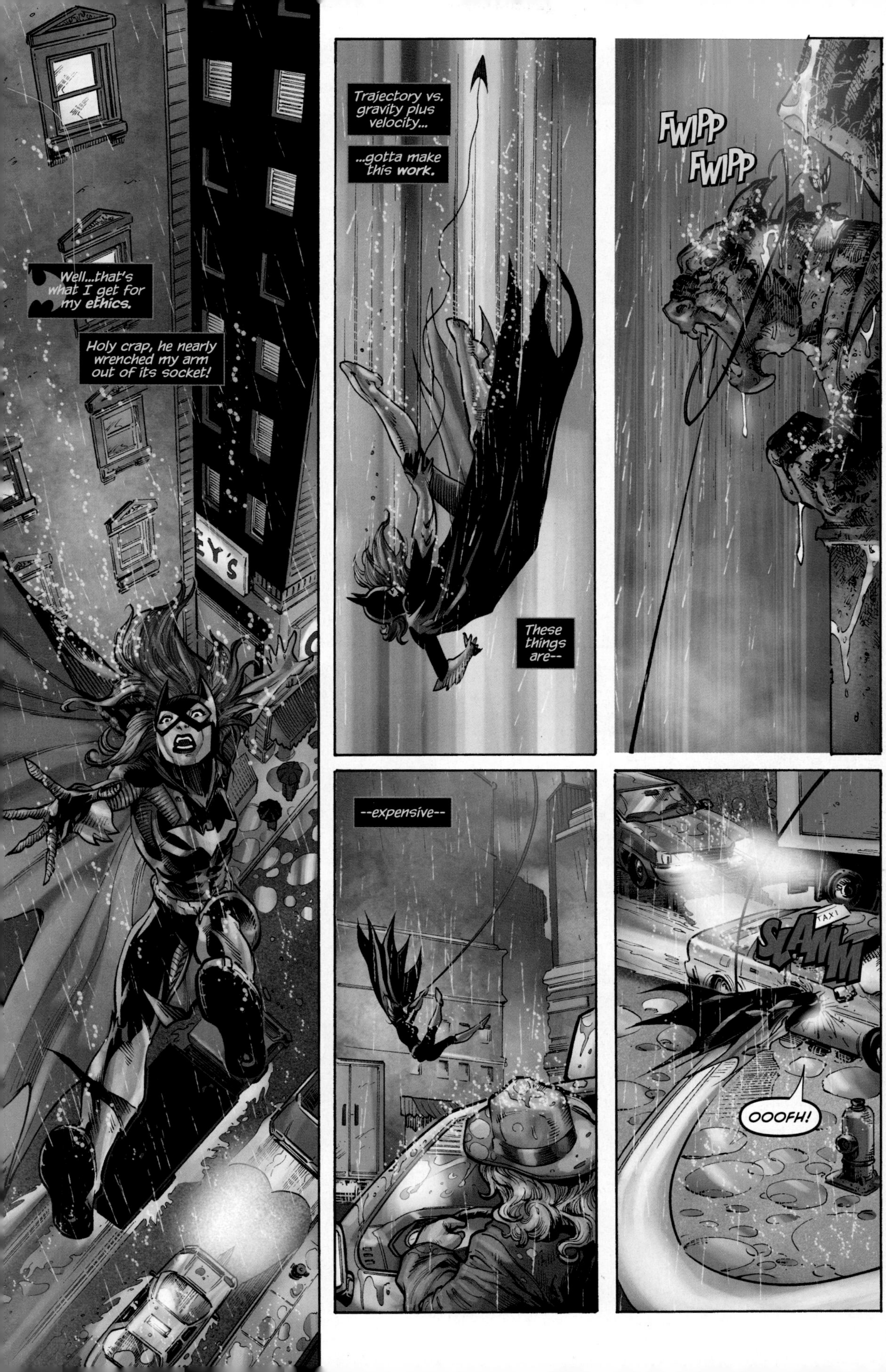

Well...that's what I get for my ethics.
Holy crap, he nearly wrenched my arm out of its socket!
EY'S
Trajectory vs. gravity plus velocity...
...gotta make this work.
These things are--
FWIPP
FWIPP
--expensive--
TAXI
SLAMM
OOOFH!

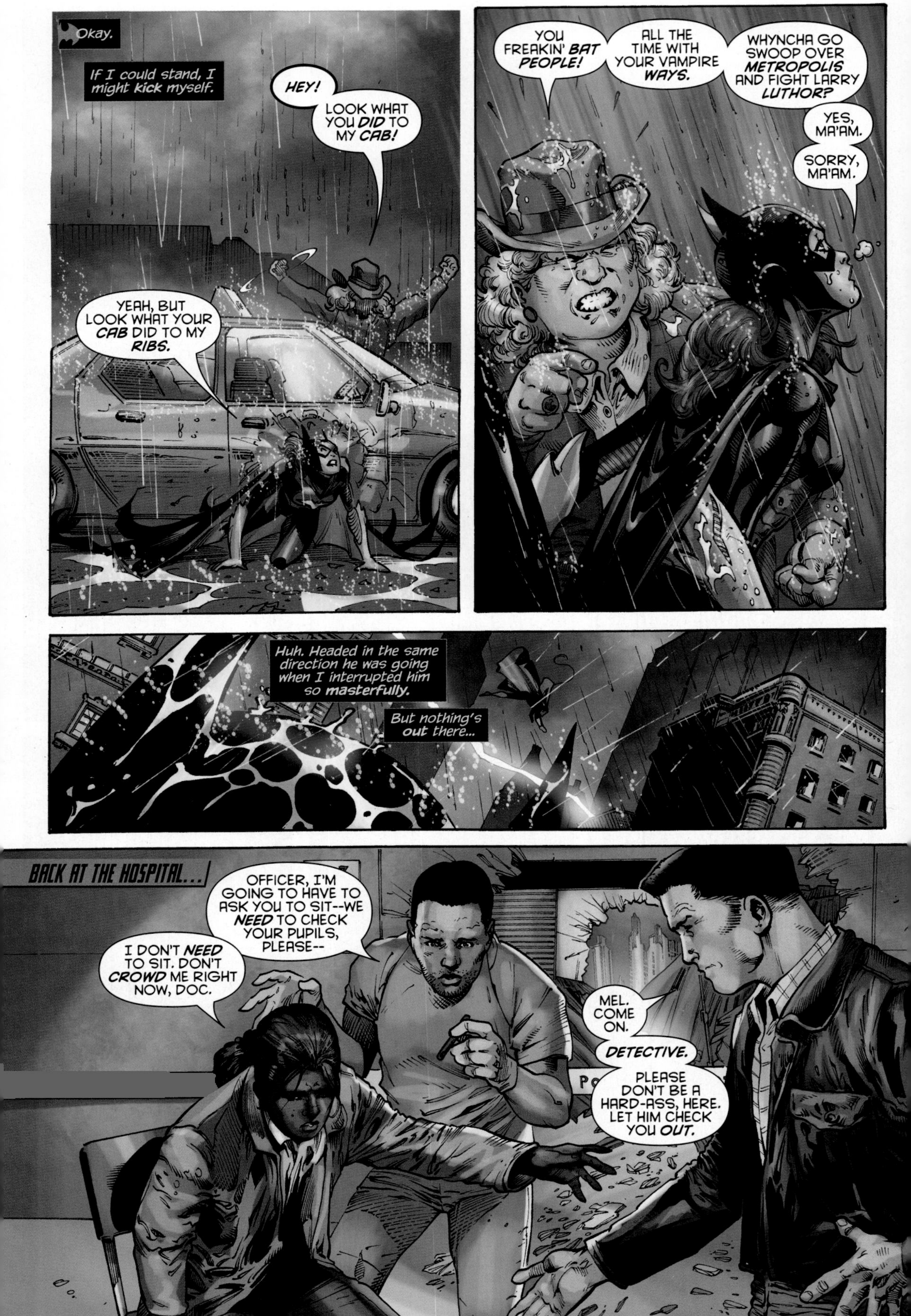
Okay.
If I could stand, I might kick myself.
HEY!
LOOK WHAT YOU DID TO MY CAB!
YEAH, BUT LOOK WHAT YOUR CAB DID TO MY RIBS.
YOU FREAKIN' BAT PEOPLE!
ALL THE TIME WITH YOUR VAMPIRE WAYS.
WHYNCHA GO SWOOP OVER METROPOLIS AND FIGHT LARRY LUTHOR?
YES, MA'AM.
SORRY, MA'AM.
Huh. Headed in the same direction he was going when I interrupted him so masterfully.
But nothing's out there...
BACK AT THE HOSPITAL...
OFFICER, I'M GOING TO HAVE TO ASK YOU TO SIT--WE NEED TO CHECK YOUR PUPILS, PLEASE--
I DON'T NEED TO SIT. DON'T CROWD ME RIGHT NOW, DOC.
MEL. COME ON.
DETECTIVE.
PLEASE DON'T BE A HARD-ASS, HERE. LET HIM CHECK YOU OUT.

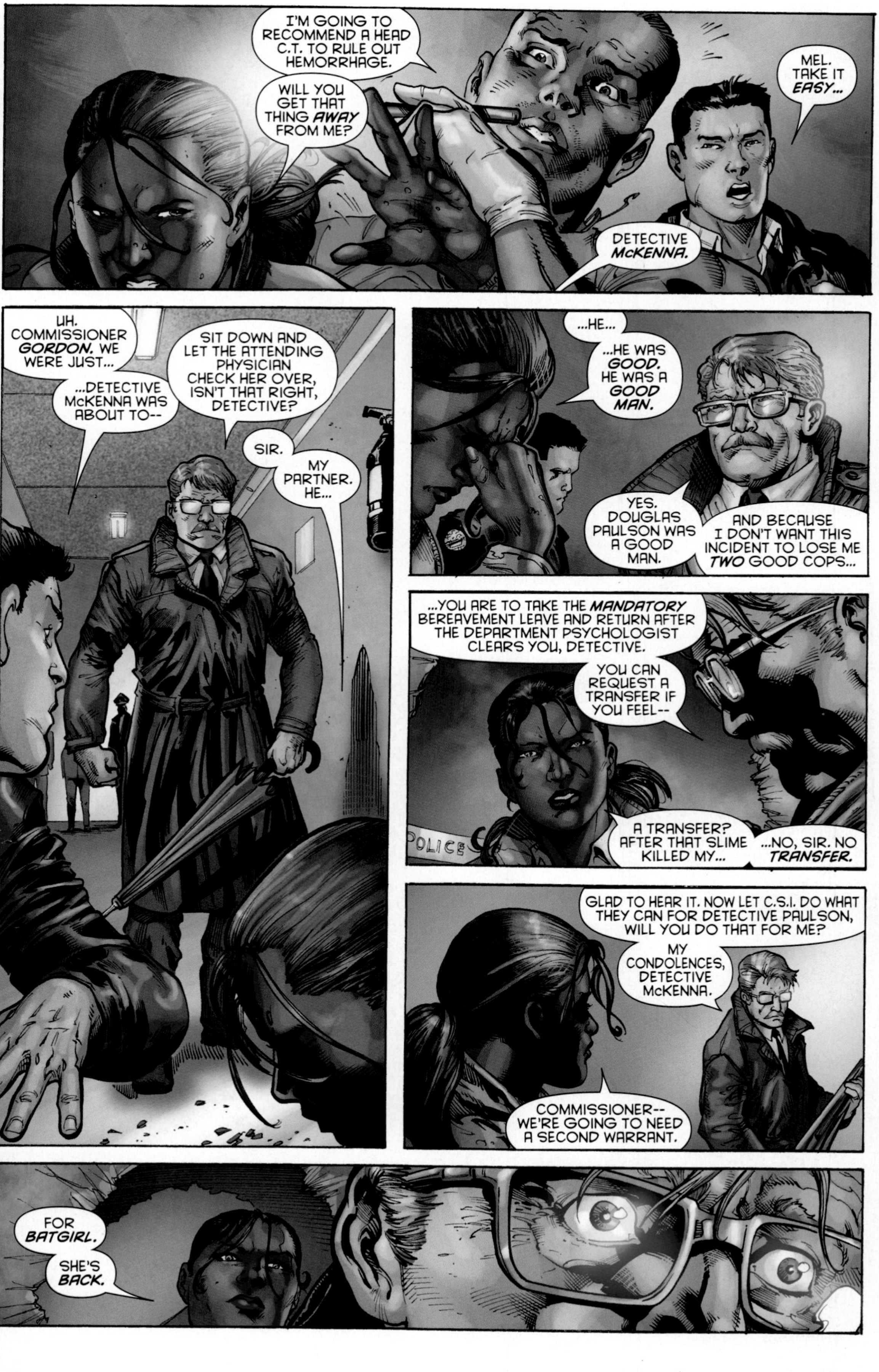

I'M GOING TO RECOMMEND A HEAD C.T. TO RULE OUT HEMORRHAGE.
WILL YOU GET THAT THING AWAY FROM ME?
MEL. TAKE IT EASY...
DETECTIVE McKENNA.
UH. COMMISSIONER GORDON. WE WERE JUST...
...DETECTIVE McKENNA WAS ABOUT TO--
SIT DOWN AND LET THE ATTENDING PHYSICIAN CHECK HER OVER, ISN'T THAT RIGHT, DETECTIVE?
SIR.
MY PARTNER. HE...
...HE...
...HE WAS GOOD. HE WAS A GOOD MAN.
YES. DOUGLAS PAULSON WAS A GOOD MAN.
AND BECAUSE I DON'T WANT THIS INCIDENT TO LOSE ME TWO GOOD COPS...
...YOU ARE TO TAKE THE MANDATORY BEREAVEMENT LEAVE AND RETURN AFTER THE DEPARTMENT PSYCHOLOGIST CLEARS YOU, DETECTIVE.
YOU CAN REQUEST A TRANSFER IF YOU FEEL--
POLICE
A TRANSFER? AFTER THAT SLIME KILLED MY...
...NO, SIR. NO TRANSFER.
GLAD TO HEAR IT. NOW LET C.S.I. DO WHAT THEY CAN FOR DETECTIVE PAULSON, WILL YOU DO THAT FOR ME?
MY CONDOLENCES, DETECTIVE McKENNA.
COMMISSIONER-- WE'RE GOING TO NEED A SECOND WARRANT.
FOR BATGIRL.
SHE'S BACK.

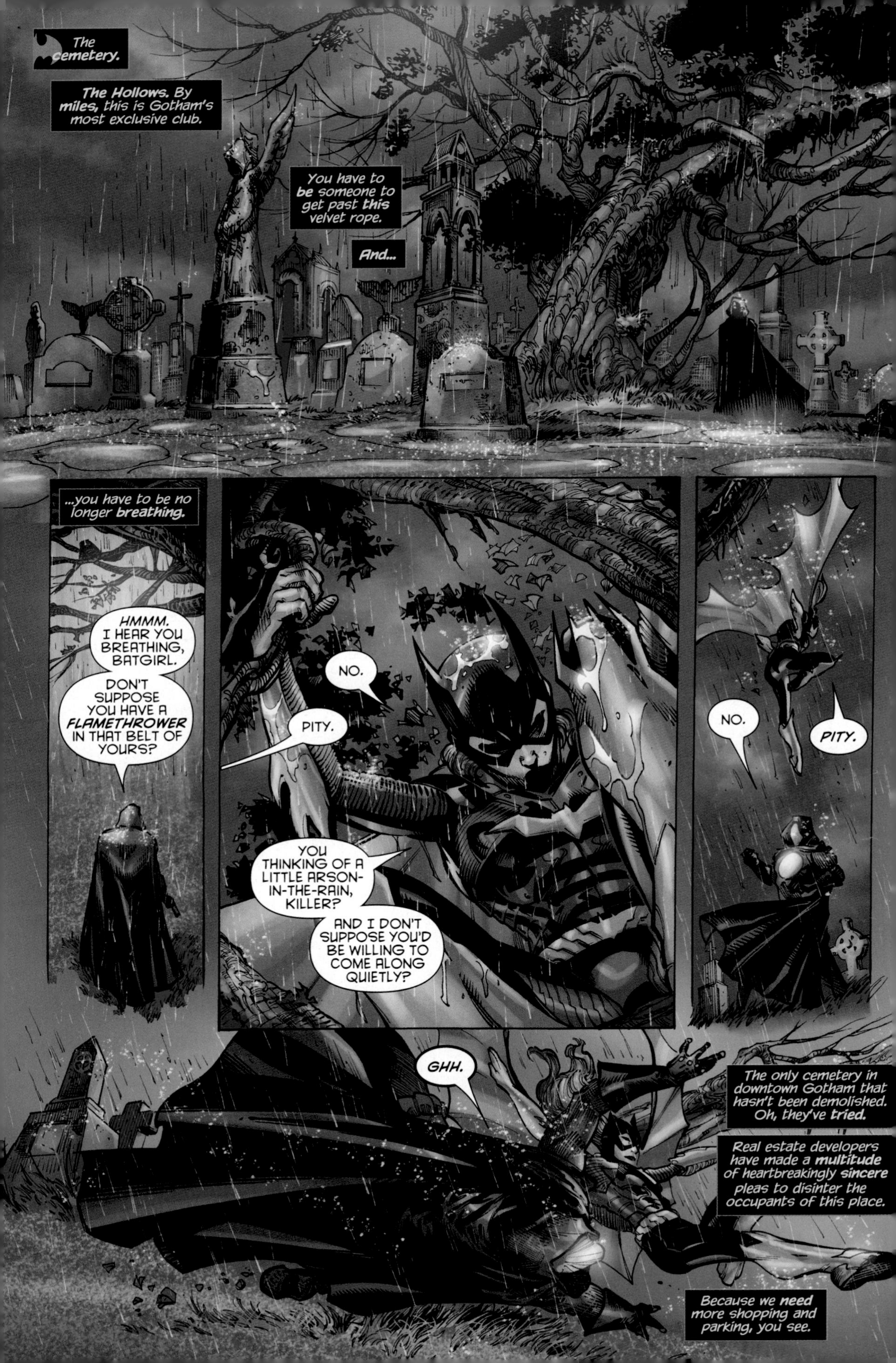
The cemetery.
The Hollows. By miles, this is Gotham's most exclusive club.
You have to be someone to get past this velvet rope.
And...
...you have to be no longer breathing.
HMMM. I HEAR YOU BREATHING, BATGIRL.
DON'T SUPPOSE YOU HAVE A FLAMETHROWER IN THAT BELT OF YOURS?
NO.
PITY.
YOU THINKING OF A LITTLE ARSON-IN-THE-RAIN, KILLER?
AND I DON'T SUPPOSE YOU'D BE WILLING TO COME ALONG QUIETLY?
NO.
PITY.
GHH.
The only cemetery in downtown Gotham that hasn't been demolished. Oh, they've tried.
Real estate developers have made a multitude of heartbreakingly sincere pleas to disinter the occupants of this place.
Because we need more shopping and parking, you see.

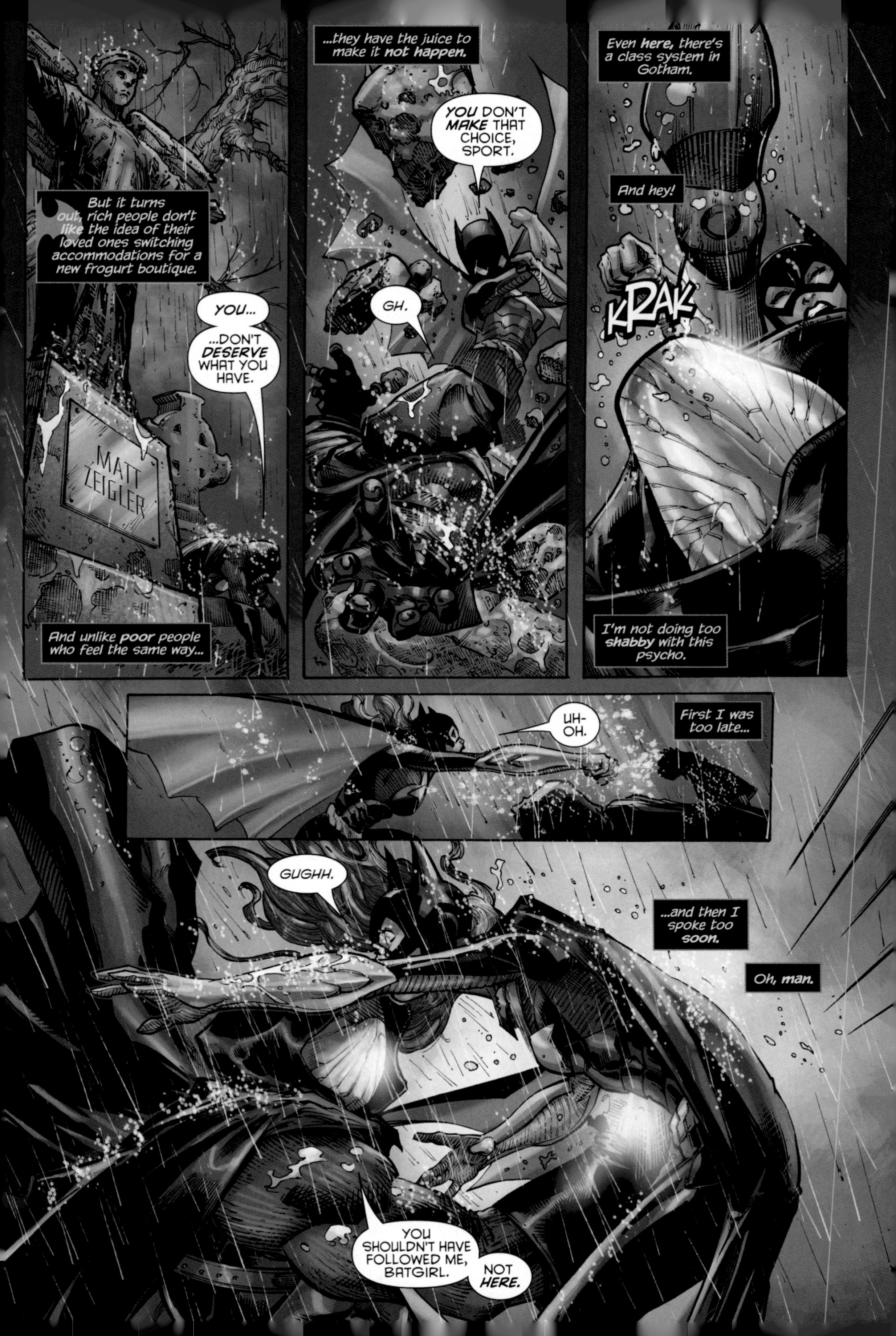

But it turns out, rich people don't like the idea of their loved ones switching accommodations for a new frogurt boutique.
YOU...
...DON'T DESERVE WHAT YOU HAVE.
MATT ZEIGLER
And unlike poor people who feel the same way...
...they have the juice to make it not happen.
YOU DON'T MAKE THAT CHOICE, SPORT.
GH.
Even here, there's a class system in Gotham.
And hey!
KRAK
I'm not doing too shabby with this psycho.
UH-OH.
First I was too late...
GUGHH.
...and then I spoke too soon.
Oh, man.
YOU SHOULDN'T HAVE FOLLOWED ME, BATGIRL.
NOT HERE.

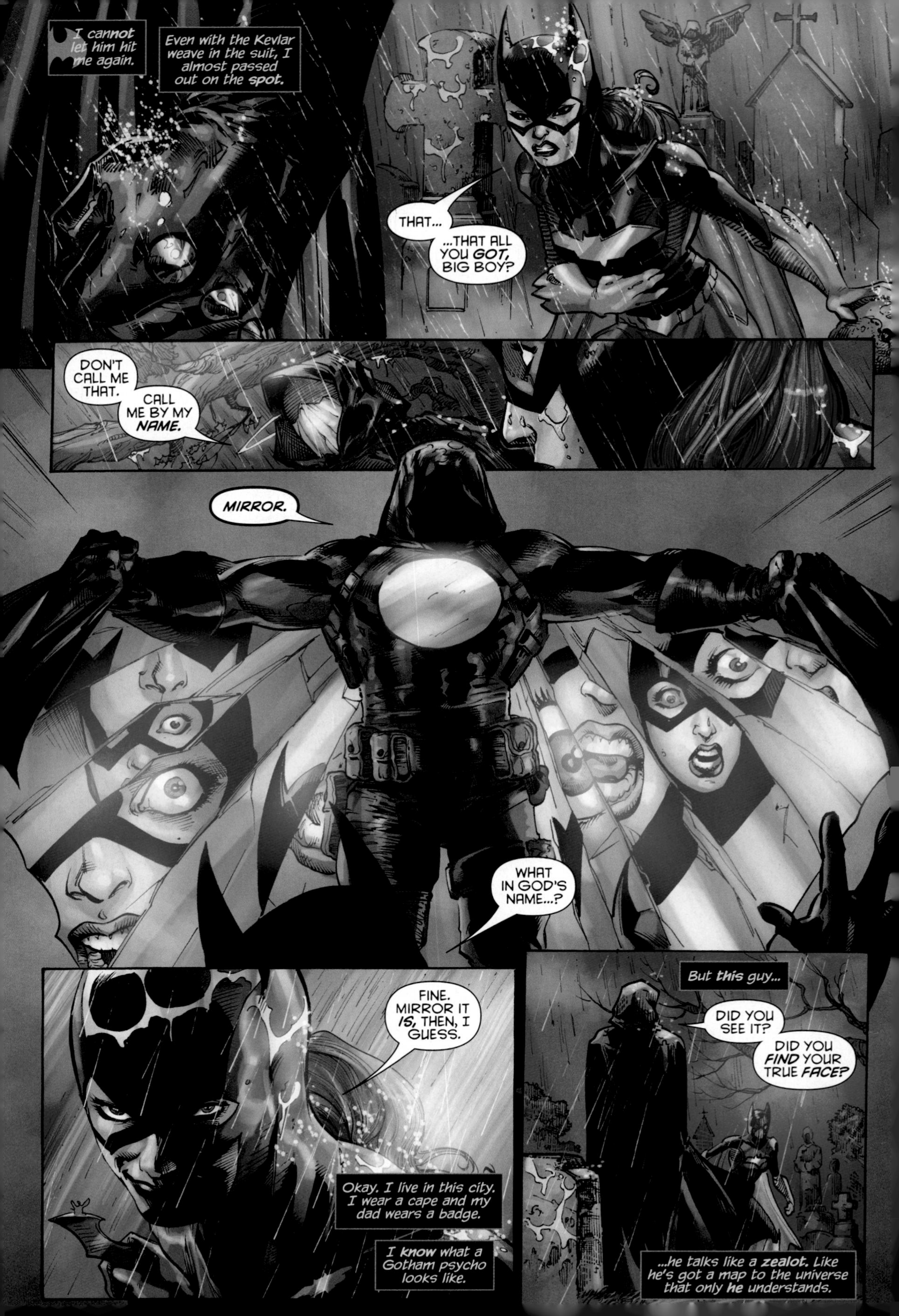
I cannot let him hit me again.
Even with the Kevlar weave in the suit, I almost passed out on the spot.
THAT...
...THAT ALL YOU GOT, BIG BOY?
DON'T CALL ME THAT.
CALL ME BY MY NAME.
MIRROR.
WHAT IN GOD'S NAME...?
FINE. MIRROR IT IS, THEN, I GUESS.
Okay. I live in this city. I wear a cape and my dad wears a badge.
I know what a Gotham psycho looks like.
But this guy...
DID YOU SEE IT?
DID YOU FIND YOUR TRUE FACE?
...he talks like a zealot. Like he's got a map to the universe that only he understands.

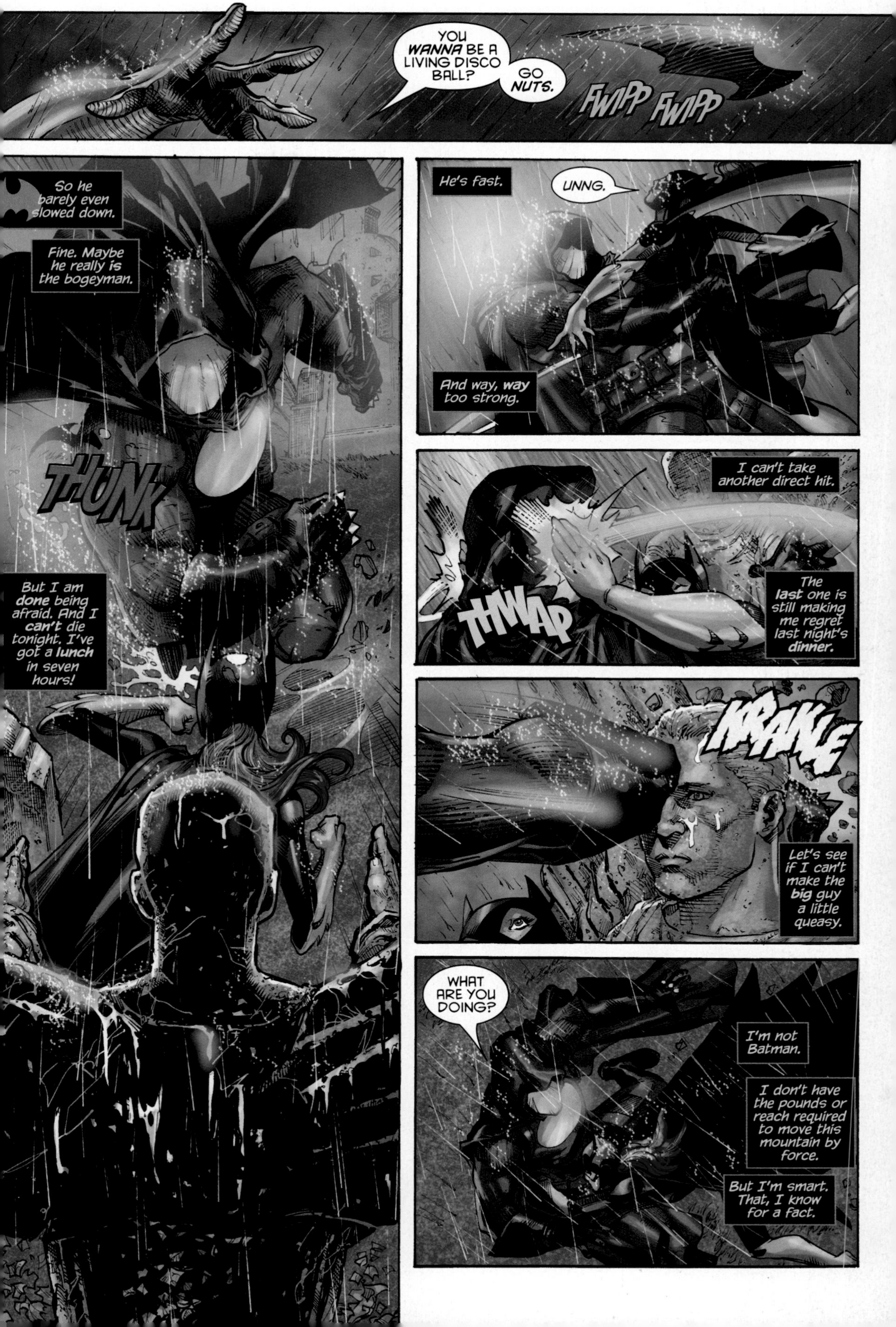

YOU WANNA BE A LIVING DISCO BALL?
GO NUTS.
FWIPP FWIPP
So he barely even slowed down.
Fine. Maybe he really is the bogeyman.
THUNK
But I am done being afraid. And I can't die tonight. I've got a lunch in seven hours!
He's fast.
UNNG.
And way, way too strong.
I can't take another direct hit.
THWAP
The last one is still making me regret last night's dinner.
KRAKLE
Let's see if I can't make the big guy a little queasy.
WHAT ARE YOU DOING?
I'm not Batman.
I don't have the pounds or reach required to move this mountain by force.
But I'm smart. That, I know for a fact.

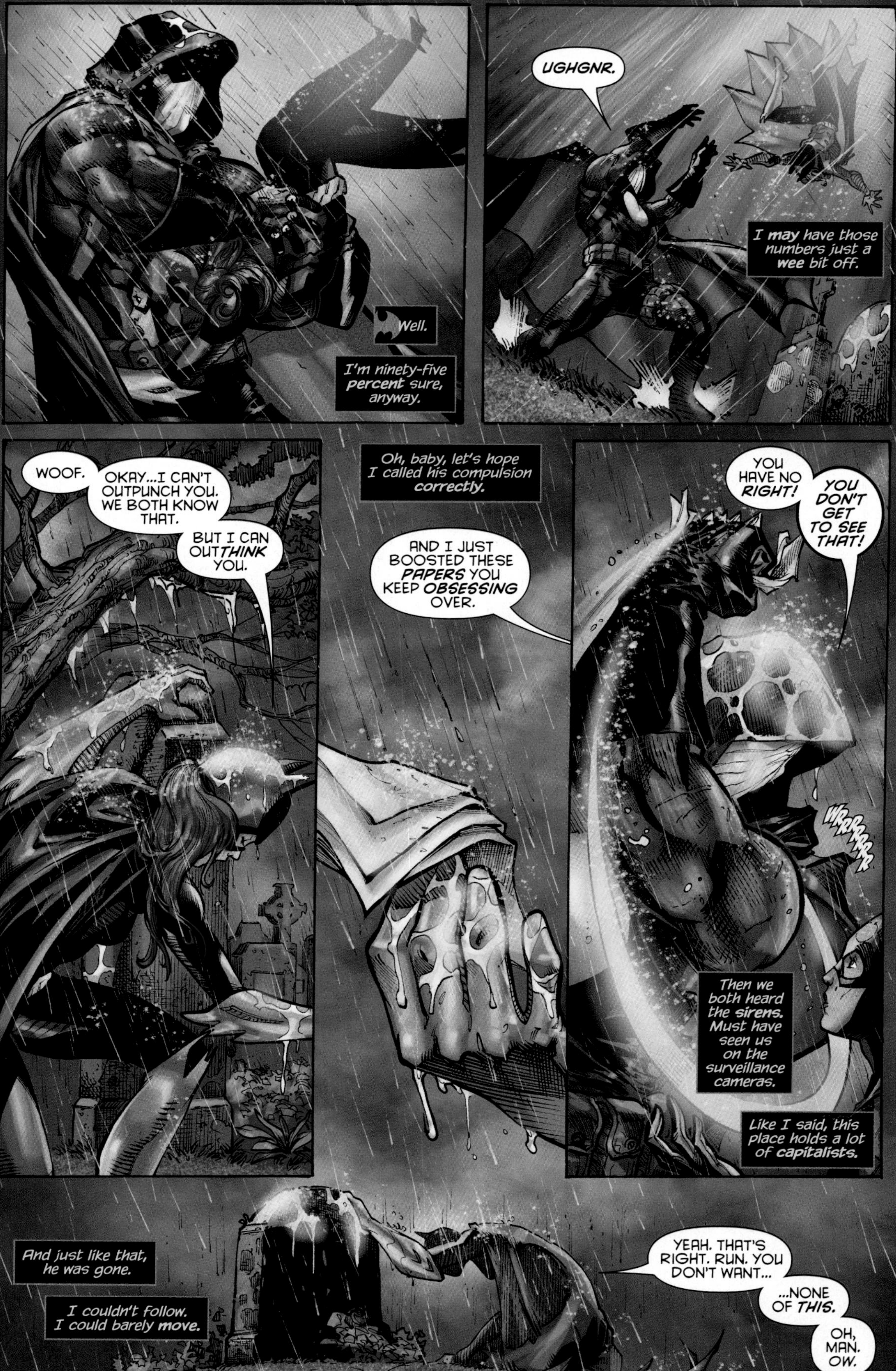
Well.
I'm ninety-five percent sure, anyway.
UGHGNR.
I may have those numbers just a wee bit off.
WOOF.
OKAY...I CAN'T OUTPUNCH YOU. WE BOTH KNOW THAT.
BUT I CAN OUTTHINK YOU.
Oh, baby, let's hope I called his compulsion correctly.
AND I JUST BOOSTED THESE PAPERS YOU KEEP OBSESSING OVER.
YOU HAVE NO RIGHT!
YOU DON'T GET TO SEE THAT!
WRRRRRRR
Then we both heard the sirens. Must have seen us on the surveillance cameras.
Like I said, this place holds a lot of capitalists.
And just like that, he was gone.
I couldn't follow. I could barely move.
YEAH. THAT'S RIGHT. RUN. YOU DON'T WANT...
...NONE OF THIS.
OH, MAN. OW.

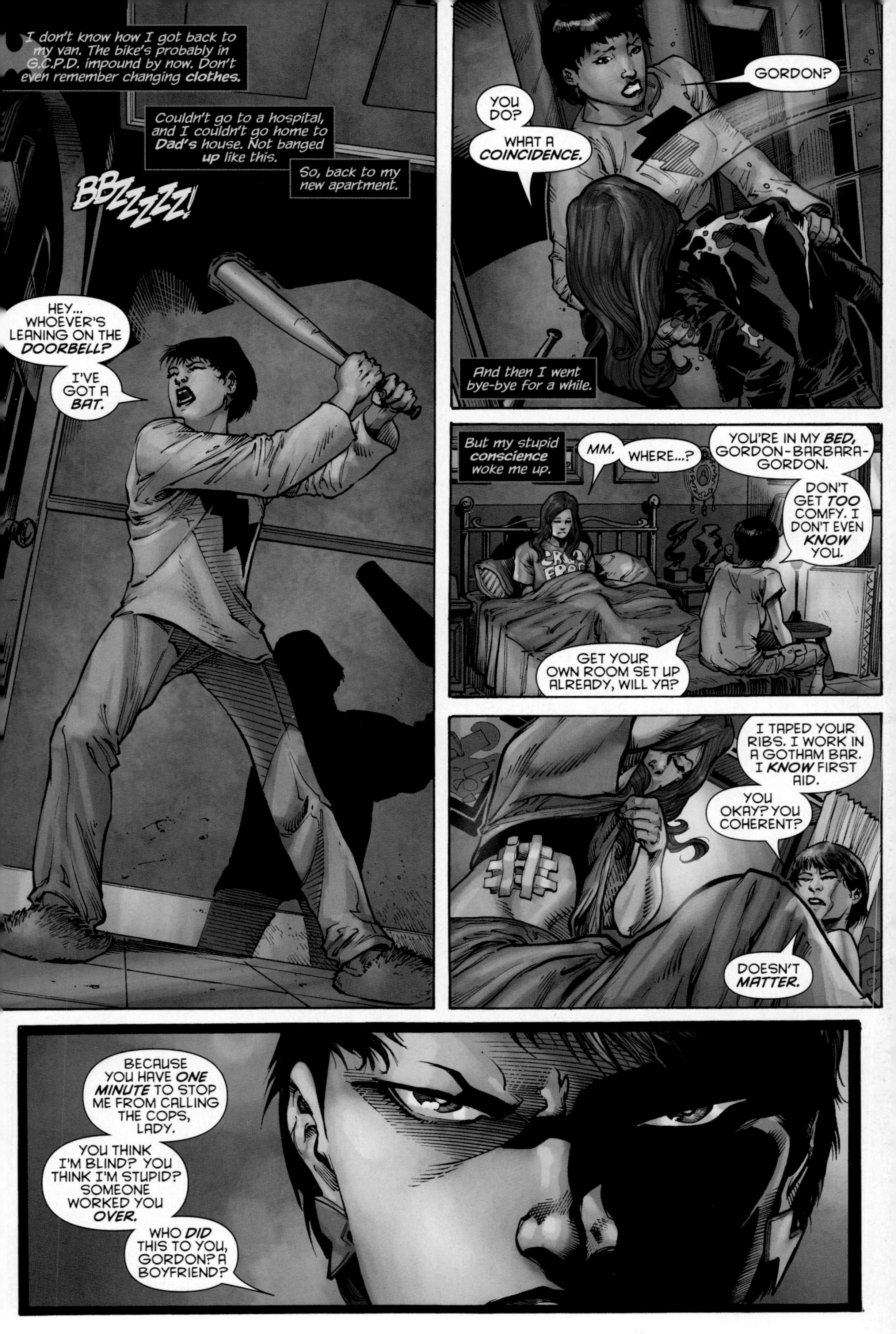

I don't know how I got back to my van. The bike's probably in G.C.P.D. impound by now. Don't even remember changing clothes.
Couldn't go to a hospital, and I couldn't go home to Dad's house. Not banged up like this.
So, back to my new apartment.
BBZZZZZ!
HEY... WHOEVER'S LEANING ON THE DOORBELL?
I'VE GOT A BAT.
GORDON?
YOU DO?
WHAT A COINCIDENCE.
And then I went bye-bye for a while.
But my stupid conscience woke me up.
MM.
WHERE...?
YOU'RE IN MY BED, GORDON-BARBARA-GORDON.
DON'T GET TOO COMFY. I DON'T EVEN KNOW YOU.
GET YOUR OWN ROOM SET UP ALREADY, WILL YA?
I TAPED YOUR RIBS. I WORK IN A GOTHAM BAR. I KNOW FIRST AID.
YOU OKAY? YOU COHERENT?
DOESN'T MATTER.
BECAUSE YOU HAVE ONE MINUTE TO STOP ME FROM CALLING THE COPS, LADY.
YOU THINK I'M BLIND? YOU THINK I'M STUPID? SOMEONE WORKED YOU OVER.
WHO DID THIS TO YOU, GORDON? A BOYFRIEND?

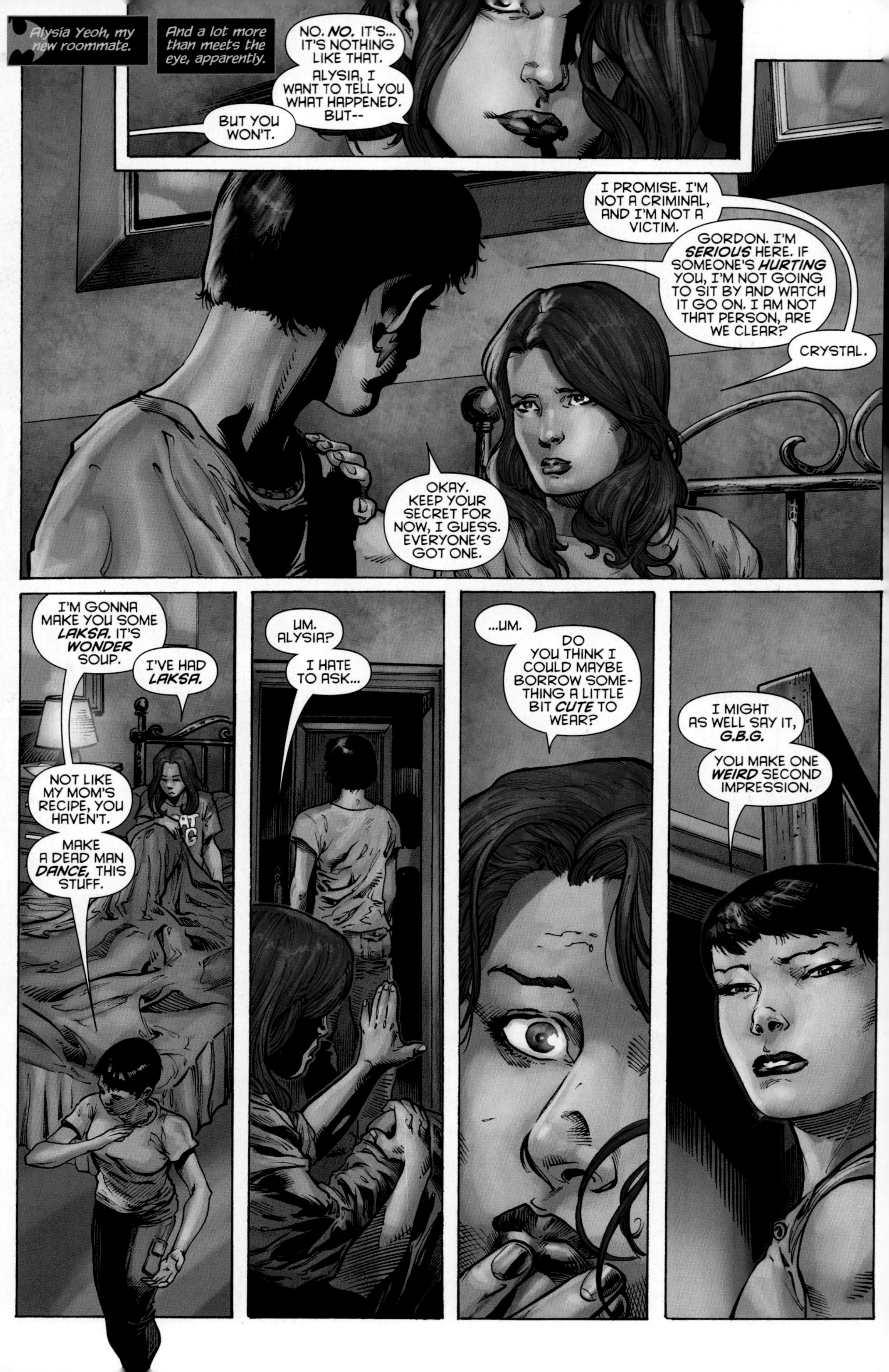
Alysia Yeoh, my new roommate.
And a lot more than meets the eye, apparently.
NO. NO. IT'S... IT'S NOTHING LIKE THAT.
ALYSIA, I WANT TO TELL YOU WHAT HAPPENED. BUT--
BUT YOU WON'T.
I PROMISE. I'M NOT A CRIMINAL, AND I'M NOT A VICTIM.
GORDON. I'M SERIOUS HERE. IF SOMEONE'S HURTING YOU, I'M NOT GOING TO SIT BY AND WATCH IT GO ON. I AM NOT THAT PERSON, ARE WE CLEAR?
CRYSTAL.
OKAY. KEEP YOUR SECRET FOR NOW, I GUESS. EVERYONE'S GOT ONE.
I'M GONNA MAKE YOU SOME LAKSA. IT'S WONDER SOUP.
I'VE HAD LAKSA.
NOT LIKE MY MOM'S RECIPE, YOU HAVEN'T.
MAKE A DEAD MAN DANCE, THIS STUFF.
UM. ALYSIA?
I HATE TO ASK...
...UM.
DO YOU THINK I COULD MAYBE BORROW SOMETHING A LITTLE BIT CUTE TO WEAR?
I MIGHT AS WELL SAY IT, G.B.G.
YOU MAKE ONE WEIRD SECOND IMPRESSION.

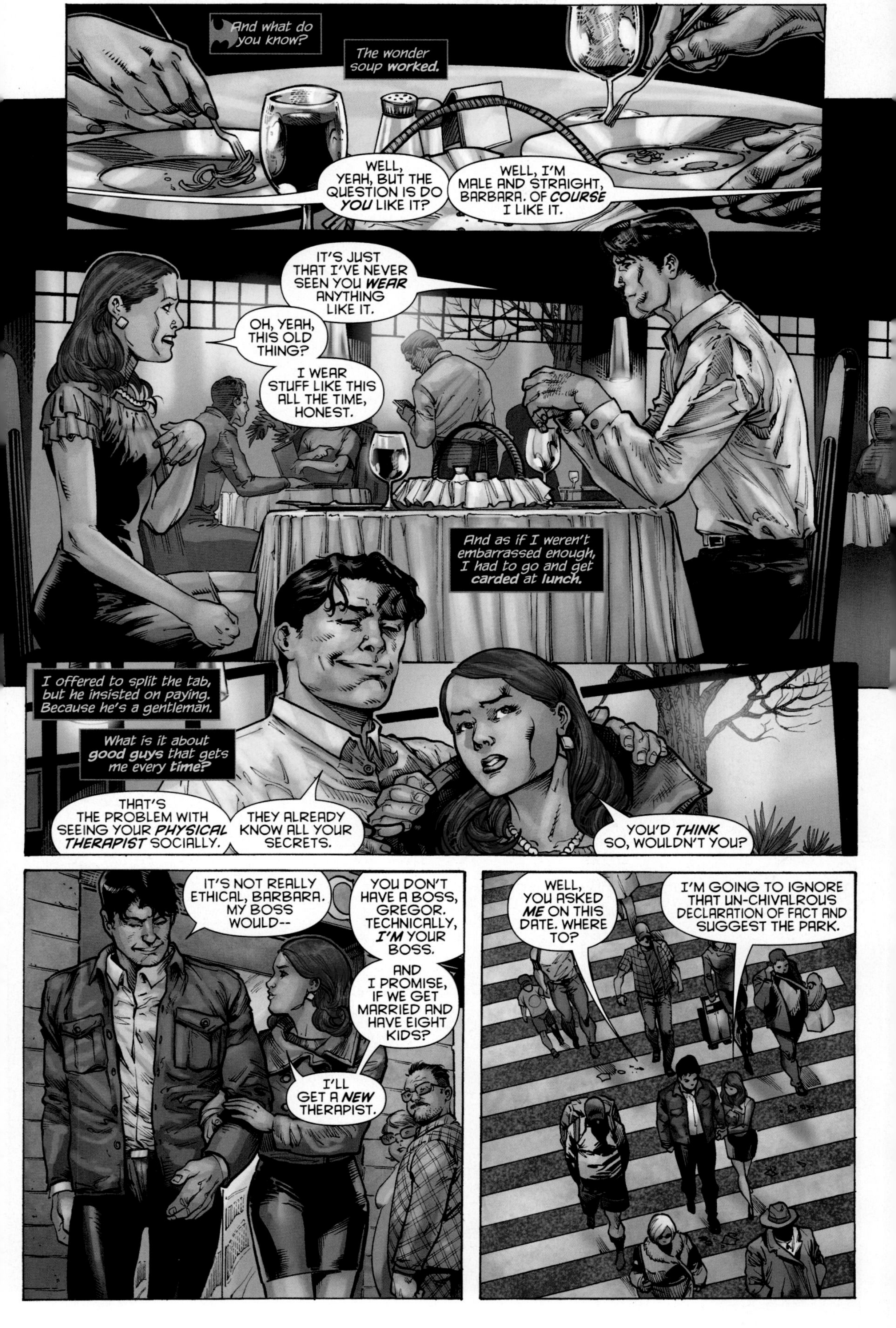
And what do you know?
The wonder soup worked.
WELL, YEAH, BUT THE QUESTION IS DO YOU LIKE IT?
WELL, I'M MALE AND STRAIGHT, BARBARA. OF COURSE I LIKE IT.
IT'S JUST THAT I'VE NEVER SEEN YOU WEAR ANYTHING LIKE IT.
OH, YEAH, THIS OLD THING?
I WEAR STUFF LIKE THIS ALL THE TIME, HONEST.
And as if I weren't embarrassed enough, I had to go and get carded at lunch.
I offered to split the tab, but he insisted on paying. Because he's a gentleman.
What is it about good guys that gets me every time?
THAT'S THE PROBLEM WITH SEEING YOUR PHYSICAL THERAPIST SOCIALLY.
THEY ALREADY KNOW ALL YOUR SECRETS.
YOU'D THINK SO, WOULDN'T YOU?
IT'S NOT REALLY ETHICAL, BARBARA. MY BOSS WOULD--
YOU DON'T HAVE A BOSS, GREGOR. TECHNICALLY, I'M YOUR BOSS.
AND I PROMISE, IF WE GET MARRIED AND HAVE EIGHT KIDS?
I'LL GET A NEW THERAPIST.
WELL, YOU ASKED ME ON THIS DATE. WHERE TO?
I'M GOING TO IGNORE THAT UN-CHIVALROUS DECLARATION OF FACT AND SUGGEST THE PARK.

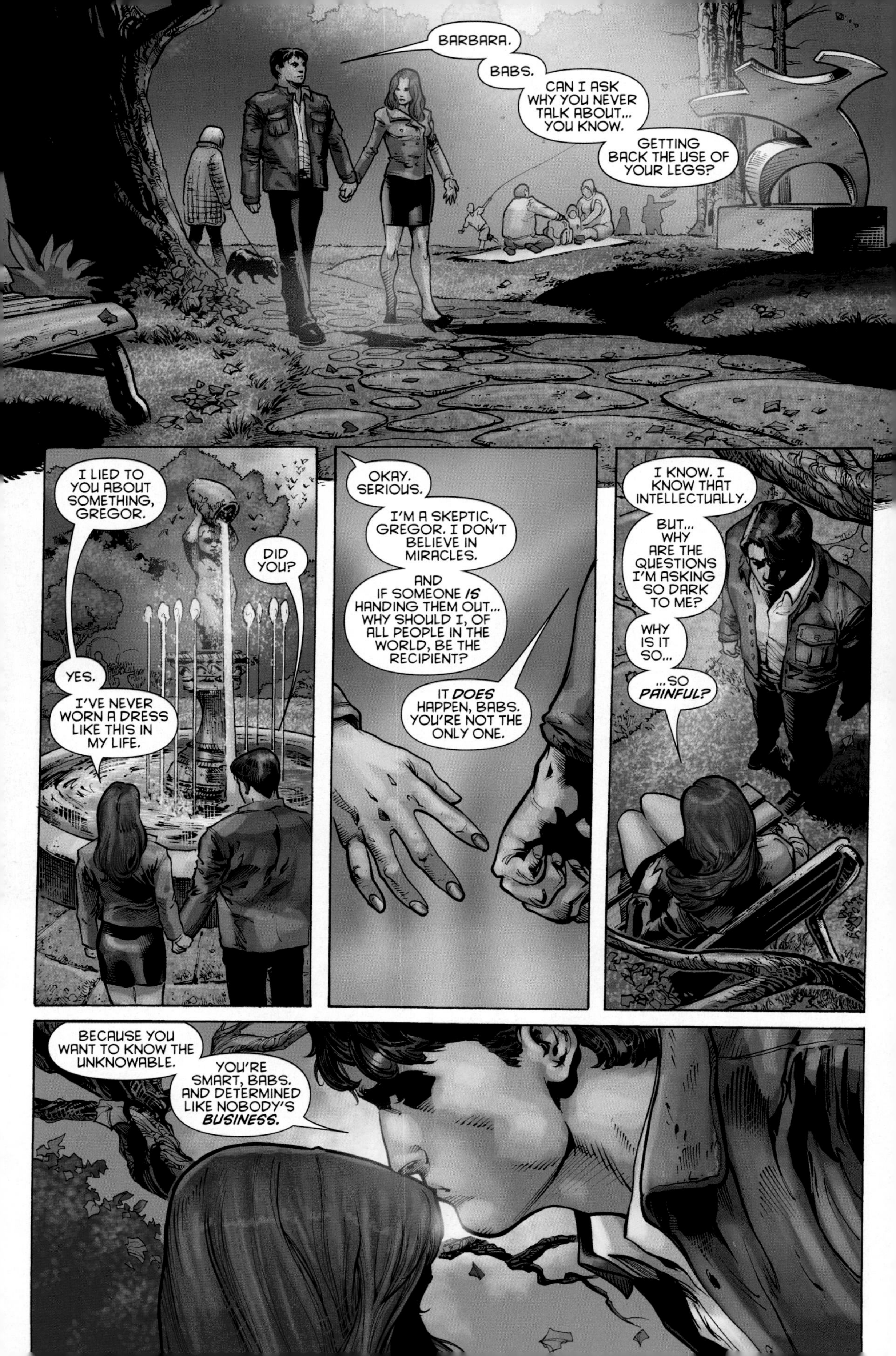
BARBARA.
BABS.
CAN I ASK WHY YOU NEVER TALK ABOUT... YOU KNOW.
GETTING BACK THE USE OF YOUR LEGS?
I LIED TO YOU ABOUT SOMETHING, GREGOR.
DID YOU?
YES.
I'VE NEVER WORN A DRESS LIKE THIS IN MY LIFE.
OKAY. SERIOUS.
I'M A SKEPTIC, GREGOR. I DON'T BELIEVE IN MIRACLES.
AND IF SOMEONE *IS* HANDING THEM OUT... WHY SHOULD I, OF ALL PEOPLE IN THE WORLD, BE THE RECIPIENT?
IT *DOES* HAPPEN, BABS. YOU'RE NOT THE ONLY ONE.
I KNOW. I KNOW THAT INTELLECTUALLY.
BUT... WHY ARE THE QUESTIONS I'M ASKING SO DARK TO ME?
WHY IS IT SO...
...SO *PAINFUL?*
BECAUSE YOU WANT TO KNOW THE UNKNOWABLE.
YOU'RE SMART, BABS. AND DETERMINED LIKE NOBODY'S *BUSINESS.*

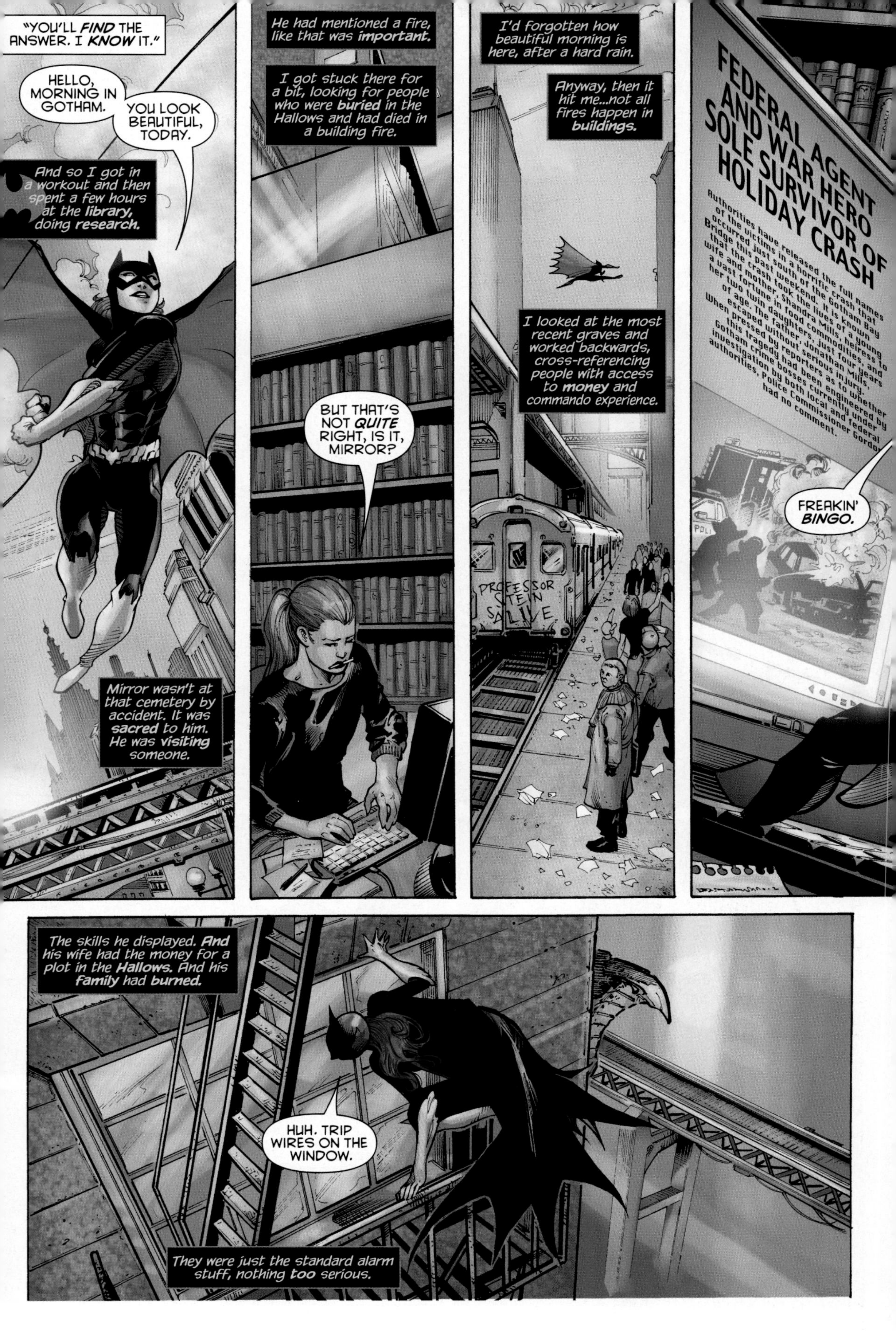
"YOU'LL FIND THE ANSWER. I KNOW IT."
HELLO, MORNING IN GOTHAM.
YOU LOOK BEAUTIFUL, TODAY.
And so I got in a workout and then spent a few hours at the library, doing research.
Mirror wasn't at that cemetery by accident. It was sacred to him. He was visiting someone.
He had mentioned a fire, like that was important.
I got stuck there for a bit, looking for people who were buried in the Hallows and had died in a building fire.
BUT THAT'S NOT QUITE RIGHT, IS IT, MIRROR?
I'd forgotten how beautiful morning is here, after a hard rain.
Anyway, then it hit me...not all fires happen in buildings.
I looked at the most recent graves and worked backwards, cross-referencing people with access to money and commando experience.
PROFESSOR STEIN SALIVE
FEDERAL AGENT AND WAR HERO SOLE SURVIVOR OF HOLIDAY CRASH
Authorities have released the full names of the victims in a horrific crash that occurred just south of the Gotham Bay Bridge this past weekend. It is known that the crash took the lives of a young wife and mother, Shandra Mills, heiress to a vast fortune in food commodities, and her two twin daughters, just four years of age. The father, Jonathan Mills, escaped without serious injury. When pressed by reporters as to whether this tragedy had been engineered by Gotham crime bosses currently under investigation by both local and federal authorities, Police Commissioner Gordon had no comment.
FREAKIN' BINGO.
The skills he displayed. And his wife had the money for a plot in the Hallows. And his family had burned.
HUH. TRIP WIRES ON THE WINDOW.
They were just the standard alarm stuff, nothing too serious.

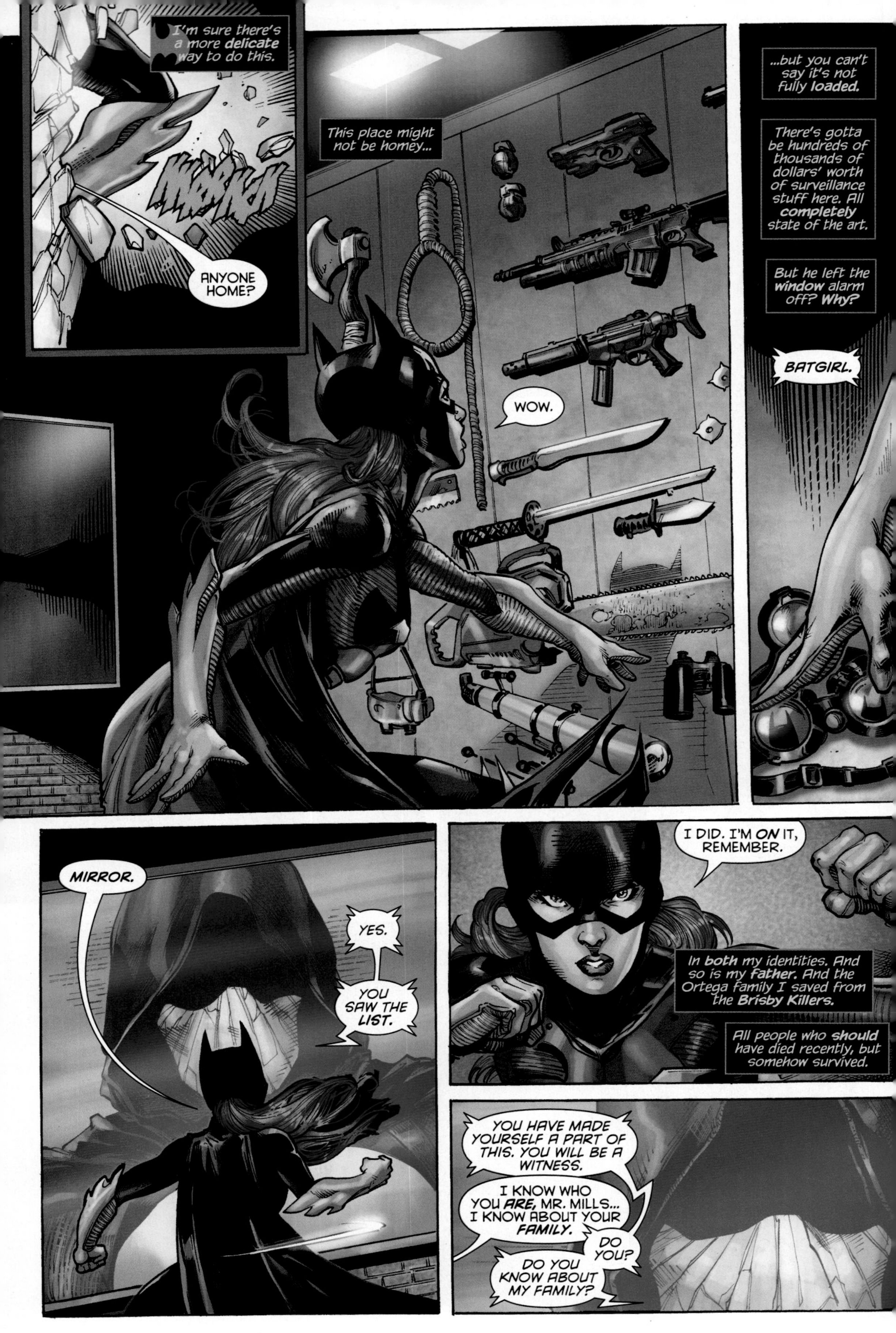

I'm sure there's a more delicate way to do this.
WHAKKK
ANYONE HOME?
This place might not be homey...
...but you can't say it's not fully loaded.
There's gotta be hundreds of thousands of dollars' worth of surveillance stuff here. All completely state of the art.
But he left the window alarm off? Why?
WOW.
BATGIRL.
MIRROR.
YES.
YOU SAW THE LIST.
I DID. I'M ON IT, REMEMBER.
In both my identities. And so is my father. And the Ortega family I saved from the Brisby Killers.
All people who should have died recently, but somehow survived.
YOU HAVE MADE YOURSELF A PART OF THIS. YOU WILL BE A WITNESS.
I KNOW WHO YOU ARE, MR. MILLS... I KNOW ABOUT YOUR FAMILY.
DO YOU?
DO YOU KNOW ABOUT MY FAMILY?

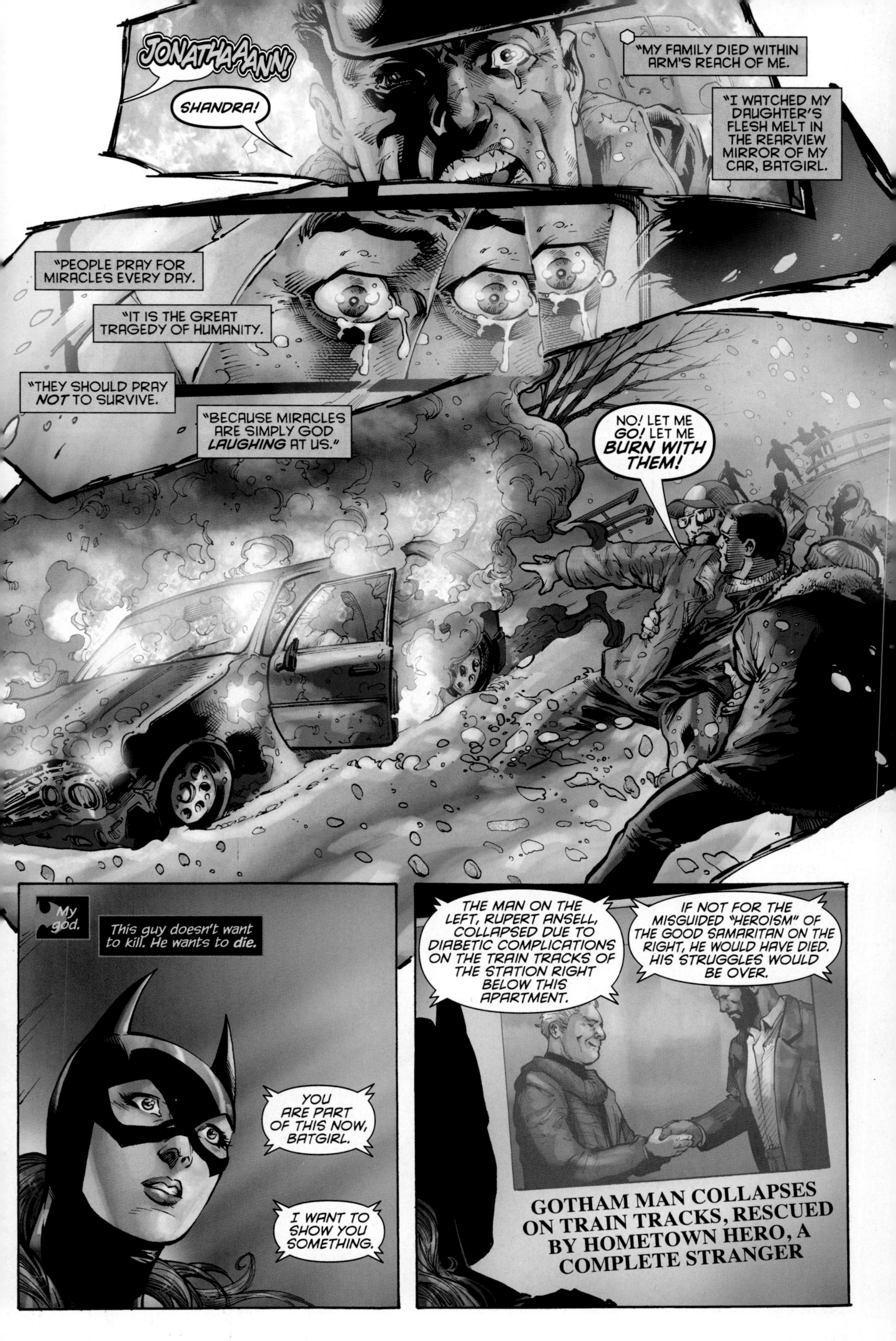
JONATHAAANN!
SHANDRA!
"MY FAMILY DIED WITHIN ARM'S REACH OF ME.
"I WATCHED MY DAUGHTER'S FLESH MELT IN THE REARVIEW MIRROR OF MY CAR, BATGIRL.
"PEOPLE PRAY FOR MIRACLES EVERY DAY.
"IT IS THE GREAT TRAGEDY OF HUMANITY.
"THEY SHOULD PRAY NOT TO SURVIVE.
"BECAUSE MIRACLES ARE SIMPLY GOD LAUGHING AT US."
NO! LET ME GO! LET ME BURN WITH THEM!
My god.
This guy doesn't want to kill. He wants to die.
YOU ARE PART OF THIS NOW, BATGIRL.
I WANT TO SHOW YOU SOMETHING.
THE MAN ON THE LEFT, RUPERT ANSELL, COLLAPSED DUE TO DIABETIC COMPLICATIONS ON THE TRAIN TRACKS OF THE STATION RIGHT BELOW THIS APARTMENT.
IF NOT FOR THE MISGUIDED "HEROISM" OF THE GOOD SAMARITAN ON THE RIGHT, HE WOULD HAVE DIED. HIS STRUGGLES WOULD BE OVER.
GOTHAM MAN COLLAPSES ON TRAIN TRACKS, RESCUED BY HOMETOWN HERO, A COMPLETE STRANGER

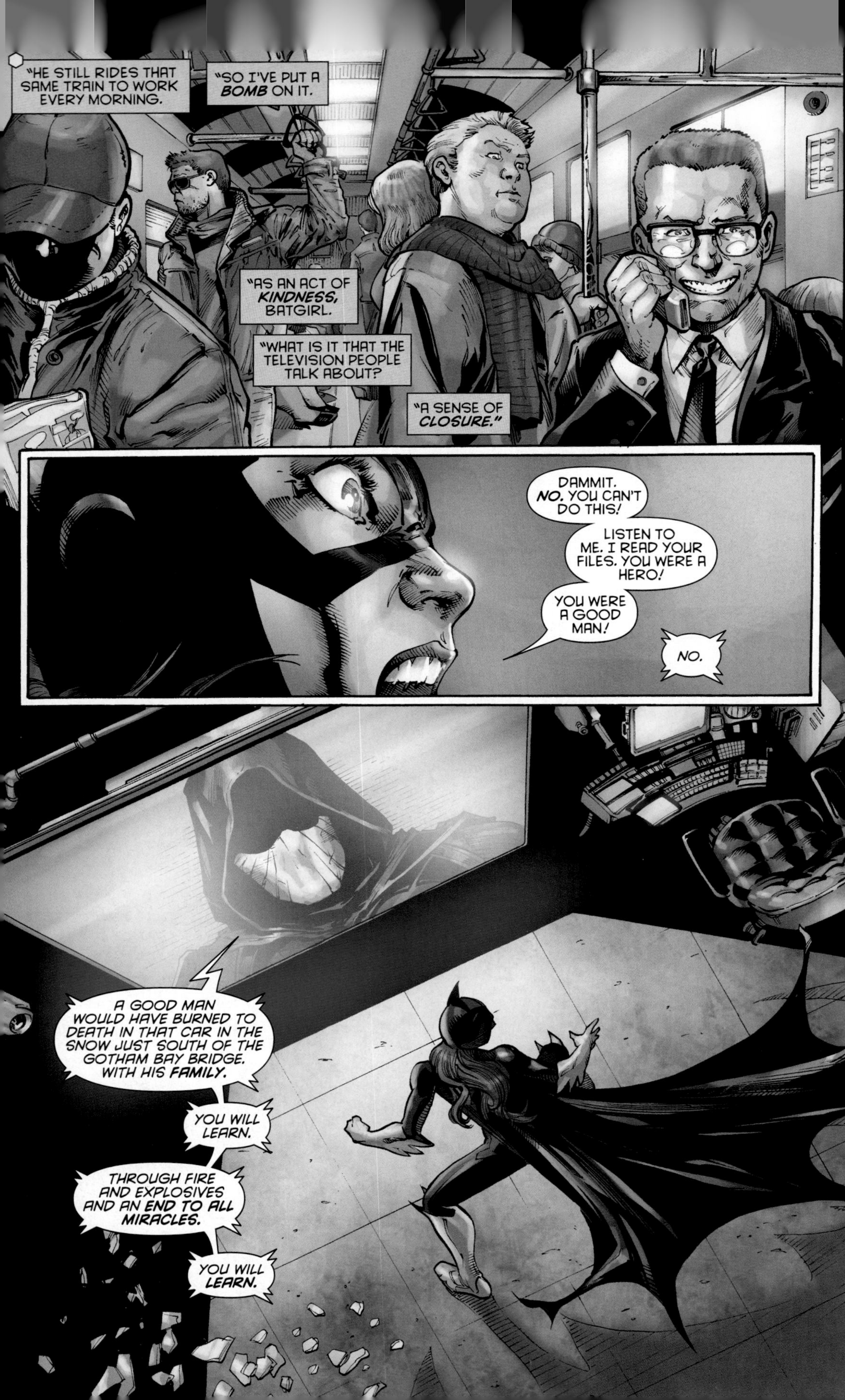
"HE STILL RIDES THAT SAME TRAIN TO WORK EVERY MORNING.
"SO I'VE PUT A **BOMB** ON IT.
"AS AN ACT OF **KINDNESS,** BATGIRL.
"WHAT IS IT THAT THE TELEVISION PEOPLE TALK ABOUT?
"A SENSE OF **CLOSURE."**
DAMMIT. **NO.** YOU CAN'T DO THIS!
LISTEN TO ME. I READ YOUR FILES. YOU WERE A HERO!
YOU WERE A GOOD MAN!
NO.
A GOOD MAN WOULD HAVE BURNED TO DEATH IN THAT CAR IN THE SNOW JUST SOUTH OF THE GOTHAM BAY BRIDGE. WITH HIS **FAMILY.**
YOU WILL LEARN.
THROUGH FIRE AND EXPLOSIVES AND AN **END TO ALL MIRACLES.**
YOU WILL **LEARN.**

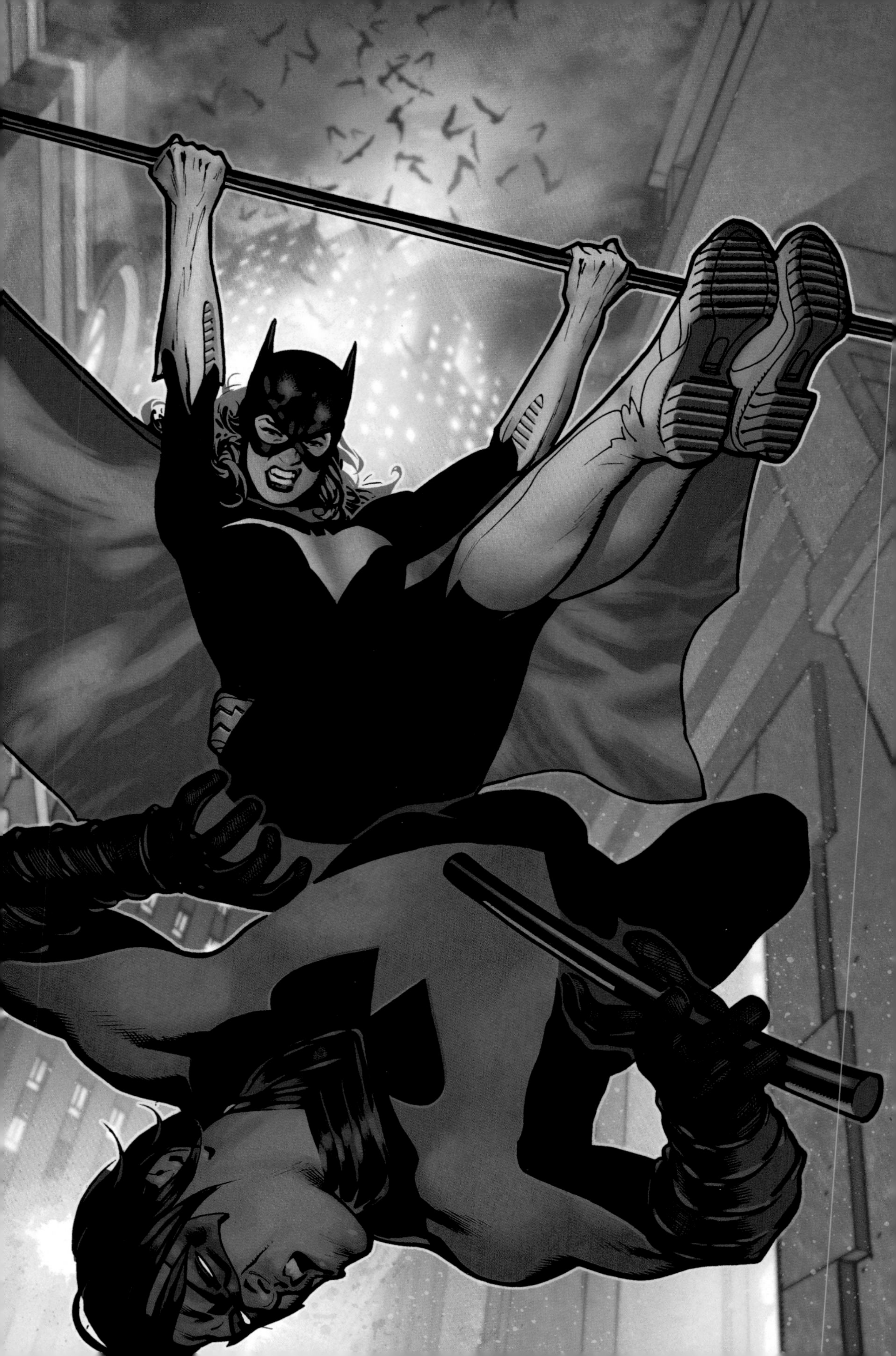

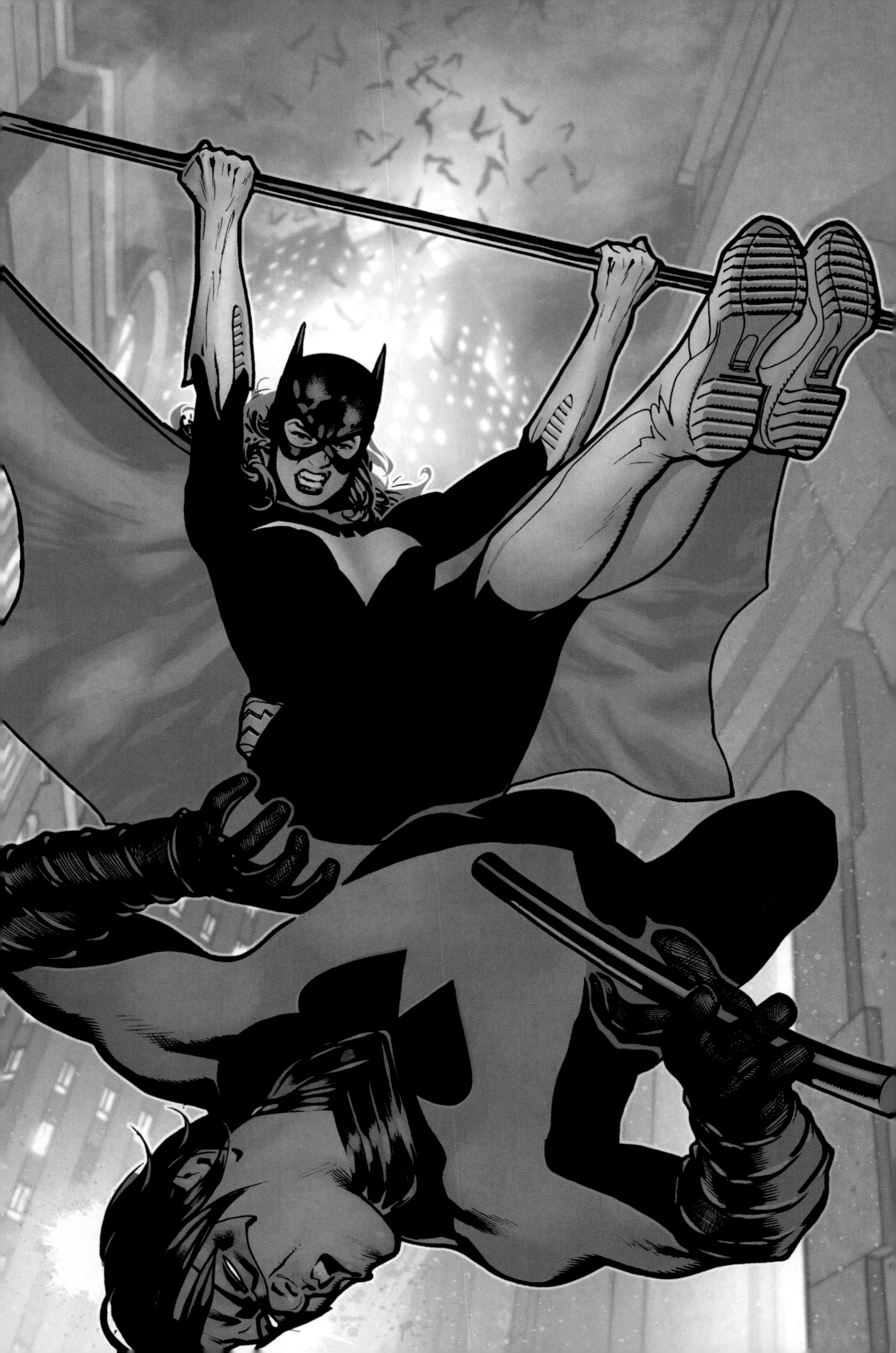

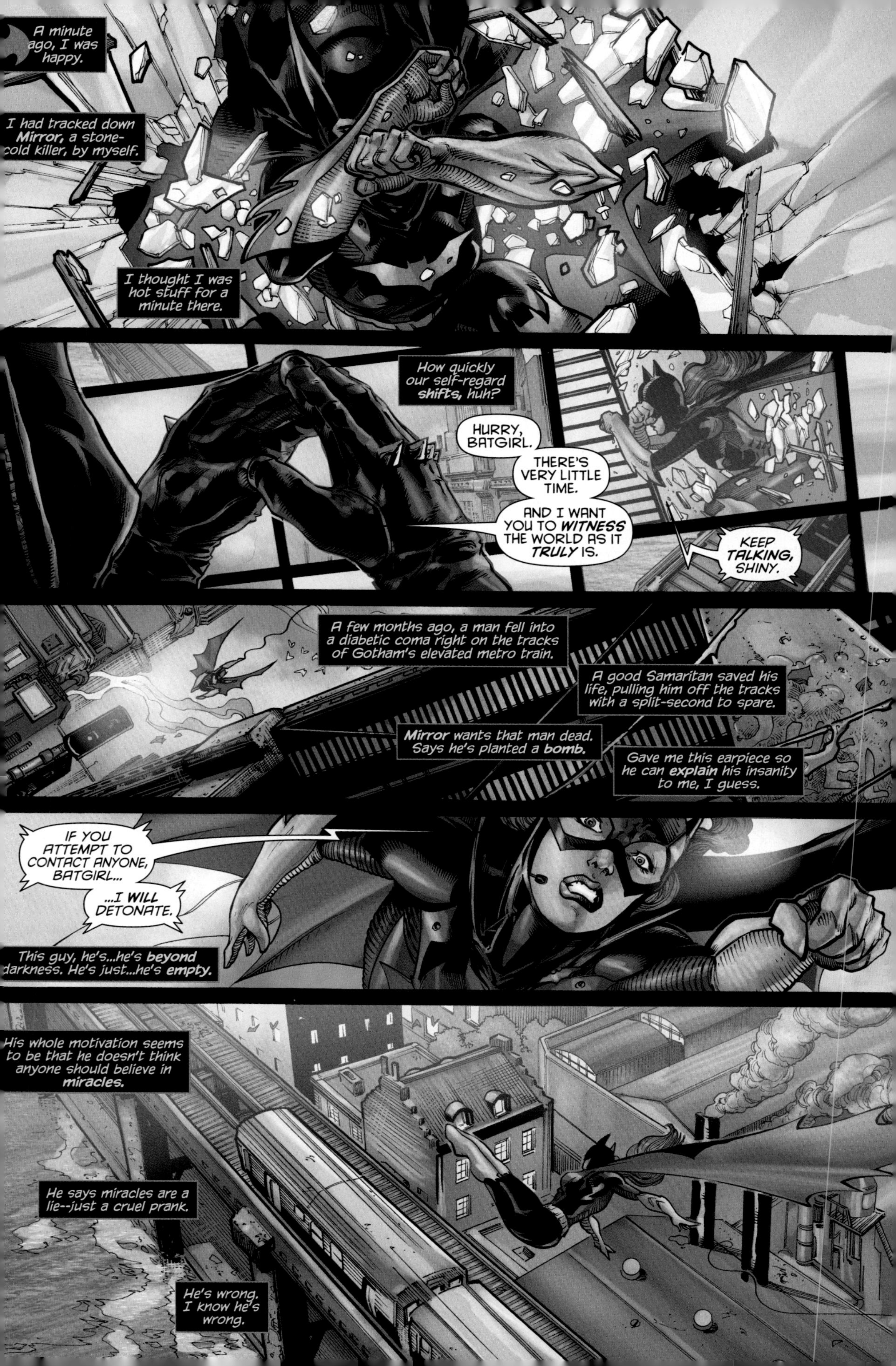

A minute ago, I was happy.
I had tracked down Mirror, a stone-cold killer, by myself.
I thought I was hot stuff for a minute there.
How quickly our self-regard shifts, huh?
HURRY, BATGIRL.
THERE'S VERY LITTLE TIME.
AND I WANT YOU TO WITNESS THE WORLD AS IT TRULY IS.
KEEP TALKING, SHINY.
A few months ago, a man fell into a diabetic coma right on the tracks of Gotham's elevated metro train.
A good Samaritan saved his life, pulling him off the tracks with a split-second to spare.
Mirror wants that man dead. Says he's planted a bomb.
Gave me this earpiece so he can explain his insanity to me, I guess.
IF YOU ATTEMPT TO CONTACT ANYONE, BATGIRL...
...I WILL DETONATE.
This guy, he's...he's beyond darkness. He's just...he's empty.
His whole motivation seems to be that he doesn't think anyone should believe in miracles.
He says miracles are a lie--just a cruel prank.
He's wrong. I know he's wrong.

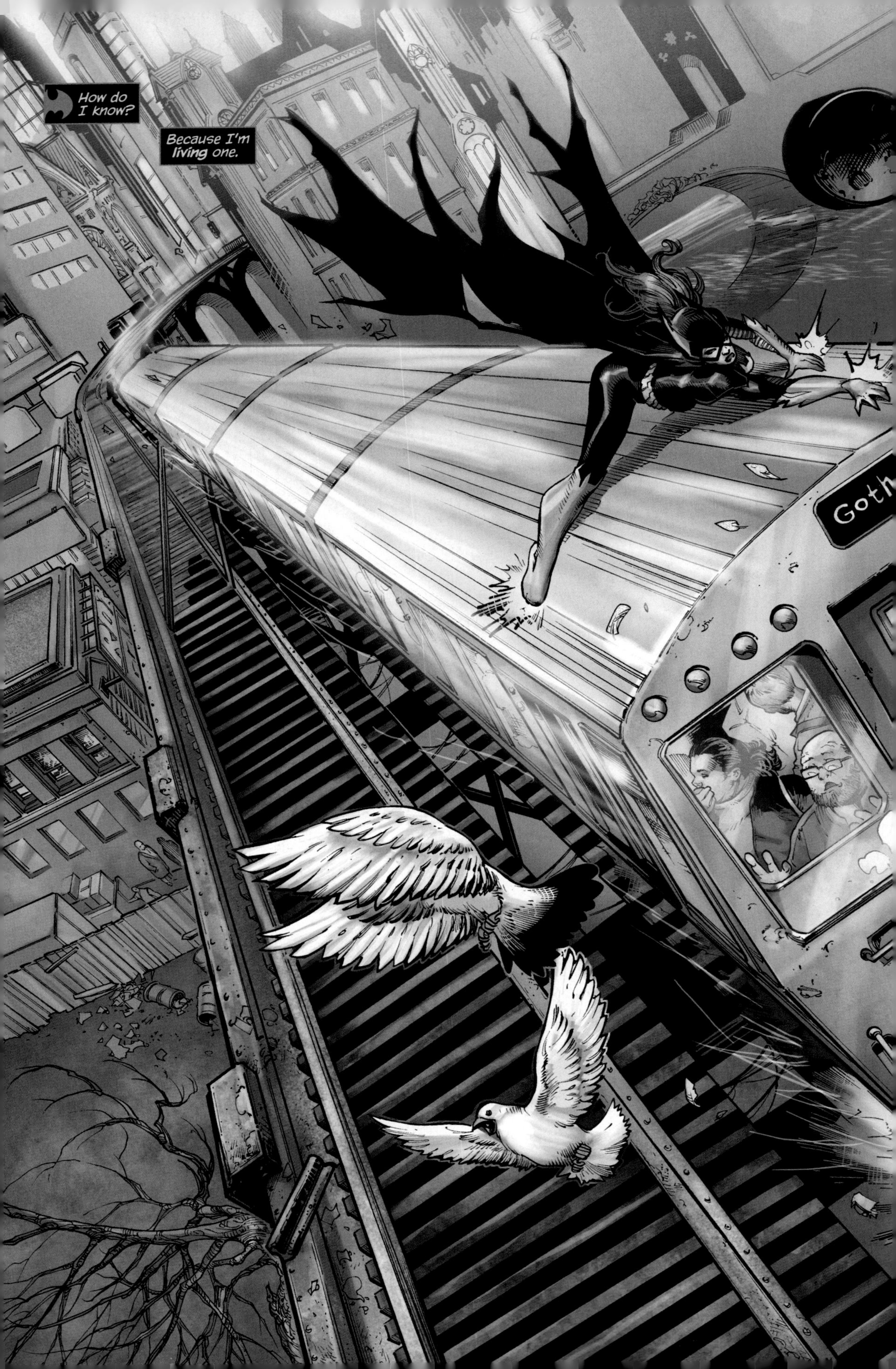

How do I know?
Because I'm *living* one.
Goth

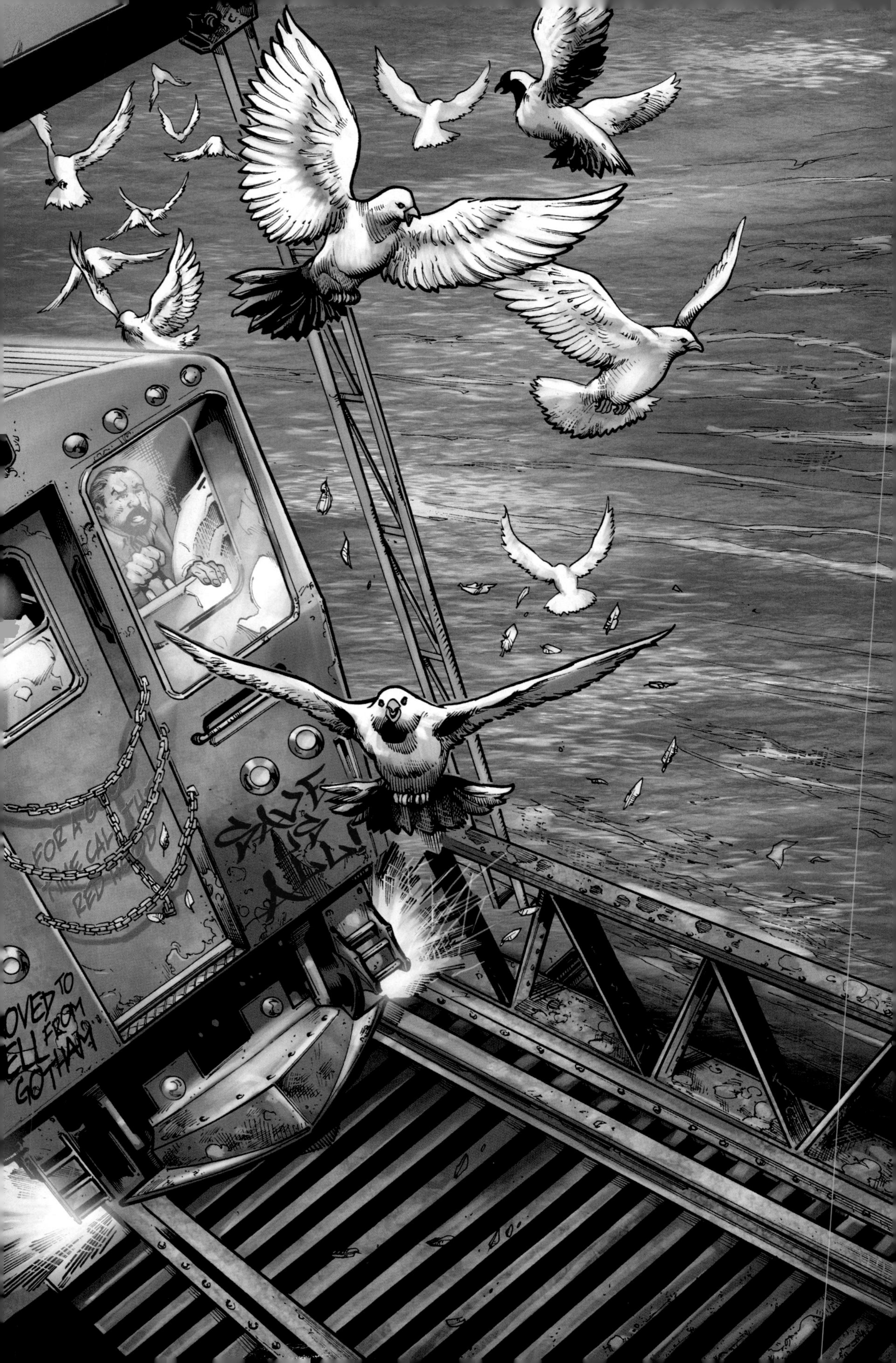
OVED TO
ELL FROM
GOTHAM

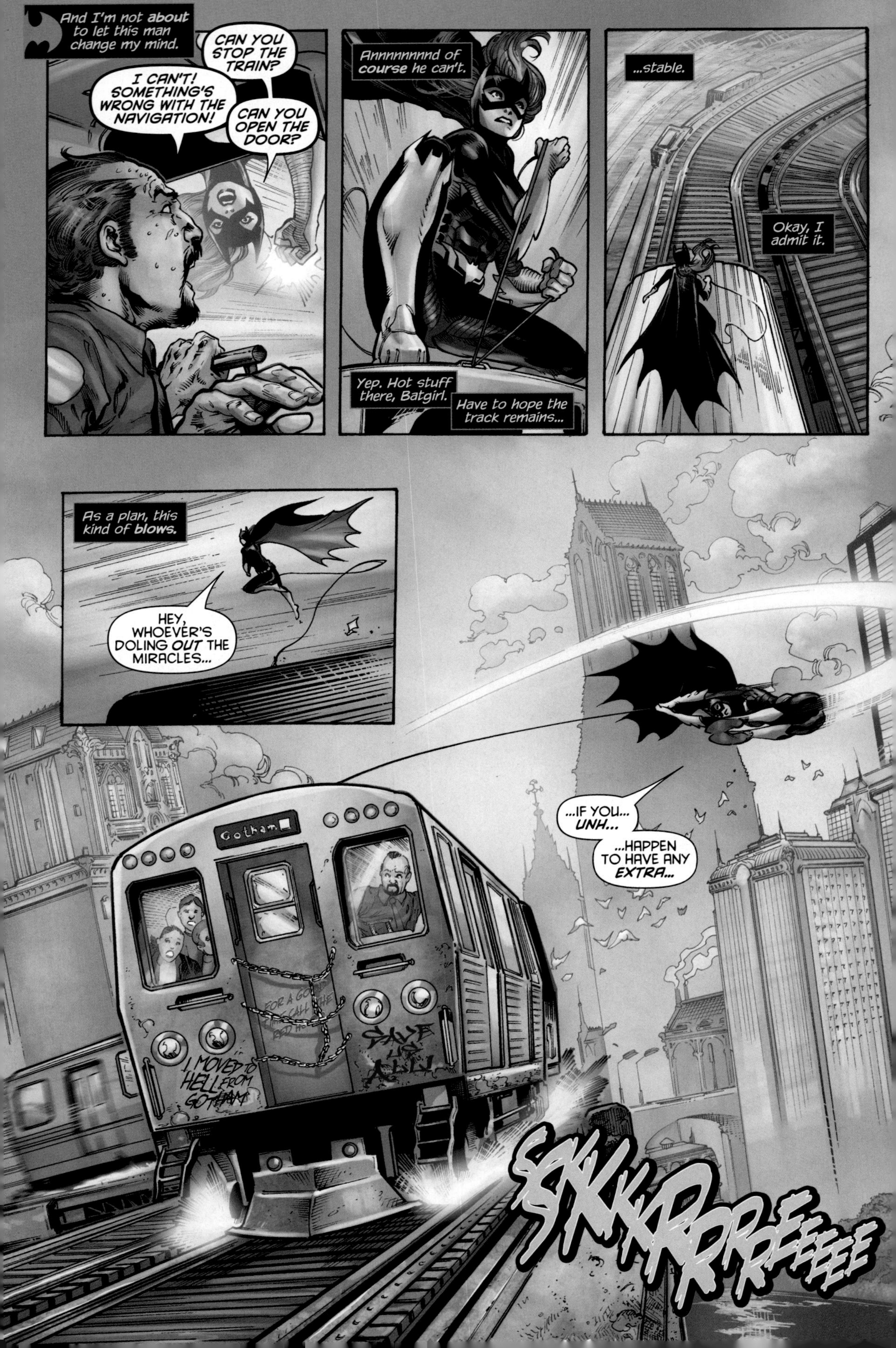
And I'm not about to let this man change my mind.
CAN YOU STOP THE TRAIN?
I CAN'T! SOMETHING'S WRONG WITH THE NAVIGATION!
CAN YOU OPEN THE DOOR?
Annnnnnnd of course he can't.
Yep. Hot stuff there, Batgirl.
Have to hope the track remains...
...stable.
Okay, I admit it.
As a plan, this kind of blows.
HEY, WHOEVER'S DOLING OUT THE MIRACLES...
...IF YOU... UNH...
...HAPPEN TO HAVE ANY EXTRA...
Gotham
I MOVED TO HELL FROM GOTHAM
SKKRRREEEEE

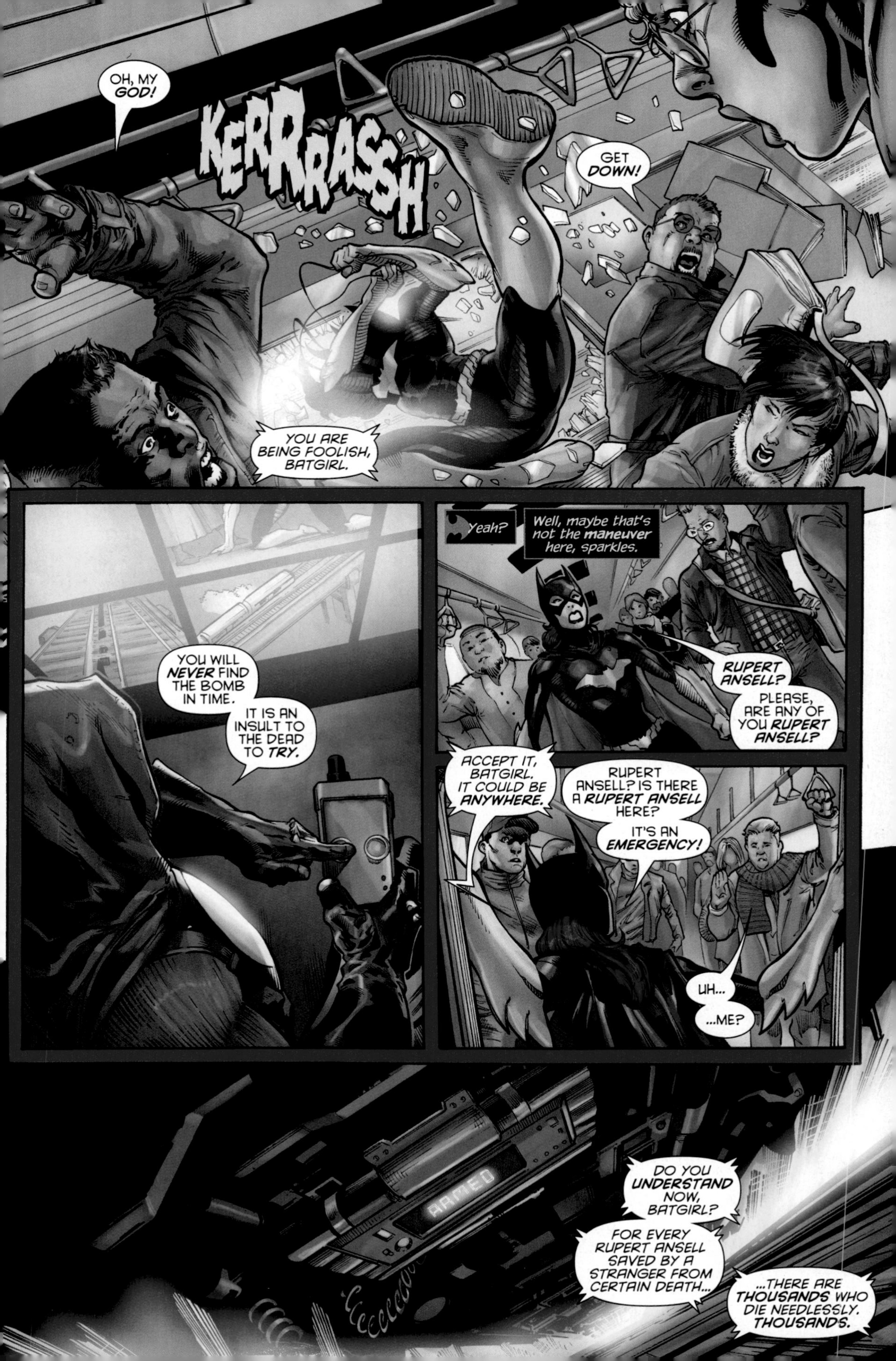
OH, MY GOD!
KERRRASSH
GET DOWN!
YOU ARE BEING FOOLISH, BATGIRL.
YOU WILL NEVER FIND THE BOMB IN TIME.
IT IS AN INSULT TO THE DEAD TO TRY.
Yeah?
Well, maybe that's not the maneuver here, sparkles.
RUPERT ANSELL?
PLEASE, ARE ANY OF YOU RUPERT ANSELL?
ACCEPT IT, BATGIRL. IT COULD BE ANYWHERE.
RUPERT ANSELL? IS THERE A RUPERT ANSELL HERE?
IT'S AN EMERGENCY!
UH...
...ME?
ARMED
DO YOU UNDERSTAND NOW, BATGIRL?
FOR EVERY RUPERT ANSELL SAVED BY A STRANGER FROM CERTAIN DEATH...
...THERE ARE THOUSANDS WHO DIE NEEDLESSLY. THOUSANDS.

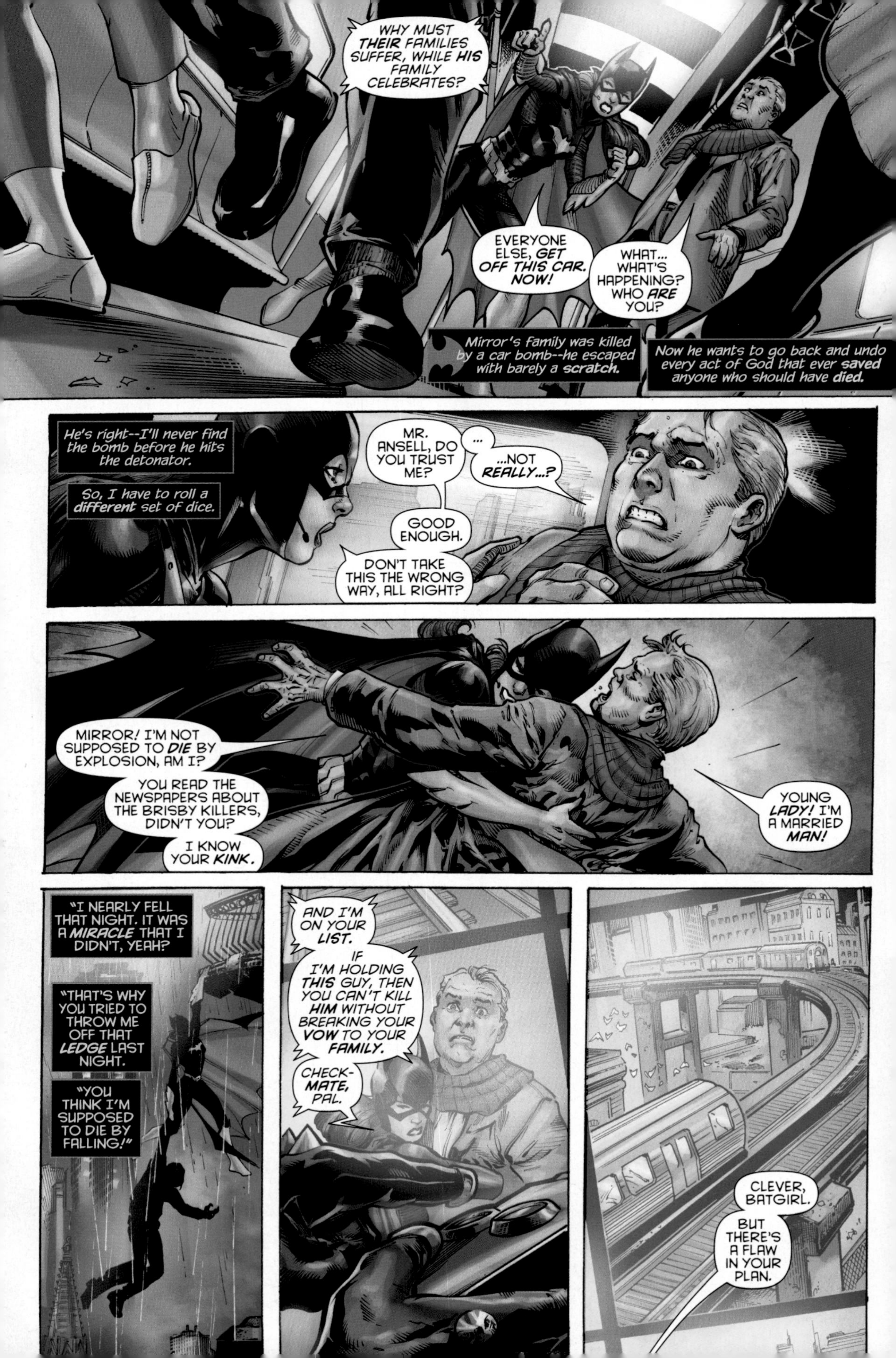
WHY MUST THEIR FAMILIES SUFFER, WHILE HIS FAMILY CELEBRATES?
EVERYONE ELSE, GET OFF THIS CAR. NOW!
WHAT... WHAT'S HAPPENING? WHO ARE YOU?
Mirror's family was killed by a car bomb--he escaped with barely a scratch.
Now he wants to go back and undo every act of God that ever saved anyone who should have died.
He's right--I'll never find the bomb before he hits the detonator.
So, I have to roll a different set of dice.
MR. ANSELL, DO YOU TRUST ME?
...
...NOT REALLY...?
GOOD ENOUGH.
DON'T TAKE THIS THE WRONG WAY, ALL RIGHT?
MIRROR! I'M NOT SUPPOSED TO DIE BY EXPLOSION, AM I?
YOU READ THE NEWSPAPERS ABOUT THE BRISBY KILLERS, DIDN'T YOU?
I KNOW YOUR KINK.
YOUNG LADY! I'M A MARRIED MAN!
"I NEARLY FELL THAT NIGHT. IT WAS A MIRACLE THAT I DIDN'T, YEAH?
"THAT'S WHY YOU TRIED TO THROW ME OFF THAT LEDGE LAST NIGHT.
"YOU THINK I'M SUPPOSED TO DIE BY FALLING!"
AND I'M ON YOUR LIST.
IF I'M HOLDING THIS GUY, THEN YOU CAN'T KILL HIM WITHOUT BREAKING YOUR VOW TO YOUR FAMILY.
CHECK-MATE, PAL.
CLEVER, BATGIRL.
BUT THERE'S A FLAW IN YOUR PLAN.

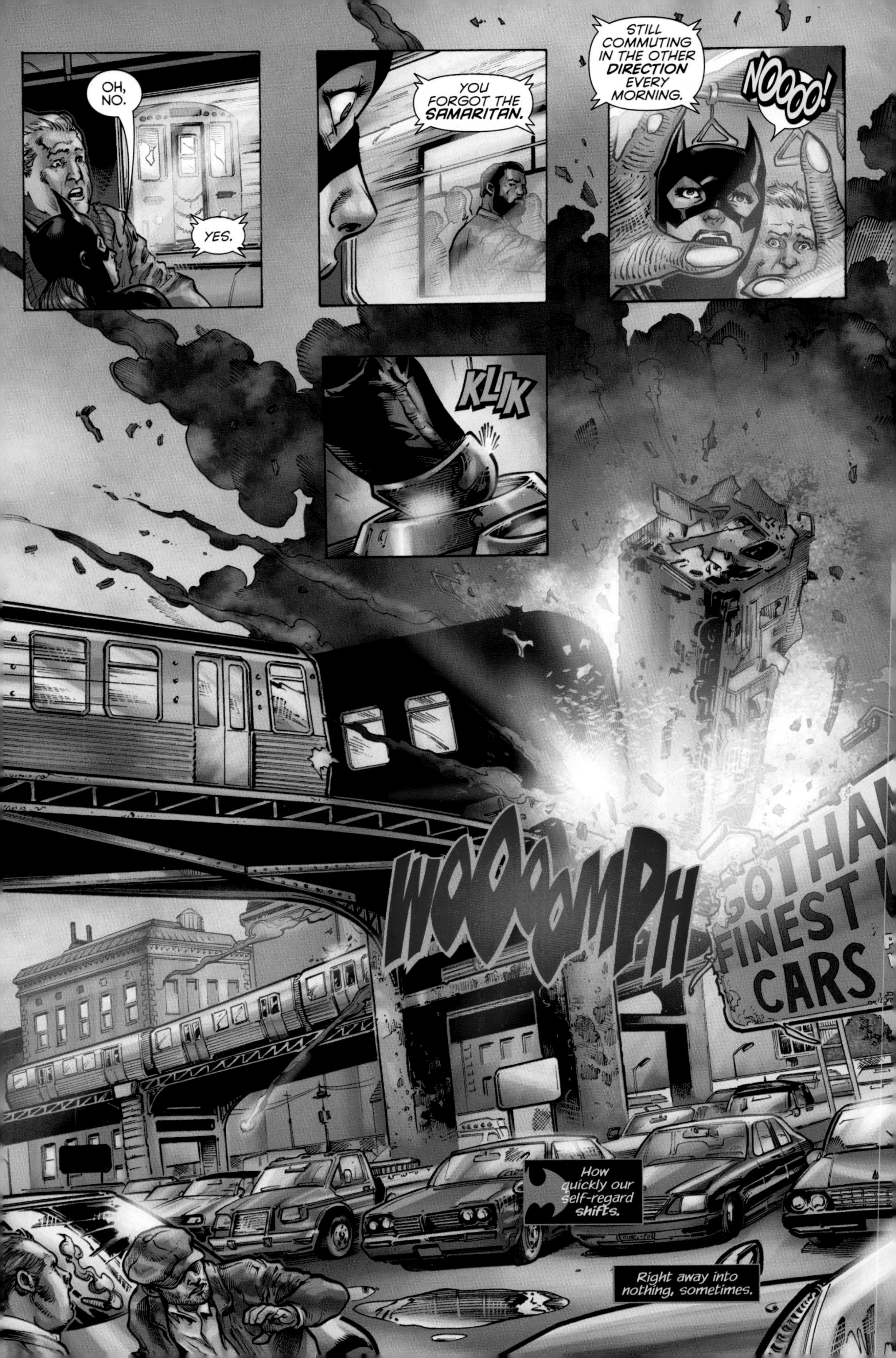
OH, NO.
YES.
YOU FORGOT THE SAMARITAN.
STILL COMMUTING IN THE OTHER DIRECTION EVERY MORNING.
NOOOO!
KLIK
WOOOOMPH
GOTHA
FINEST
CARS
How quickly our self-regard shifts.
Right away into nothing, sometimes.

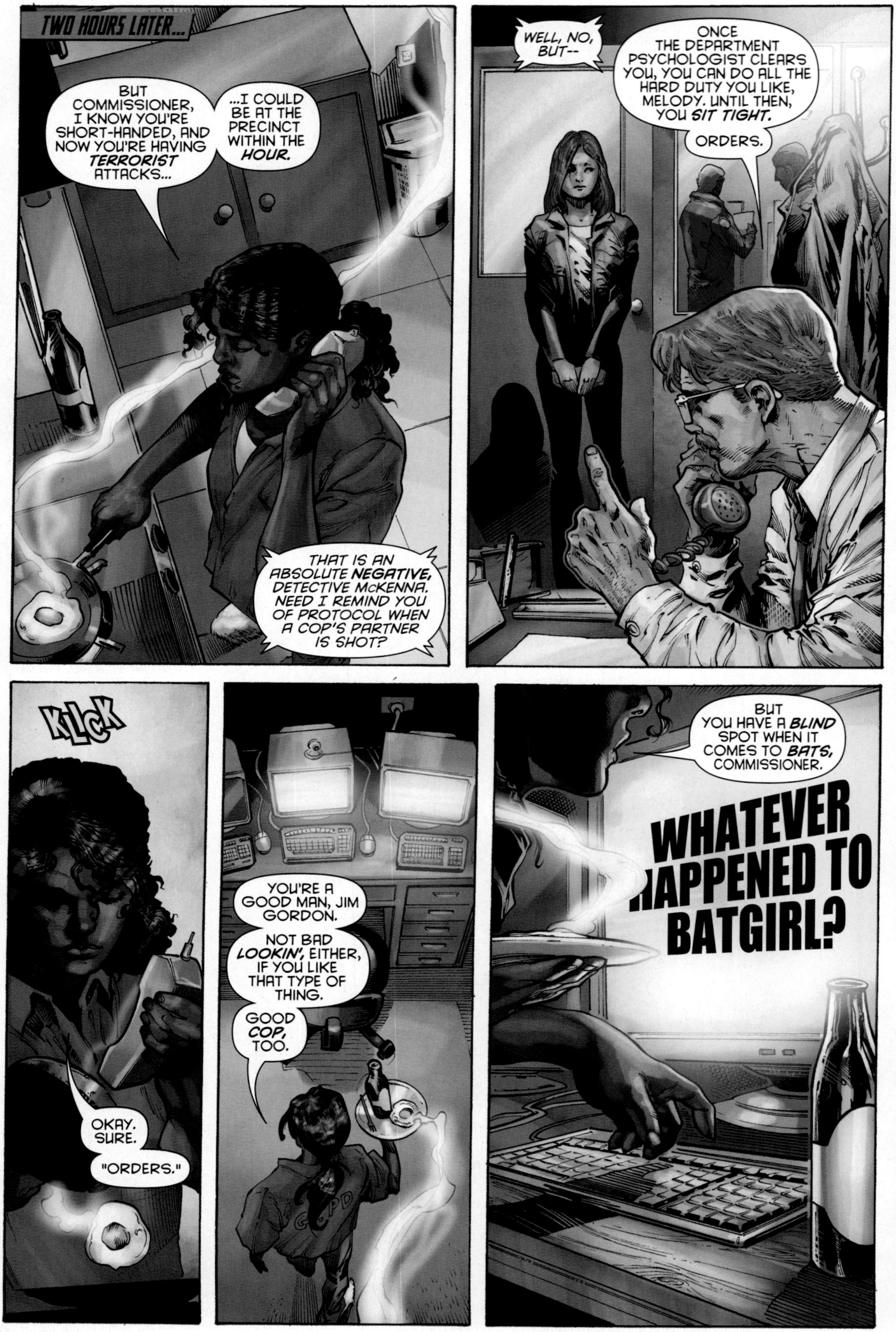
TWO HOURS LATER...
BUT COMMISSIONER, I KNOW YOU'RE SHORT-HANDED, AND NOW YOU'RE HAVING TERRORIST ATTACKS...
...I COULD BE AT THE PRECINCT WITHIN THE HOUR.
THAT IS AN ABSOLUTE NEGATIVE, DETECTIVE McKENNA. NEED I REMIND YOU OF PROTOCOL WHEN A COP'S PARTNER IS SHOT?
WELL, NO, BUT--
ONCE THE DEPARTMENT PSYCHOLOGIST CLEARS YOU, YOU CAN DO ALL THE HARD DUTY YOU LIKE, MELODY. UNTIL THEN, YOU SIT TIGHT.
ORDERS.
KLICK
OKAY. SURE.
"ORDERS."
YOU'RE A GOOD MAN, JIM GORDON.
NOT BAD LOOKIN', EITHER, IF YOU LIKE THAT TYPE OF THING.
GOOD COP, TOO.
BUT YOU HAVE A BLIND SPOT WHEN IT COMES TO BATS, COMMISSIONER.
WHATEVER HAPPENED TO BATGIRL?

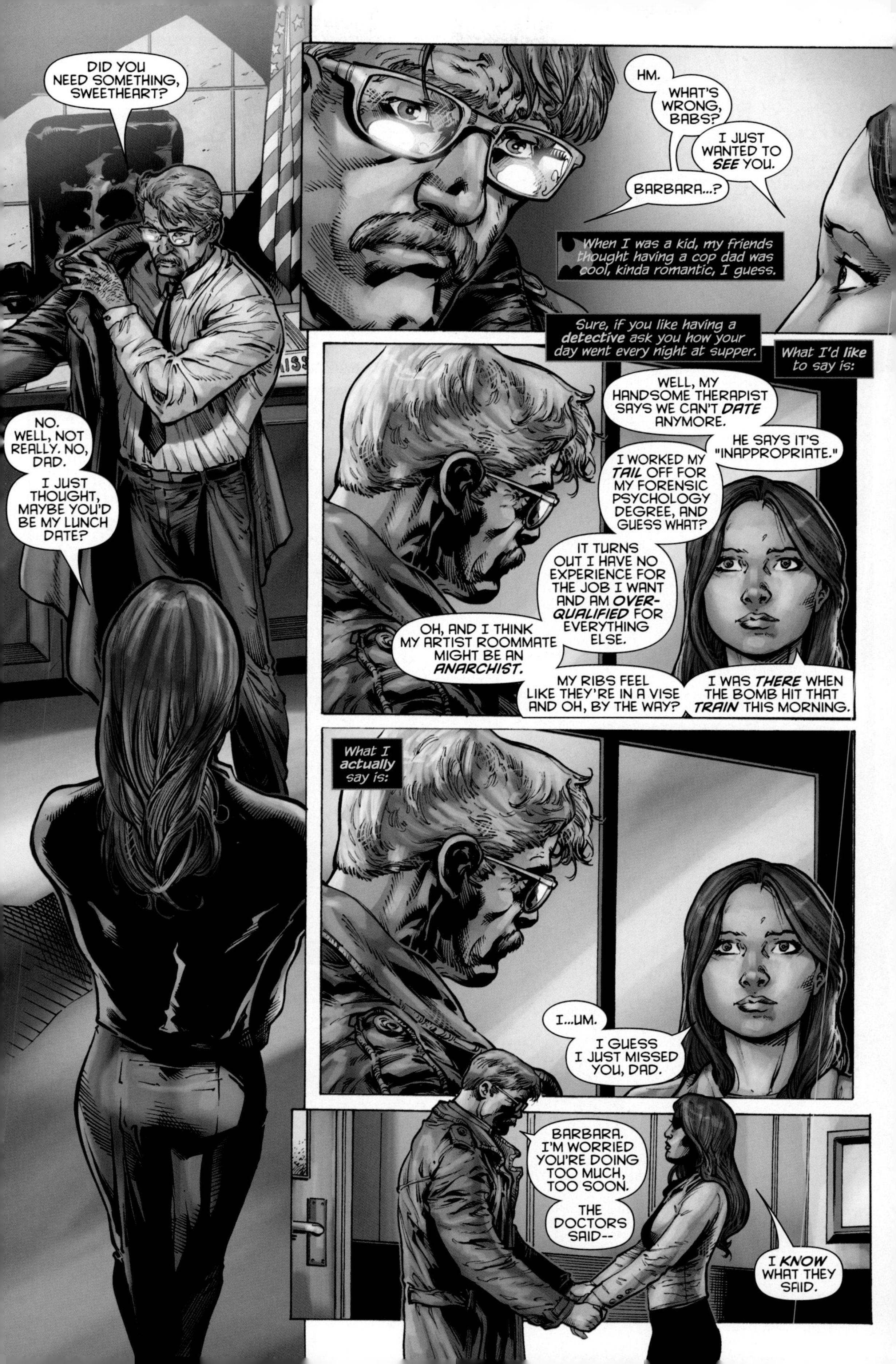

DID YOU NEED SOMETHING, SWEETHEART?
NO. WELL, NOT REALLY. NO, DAD.
I JUST THOUGHT, MAYBE YOU'D BE MY LUNCH DATE?
HM.
WHAT'S WRONG, BABS?
I JUST WANTED TO SEE YOU.
BARBARA...?
When I was a kid, my friends thought having a cop dad was cool, kinda romantic, I guess.
Sure, if you like having a detective ask you how your day went every night at supper.
What I'd like to say is:
WELL, MY HANDSOME THERAPIST SAYS WE CAN'T DATE ANYMORE.
HE SAYS IT'S "INAPPROPRIATE."
I WORKED MY TAIL OFF FOR MY FORENSIC PSYCHOLOGY DEGREE, AND GUESS WHAT?
IT TURNS OUT I HAVE NO EXPERIENCE FOR THE JOB I WANT AND AM OVER-QUALIFIED FOR EVERYTHING ELSE.
OH, AND I THINK MY ARTIST ROOMMATE MIGHT BE AN ANARCHIST.
MY RIBS FEEL LIKE THEY'RE IN A VISE AND OH, BY THE WAY?
I WAS THERE WHEN THE BOMB HIT THAT TRAIN THIS MORNING.
What I actually say is:
I...UM.
I GUESS I JUST MISSED YOU, DAD.
BARBARA. I'M WORRIED YOU'RE DOING TOO MUCH, TOO SOON.
THE DOCTORS SAID--
I KNOW WHAT THEY SAID.

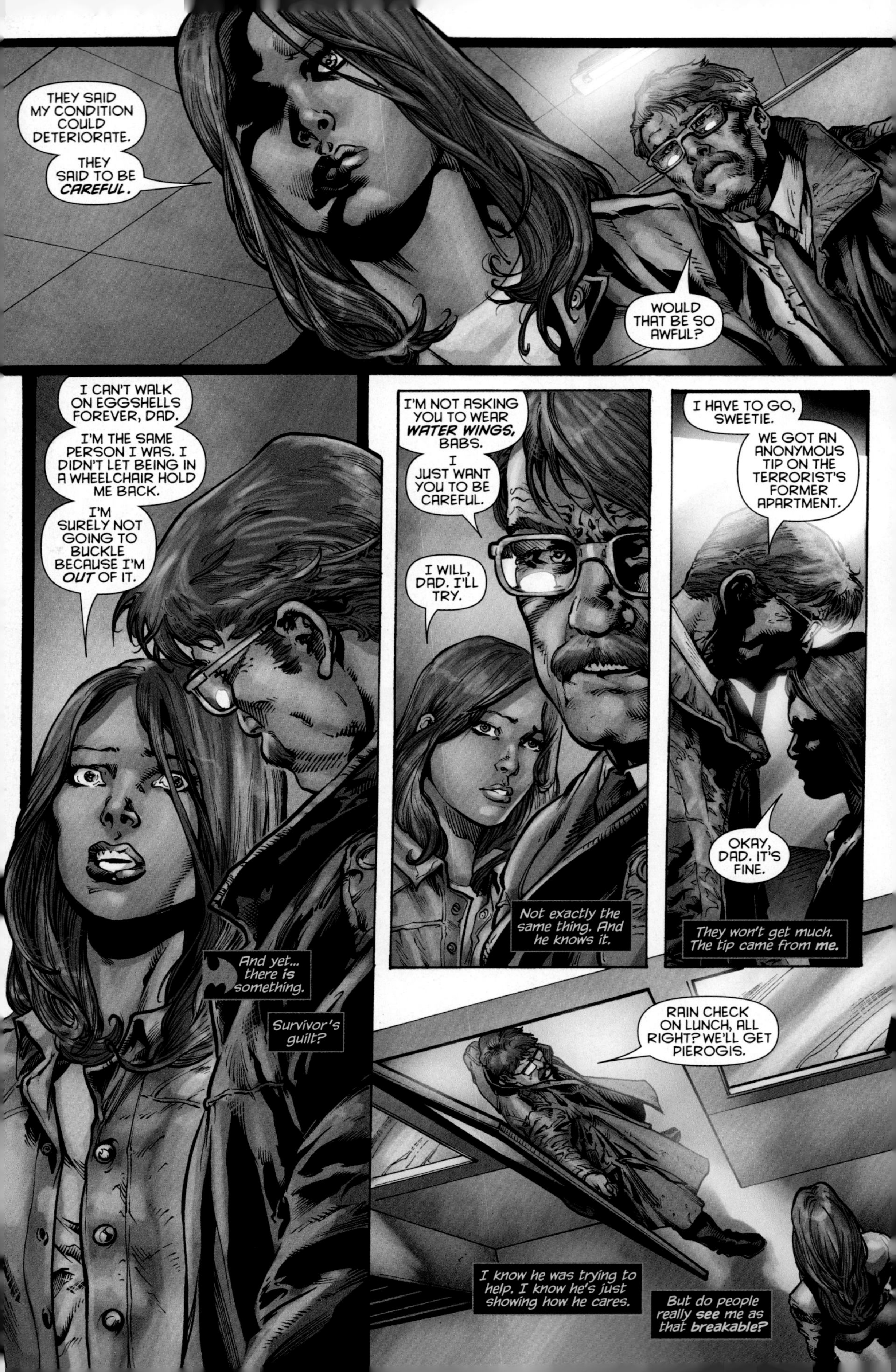

THEY SAID MY CONDITION COULD DETERIORATE.
THEY SAID TO BE CAREFUL.
WOULD THAT BE SO AWFUL?
I CAN'T WALK ON EGGSHELLS FOREVER, DAD.
I'M THE SAME PERSON I WAS. I DIDN'T LET BEING IN A WHEELCHAIR HOLD ME BACK.
I'M SURELY NOT GOING TO BUCKLE BECAUSE I'M OUT OF IT.
And yet... there is something.
Survivor's guilt?
I'M NOT ASKING YOU TO WEAR WATER WINGS, BABS.
I JUST WANT YOU TO BE CAREFUL.
I WILL, DAD. I'LL TRY.
Not exactly the same thing. And he knows it.
I HAVE TO GO, SWEETIE.
WE GOT AN ANONYMOUS TIP ON THE TERRORIST'S FORMER APARTMENT.
OKAY, DAD. IT'S FINE.
They won't get much. The tip came from me.
RAIN CHECK ON LUNCH, ALL RIGHT? WE'LL GET PIEROGIS.
I know he was trying to help. I know he's just showing how he cares.
But do people really see me as that breakable?

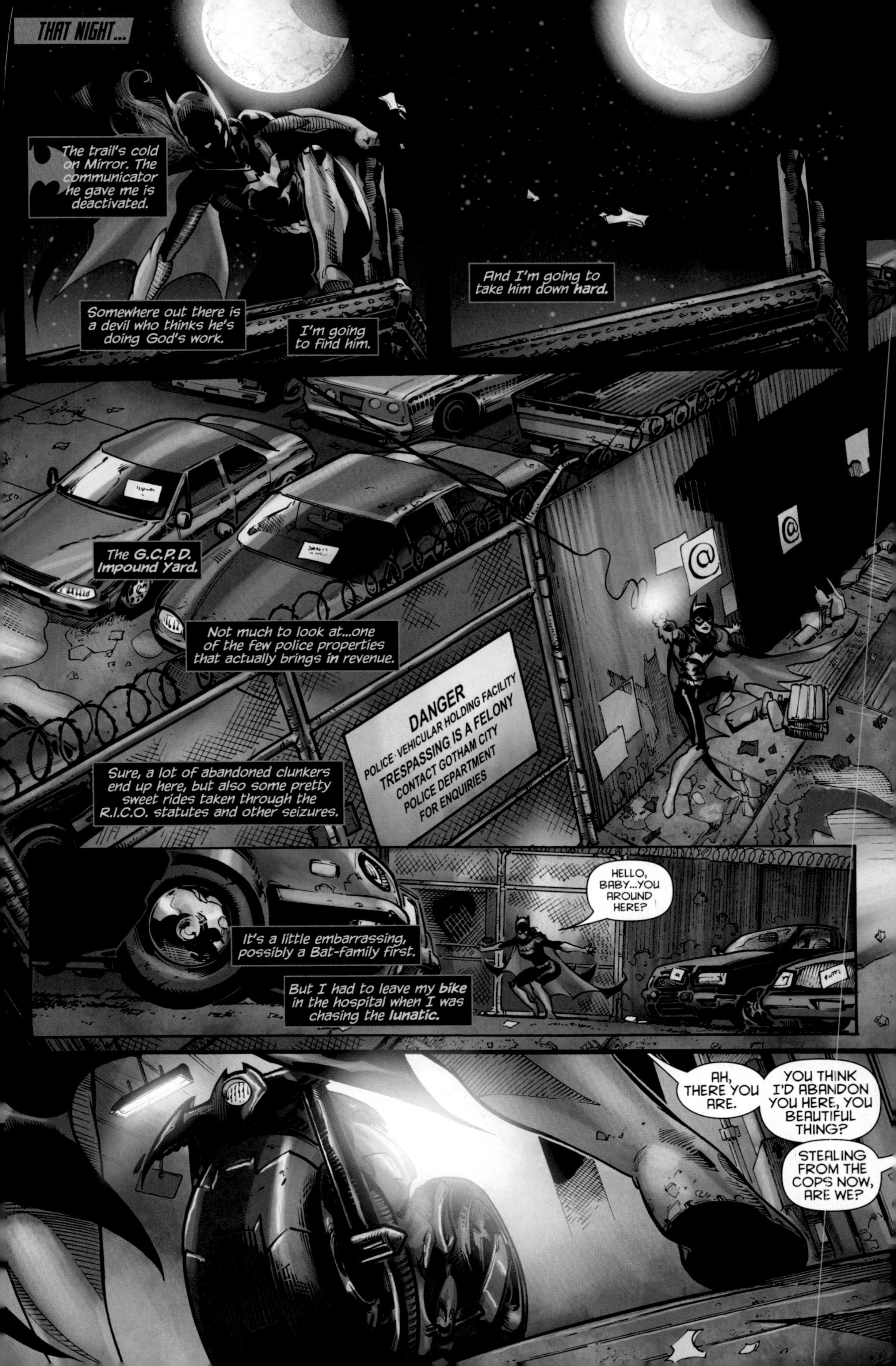
THAT NIGHT...
The trail's cold on Mirror. The communicator he gave me is deactivated.
Somewhere out there is a devil who thinks he's doing God's work.
I'm going to find him.
And I'm going to take him down hard.
The G.C.P.D. Impound Yard.
Not much to look at...one of the few police properties that actually brings in revenue.
DANGER
POLICE · VEHICULAR HOLDING FACILITY
TRESPASSING IS A FELONY
CONTACT GOTHAM CITY
POLICE DEPARTMENT
FOR ENQUIRIES
Sure, a lot of abandoned clunkers end up here, but also some pretty sweet rides taken through the R.I.C.O. statutes and other seizures.
It's a little embarrassing, possibly a Bat-family first.
HELLO, BABY...YOU AROUND HERE?
But I had to leave my bike in the hospital when I was chasing the lunatic.
AH, THERE YOU ARE.
YOU THINK I'D ABANDON YOU HERE, YOU BEAUTIFUL THING?
STEALING FROM THE COPS NOW, ARE WE?

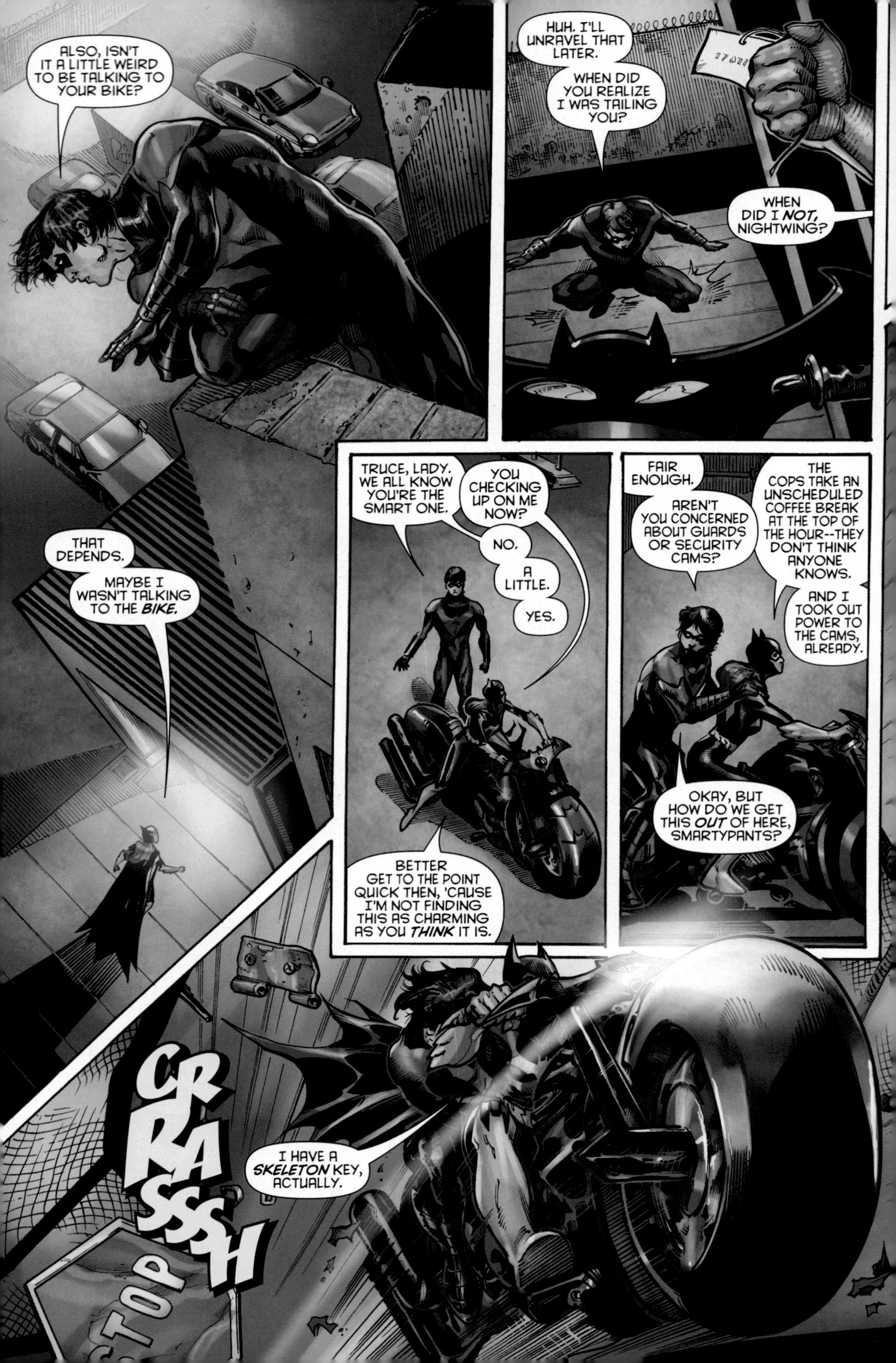

ALSO, ISN'T IT A LITTLE WEIRD TO BE TALKING TO YOUR BIKE?
THAT DEPENDS.
MAYBE I WASN'T TALKING TO THE *BIKE.*
HUH. I'LL UNRAVEL THAT LATER.
WHEN DID YOU REALIZE I WAS TAILING YOU?
WHEN DID I *NOT,* NIGHTWING?
TRUCE, LADY. WE ALL KNOW YOU'RE THE SMART ONE.
YOU CHECKING UP ON ME NOW?
NO.
A LITTLE.
YES.
BETTER GET TO THE POINT QUICK THEN, 'CAUSE I'M NOT FINDING THIS AS CHARMING AS YOU *THINK* IT IS.
FAIR ENOUGH.
AREN'T YOU CONCERNED ABOUT GUARDS OR SECURITY CAMS?
THE COPS TAKE AN UNSCHEDULED COFFEE BREAK AT THE TOP OF THE HOUR--THEY DON'T THINK ANYONE KNOWS.
AND I TOOK OUT POWER TO THE CAMS, ALREADY.
OKAY, BUT HOW DO WE GET THIS *OUT* OF HERE, SMARTYPANTS?
CRRASSSH
I HAVE A *SKELETON* KEY, ACTUALLY.
STOP

I can't help thinking that I've traded one set of wheels for another. It's nice.

Wind in my hair.

Former Boy Wonder wrapped around me.

Painfully nice.

YOU OKAY?

Makes me think of something other than trains and explosions.

For a little while.

I'VE BEEN SHOT OUT OF CANNONS, BATGIRL. I'M OKAY.

I MIGHT BE A LITTLE BIT BETTER THAN OKAY, TO BE HONEST.

I was thinking the same thing, actually. But I'm not going to tell *him* that, yet.

HEARD YOU'RE HANGING OUT IN OLD GOTHAM?

YEAH. IT'S... TROUBLED.

BUT HALY'S CIRCUS IS BACK IN TOWN--HOW ODD IS THAT?

I didn't like him when I first met him, a few years ago. Not really.

Hard to believe that, now.

SO, WHY *ARE* YOU HERE, RICHARD?

WELL, IT'S THAT WE...I MEAN, I...

COME ON, BABS, YOU'RE *RECOVERING.*

AND YOU BOTH, I MEAN, YOU...THAT WORRIES YOU?

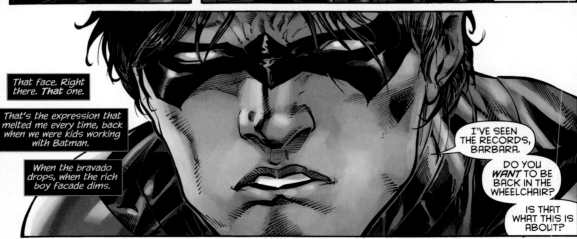

That face. Right there. *That* one.

That's the expression that melted me every time, back when we were kids working with Batman.

When the bravado drops, when the rich boy facade dims.

I'VE SEEN THE RECORDS, BARBARA.

DO YOU *WANT* TO BE BACK IN THE WHEELCHAIR?

IS THAT WHAT THIS IS ABOUT?

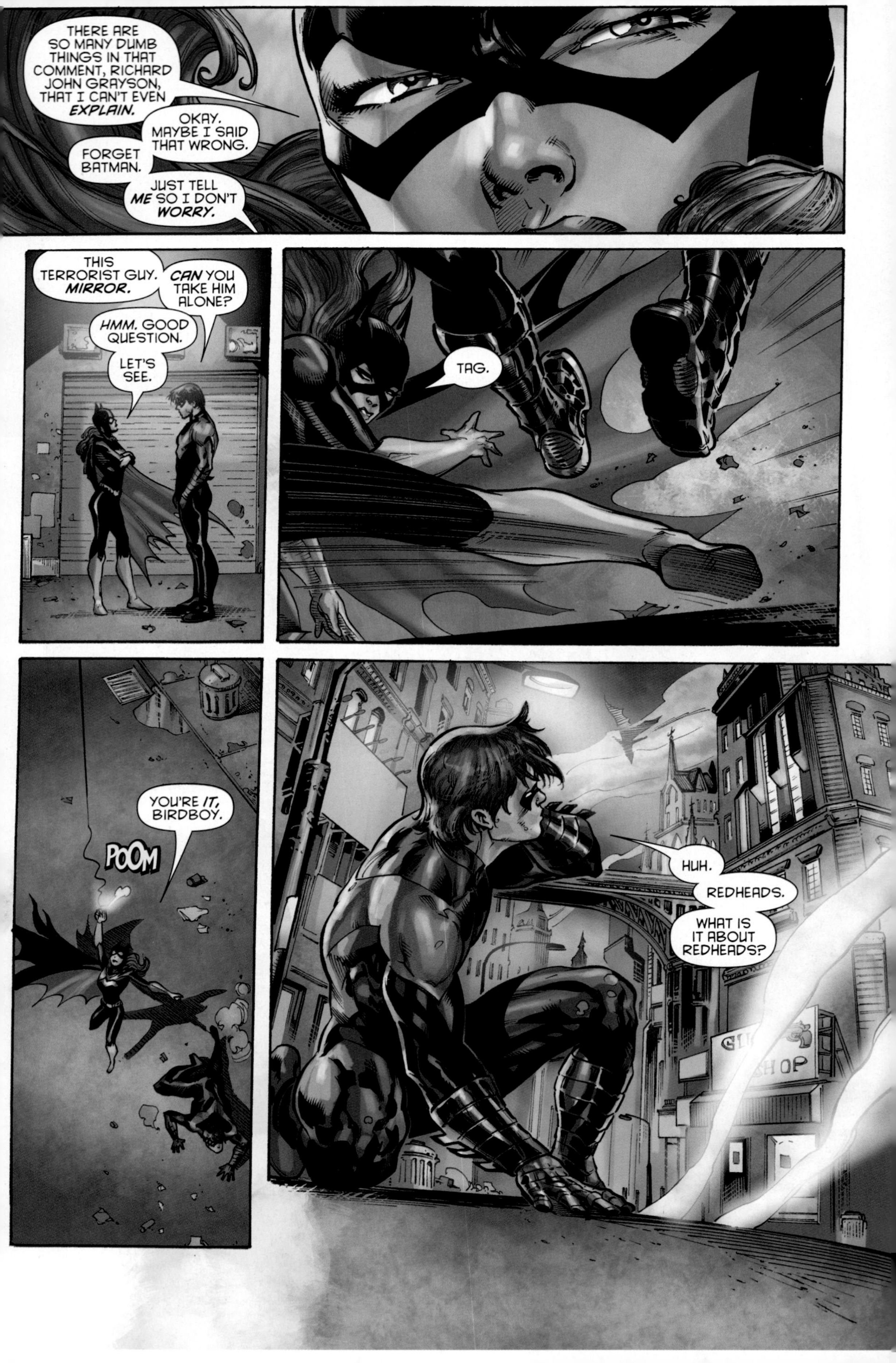
THERE ARE SO MANY DUMB THINGS IN THAT COMMENT, RICHARD JOHN GRAYSON, THAT I CAN'T EVEN *EXPLAIN.*
OKAY. MAYBE I SAID THAT WRONG.
FORGET BATMAN.
JUST TELL *ME* SO I DON'T *WORRY.*
THIS TERRORIST GUY. *MIRROR.*
CAN YOU TAKE HIM ALONE?
HMM. GOOD QUESTION.
LET'S SEE.
TAG.
YOU'RE *IT,* BIRDBOY.
POOM
HUH.
REDHEADS.
WHAT IS IT ABOUT REDHEADS?

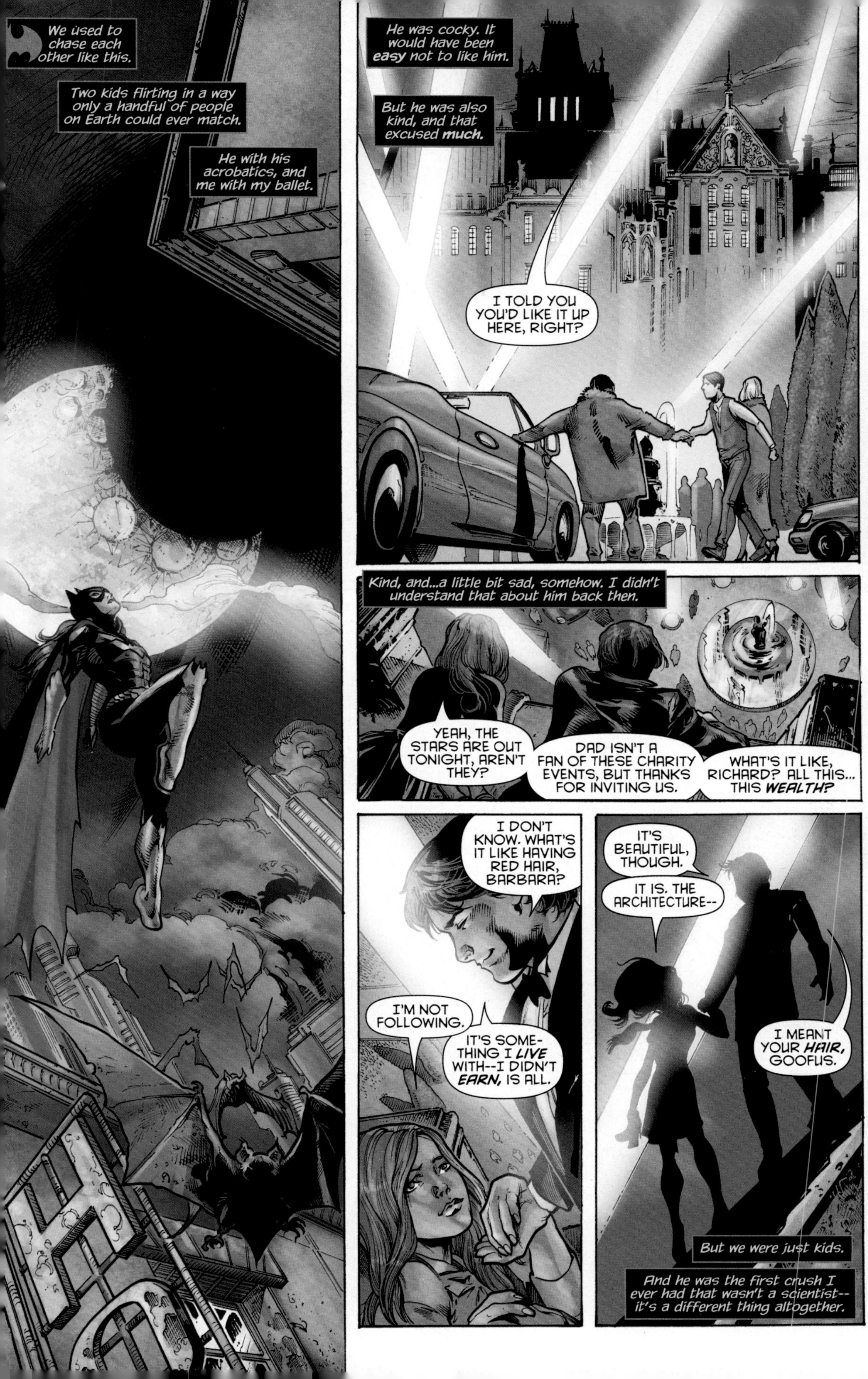

We used to chase each other like this.
Two kids flirting in a way only a handful of people on Earth could ever match.
He with his acrobatics, and me with my ballet.
He was cocky. It would have been easy not to like him.
But he was also kind, and that excused much.
I TOLD YOU YOU'D LIKE IT UP HERE, RIGHT?
Kind, and...a little bit sad, somehow. I didn't understand that about him back then.
YEAH, THE STARS ARE OUT TONIGHT, AREN'T THEY?
DAD ISN'T A FAN OF THESE CHARITY EVENTS, BUT THANKS FOR INVITING US.
WHAT'S IT LIKE, RICHARD? ALL THIS... THIS WEALTH?
I DON'T KNOW. WHAT'S IT LIKE HAVING RED HAIR, BARBARA?
I'M NOT FOLLOWING.
IT'S SOMETHING I LIVE WITH--I DIDN'T EARN, IS ALL.
IT'S BEAUTIFUL, THOUGH.
IT IS. THE ARCHITECTURE--
I MEANT YOUR HAIR, GOOFUS.
But we were just kids.
And he was the first crush I ever had that wasn't a scientist--it's a different thing altogether.

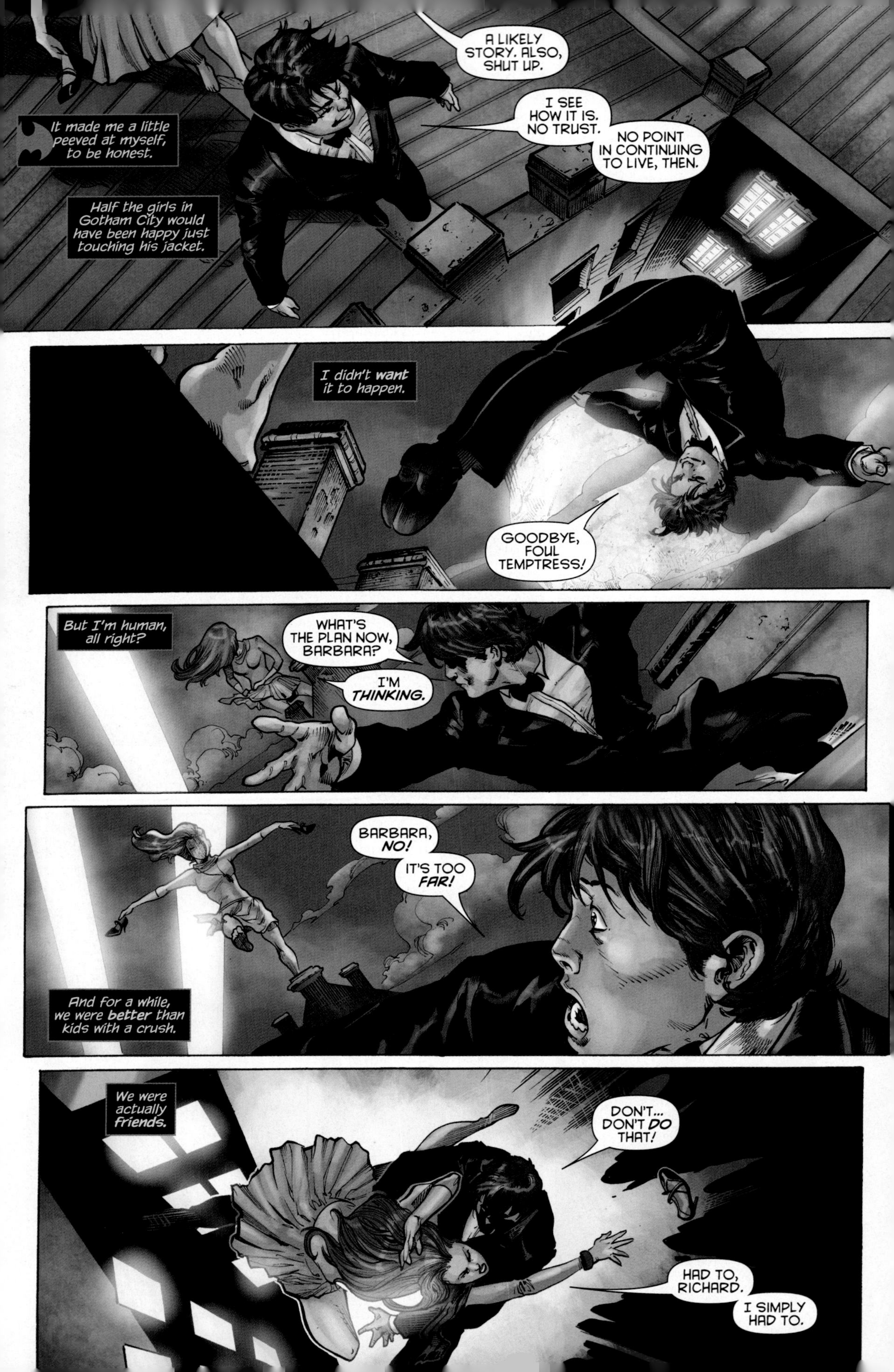
A LIKELY STORY. ALSO, SHUT UP.
It made me a little peeved at myself, to be honest.
I SEE HOW IT IS. NO TRUST.
NO POINT IN CONTINUING TO LIVE, THEN.
Half the girls in Gotham City would have been happy just touching his jacket.
I didn't **want** it to happen.
GOODBYE, FOUL TEMPTRESS!
But I'm human, all right?
WHAT'S THE PLAN NOW, BARBARA?
I'M *THINKING.*
BARBARA, *NO!*
IT'S TOO *FAR!*
And for a while, we were **better** than kids with a crush.
We were actually **friends.**
DON'T... DON'T *DO* THAT!
HAD TO, RICHARD.
I SIMPLY HAD TO.

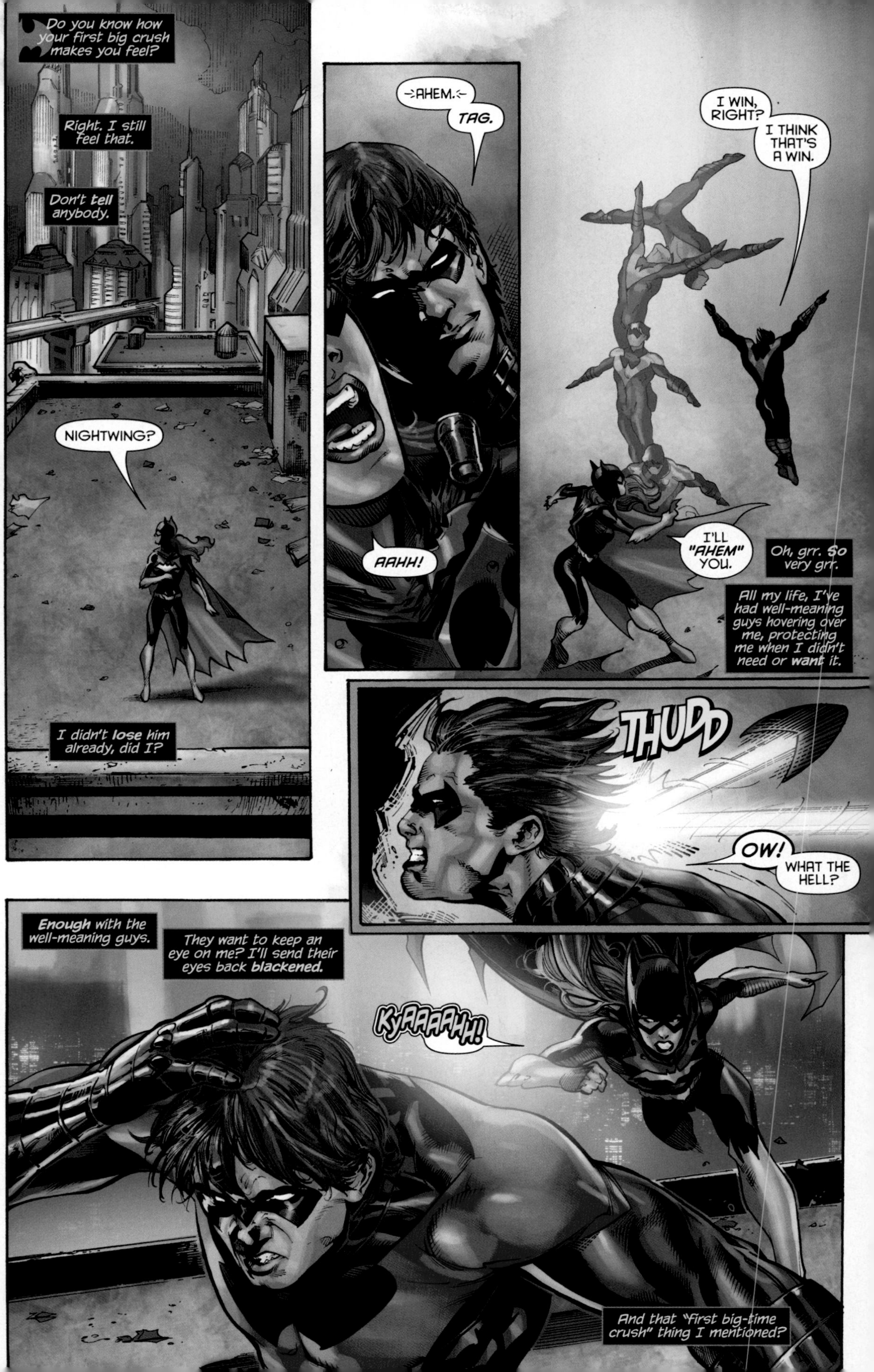
Do you know how your first big crush makes you feel?
Right. I still feel that.
Don't tell anybody.
NIGHTWING?
I didn't lose him already, did I?
-AHEM.-
TAG.
AAHH!
I WIN, RIGHT?
I THINK THAT'S A WIN.
I'LL "AHEM" YOU.
Oh, grr. So very grr.
All my life, I've had well-meaning guys hovering over me, protecting me when I didn't need or want it.
THUDD
OW!
WHAT THE HELL?
Enough with the well-meaning guys.
They want to keep an eye on me? I'll send their eyes back blackened.
KyAAAAHH!
And that "first big-time crush" thing I mentioned?

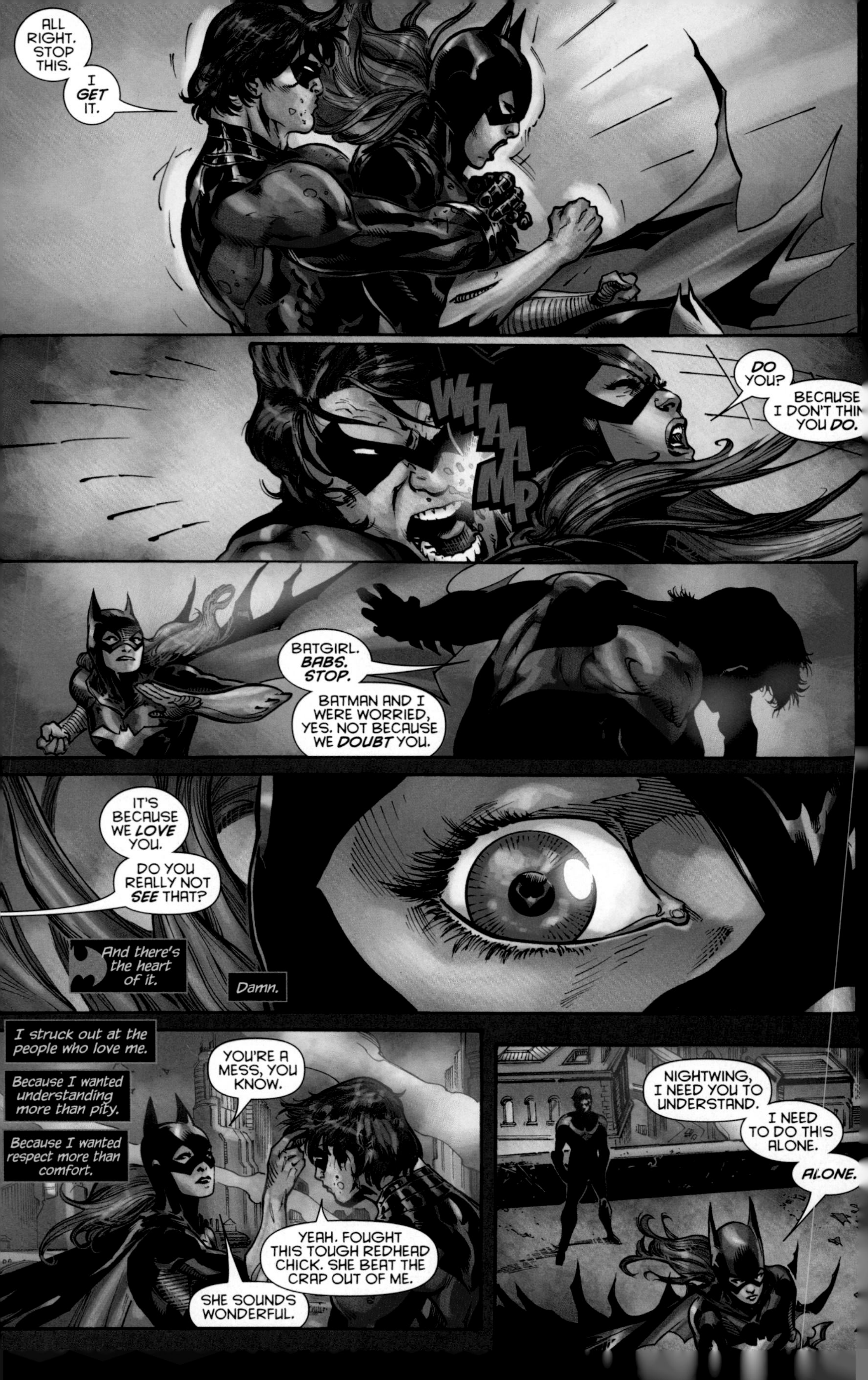
ALL RIGHT. STOP THIS.
I GET IT.
WHHAAAMP
DO YOU?
BECAUSE I DON'T THIN YOU DO.
BATGIRL. BABS. STOP.
BATMAN AND I WERE WORRIED, YES. NOT BECAUSE WE DOUBT YOU.
IT'S BECAUSE WE LOVE YOU.
DO YOU REALLY NOT SEE THAT?
And there's the heart of it.
Damn.
I struck out at the people who love me.
Because I wanted understanding more than pity.
Because I wanted respect more than comfort.
YOU'RE A MESS, YOU KNOW.
YEAH. FOUGHT THIS TOUGH REDHEAD CHICK. SHE BEAT THE CRAP OUT OF ME.
SHE SOUNDS WONDERFUL.
NIGHTWING, I NEED YOU TO UNDERSTAND.
I NEED TO DO THIS ALONE.
ALONE.

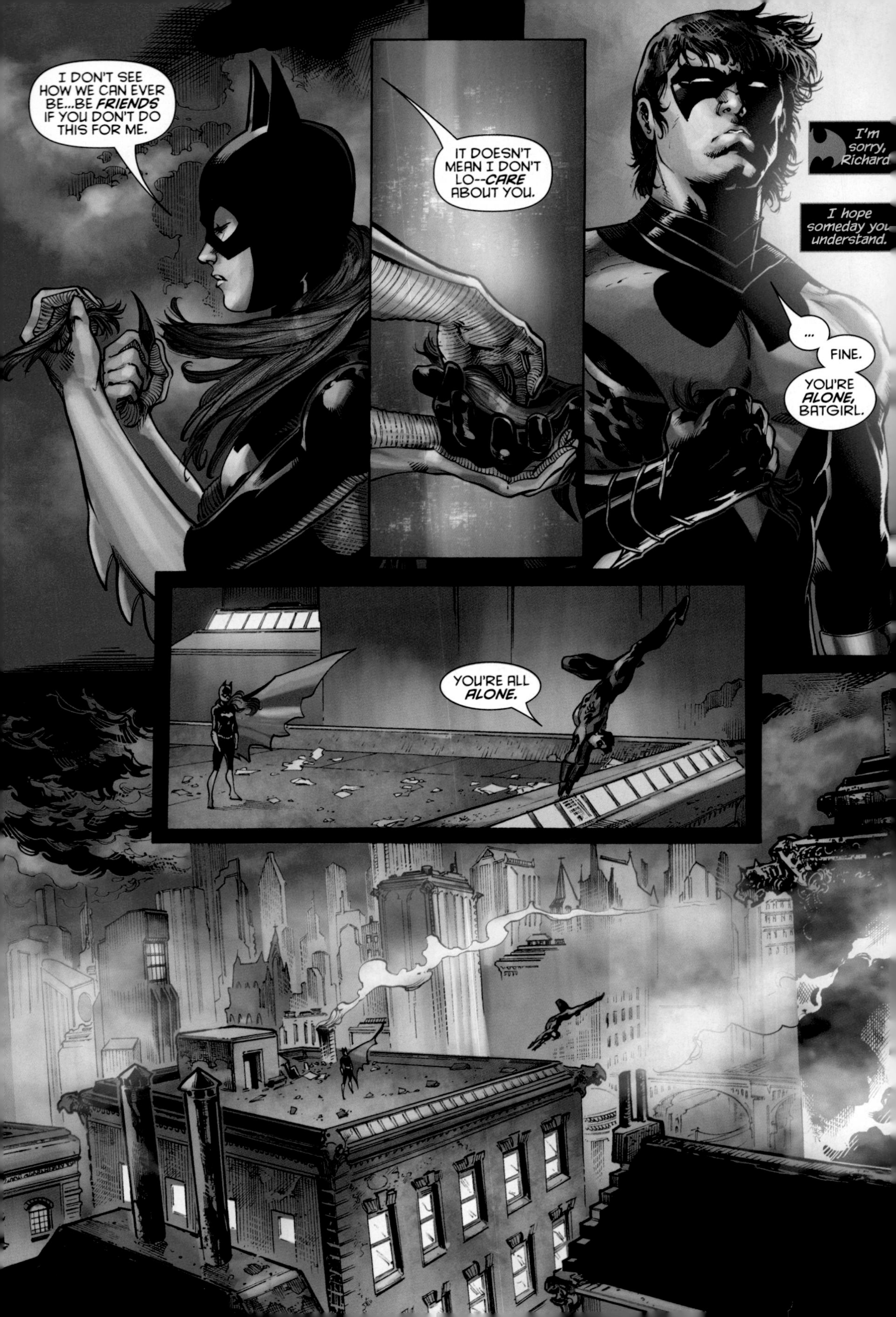
I DON'T SEE HOW WE CAN EVER BE...BE FRIENDS IF YOU DON'T DO THIS FOR ME.
IT DOESN'T MEAN I DON'T LO--CARE ABOUT YOU.
I'm sorry, Richard
I hope someday you understand.
...
FINE.
YOU'RE ALONE, BATGIRL.
YOU'RE ALL ALONE.

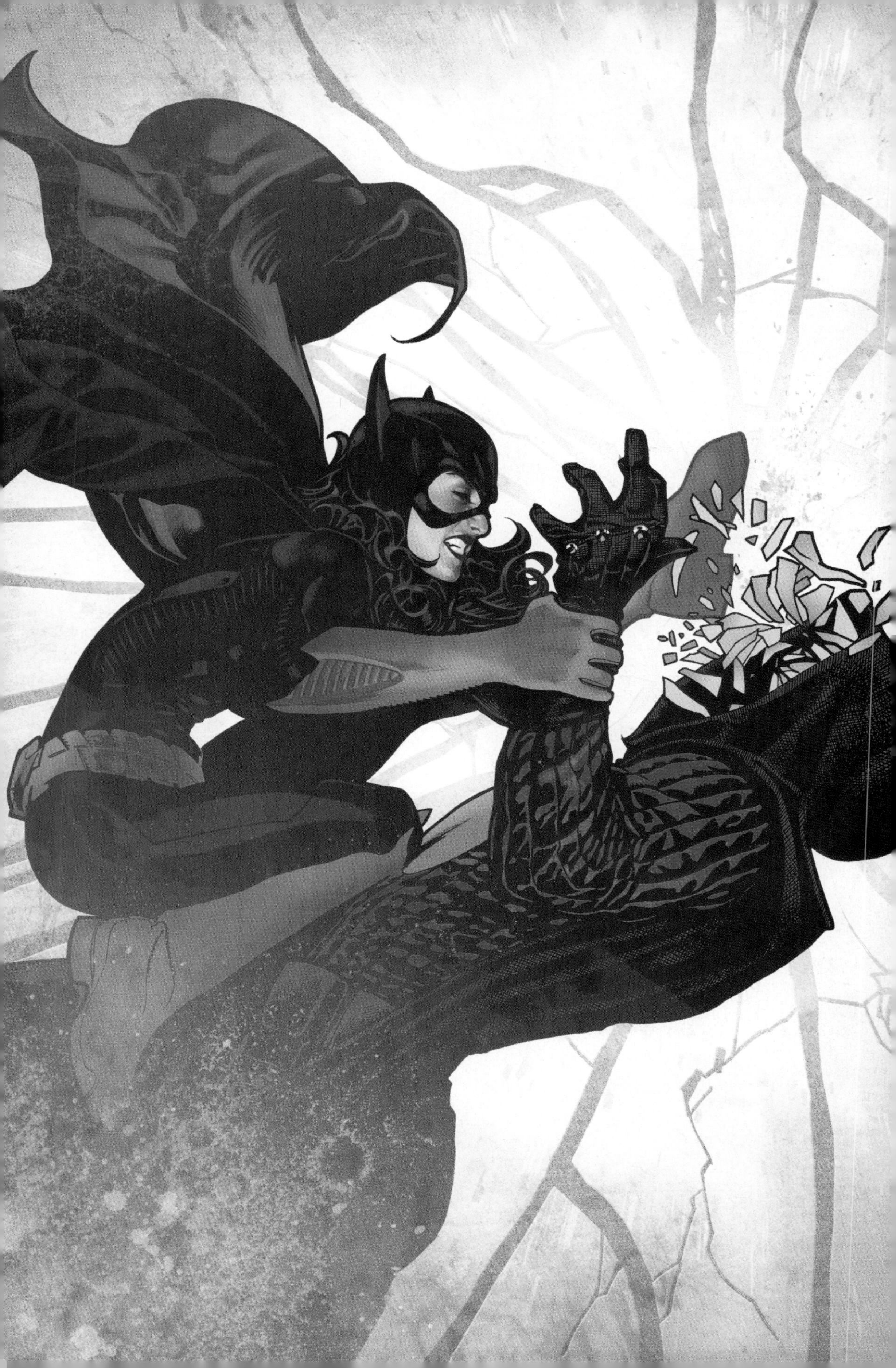

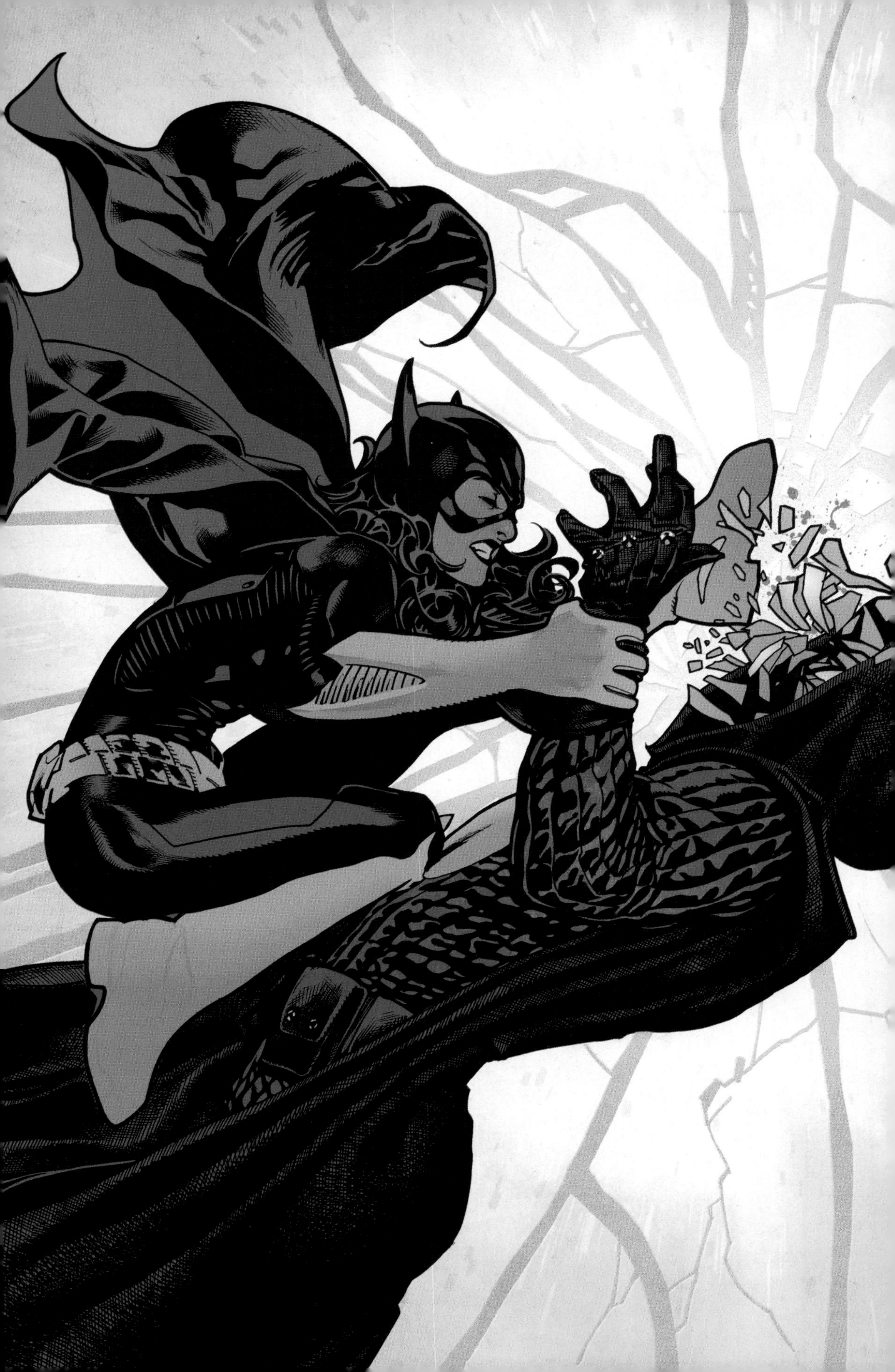

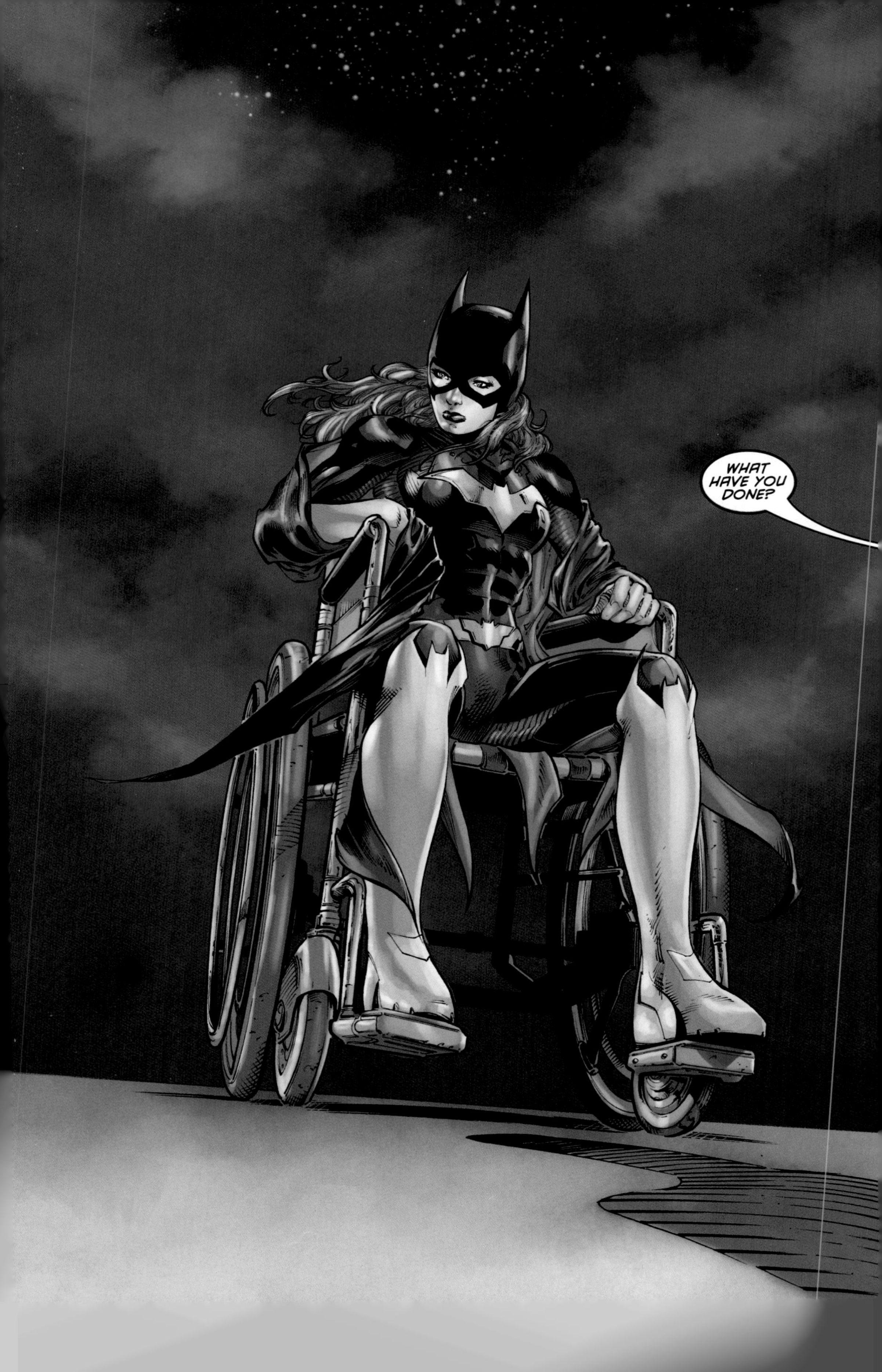
WHAT HAVE YOU DONE?

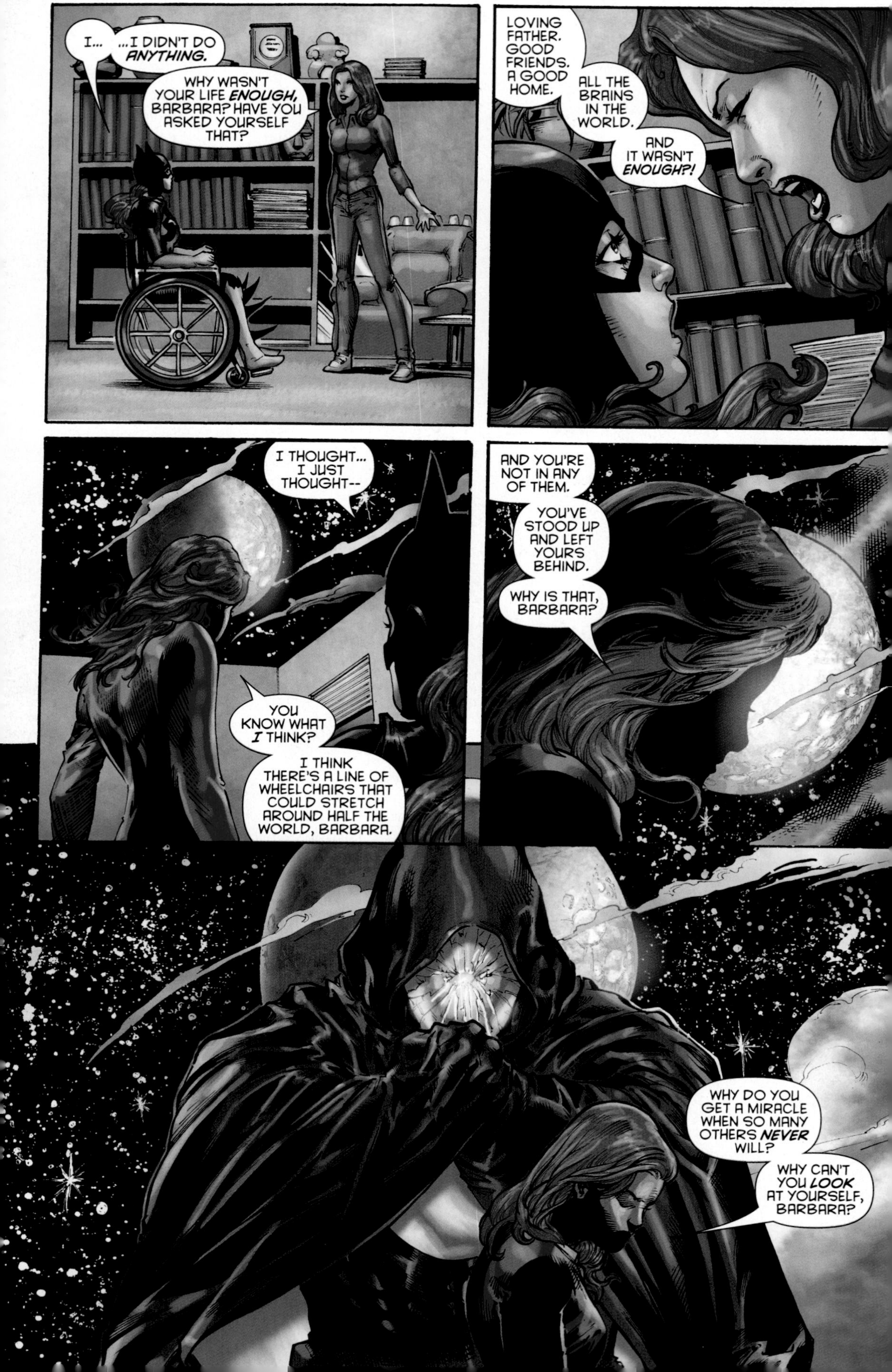
I...
...I DIDN'T DO ANYTHING.
WHY WASN'T YOUR LIFE ENOUGH, BARBARA? HAVE YOU ASKED YOURSELF THAT?
LOVING FATHER. GOOD FRIENDS. A GOOD HOME.
ALL THE BRAINS IN THE WORLD.
AND IT WASN'T ENOUGH?!
I THOUGHT... I JUST THOUGHT--
YOU KNOW WHAT I THINK?
I THINK THERE'S A LINE OF WHEELCHAIRS THAT COULD STRETCH AROUND HALF THE WORLD, BARBARA.
AND YOU'RE NOT IN ANY OF THEM.
YOU'VE STOOD UP AND LEFT YOURS BEHIND.
WHY IS THAT, BARBARA?
WHY DO YOU GET A MIRACLE WHEN SO MANY OTHERS NEVER WILL?
WHY CAN'T YOU LOOK AT YOURSELF, BARBARA?

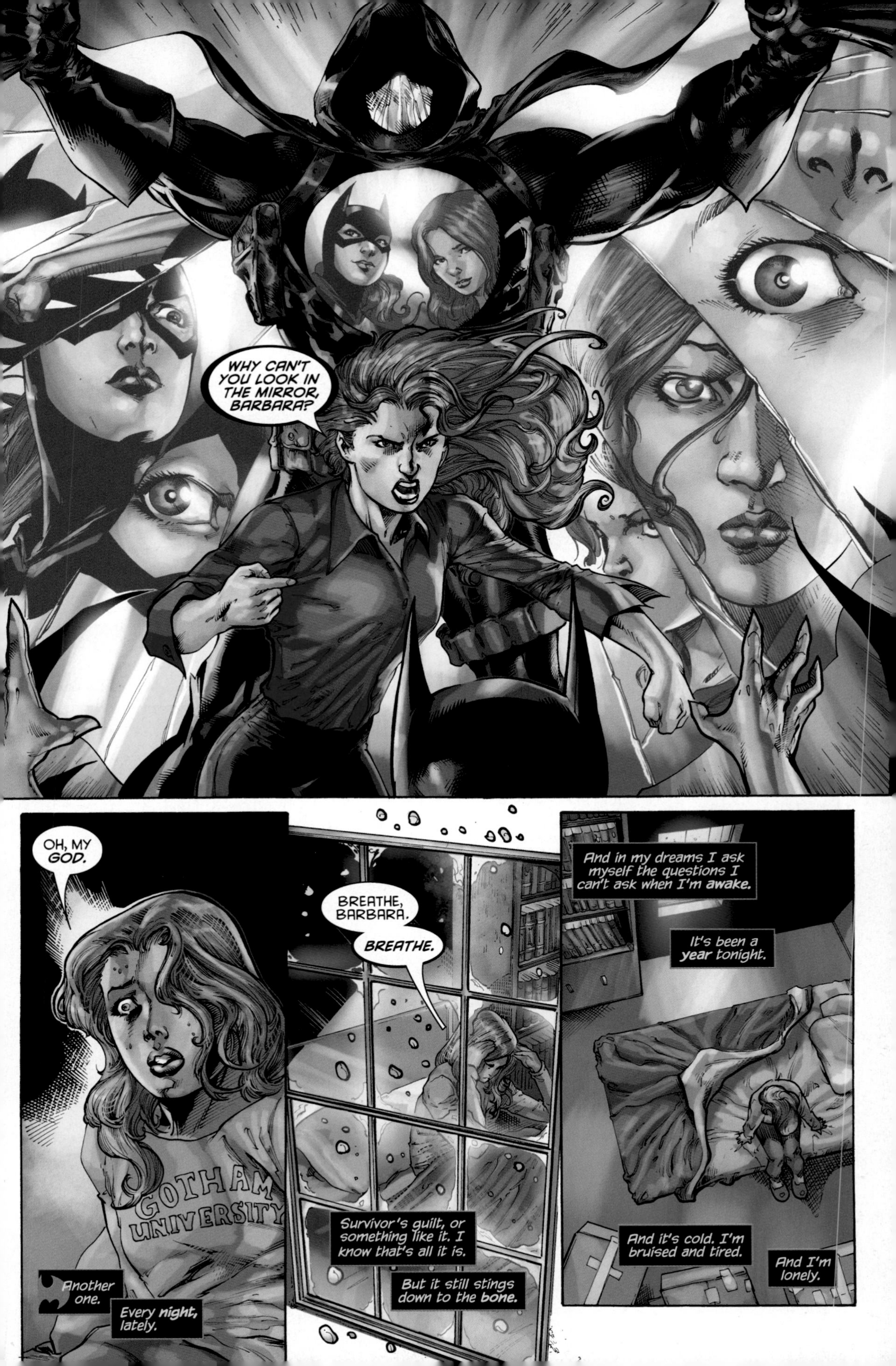
WHY CAN'T YOU LOOK IN THE MIRROR, BARBARA?
OH, MY GOD.
GOTHAM UNIVERSITY
Another one.
Every night, lately.
BREATHE, BARBARA.
BREATHE.
Survivor's guilt, or something like it. I know that's all it is.
But it still stings down to the bone.
And in my dreams I ask myself the questions I can't ask when I'm awake.
It's been a year tonight.
And it's cold. I'm bruised and tired.
And I'm lonely.

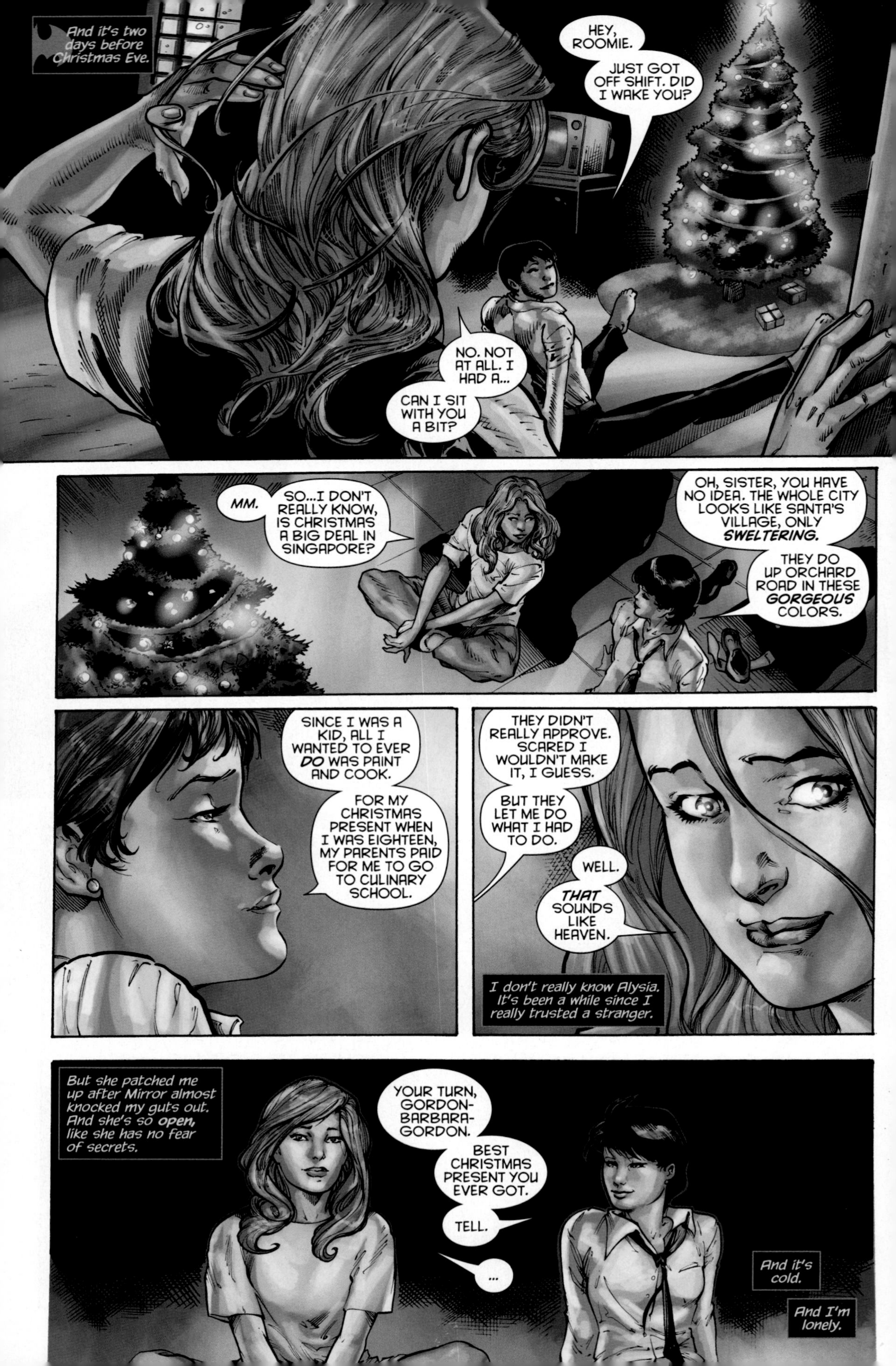

And it's two days before Christmas Eve.
HEY, ROOMIE.
JUST GOT OFF SHIFT. DID I WAKE YOU?
NO. NOT AT ALL. I HAD A...
CAN I SIT WITH YOU A BIT?
MM.
SO...I DON'T REALLY KNOW, IS CHRISTMAS A BIG DEAL IN SINGAPORE?
OH, SISTER, YOU HAVE NO IDEA. THE WHOLE CITY LOOKS LIKE SANTA'S VILLAGE, ONLY SWELTERING.
THEY DO UP ORCHARD ROAD IN THESE GORGEOUS COLORS.
SINCE I WAS A KID, ALL I WANTED TO EVER DO WAS PAINT AND COOK.
FOR MY CHRISTMAS PRESENT WHEN I WAS EIGHTEEN, MY PARENTS PAID FOR ME TO GO TO CULINARY SCHOOL.
THEY DIDN'T REALLY APPROVE. SCARED I WOULDN'T MAKE IT, I GUESS.
BUT THEY LET ME DO WHAT I HAD TO DO.
WELL.
THAT SOUNDS LIKE HEAVEN.
I don't really know Alysia. It's been a while since I really trusted a stranger.
But she patched me up after Mirror almost knocked my guts out. And she's so open, like she has no fear of secrets.
YOUR TURN, GORDON-BARBARA-GORDON.
BEST CHRISTMAS PRESENT YOU EVER GOT.
TELL.
...
And it's cold.
And I'm lonely.

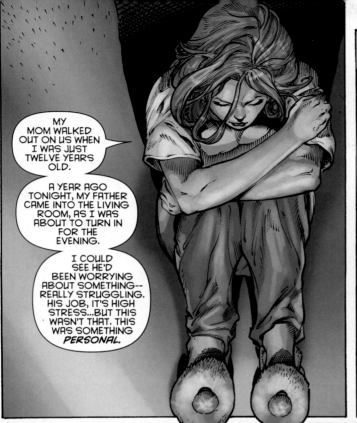

MY MOM WALKED OUT ON US WHEN I WAS JUST TWELVE YEARS OLD.

A YEAR AGO TONIGHT, MY FATHER CAME INTO THE LIVING ROOM, AS I WAS ABOUT TO TURN IN FOR THE EVENING.

I COULD SEE HE'D BEEN WORRYING ABOUT SOMETHING-- REALLY STRUGGLING. HIS JOB, IT'S HIGH STRESS...BUT THIS WASN'T THAT. THIS WAS SOMETHING *PERSONAL*.

"THERE'S A CLINIC IN SOUTH AFRICA, BARBARA."

THAT'S ALL HE COULD SAY.

HE DIDN'T SAY "CURE." THAT WORD WAS SORT OF TABOO IN OUR HOUSE. JUST THAT THERE WAS A CLINIC.

SO THE WHEELCHAIR RAMP IN YOUR VAN--IT'S NOT FOR *FAMILY*, IS IT?

NO.

IT WAS MINE.

YOU STILL KEEP IT A YEAR LATER?

She's astute, too.

Don't know if that's good or bad.

What was I thinking?

I don't even know this girl.

OKAY. IF WE'RE TELLING *BIG* TIME SECRETS, I HAVE ONE.

ALYSIA, I HAVE TO GO. RAIN CHECK, OKAY?

I HAVE SOME STUFF I HAVE TO...I HAVE THINGS TO DO.

DID I SAY SOMETHING?

IT'S NOT YOU, IT'S OKAY, I JUST--

MAN, YOU DO MYSTERIOUS LIKE YOU WERE *BORN* INTO IT.

BARBARA!

DON'T YOU THINK YOU'D BETTER PUT SOME *SHOES* ON OR SOMETHING THERE, SPEEDY?

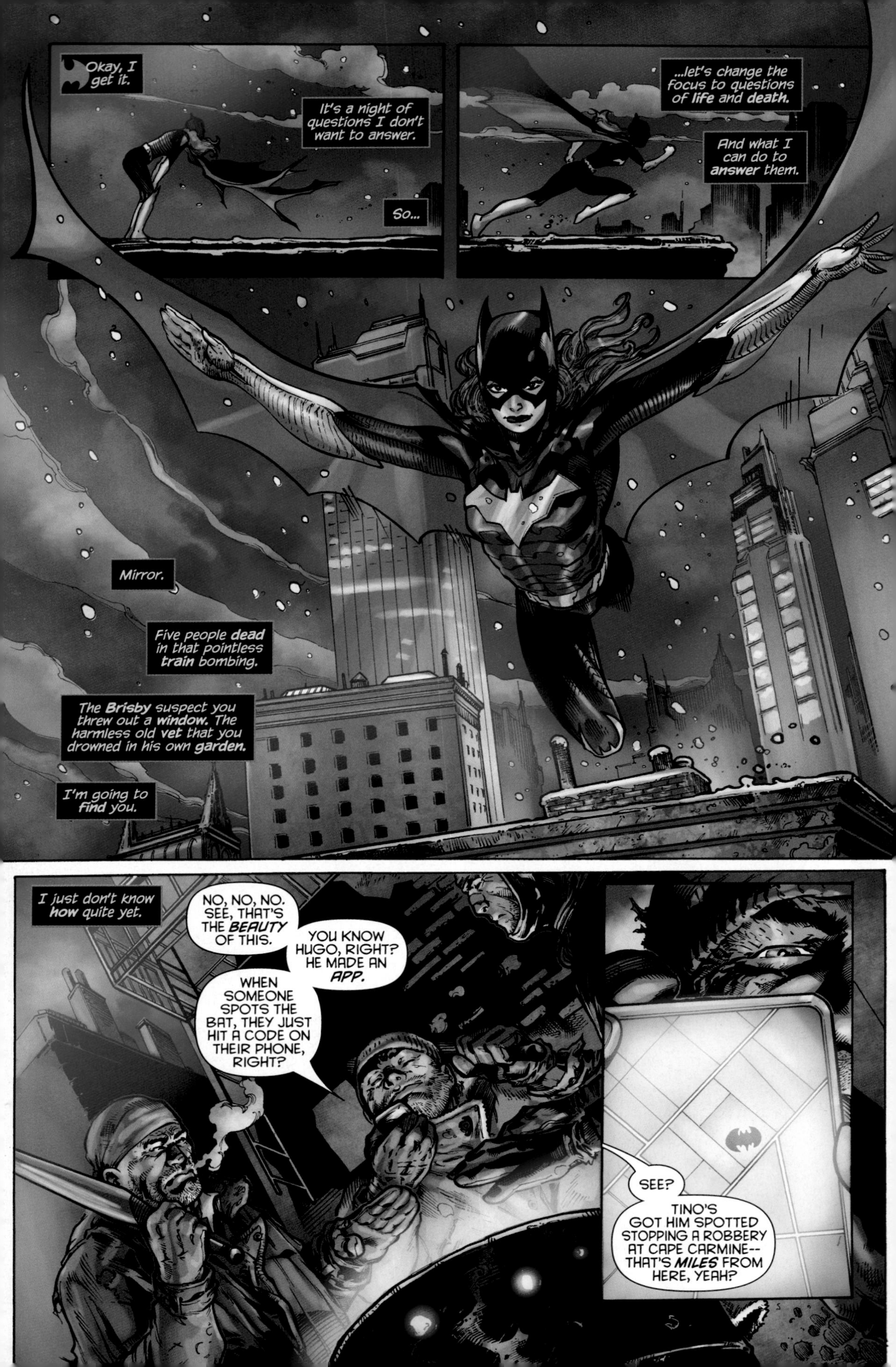
Okay, I get it.
It's a night of questions I don't want to answer.
So...
...let's change the focus to questions of **life** and **death.**
And what I can do to **answer** them.
Mirror.
Five people **dead** in that pointless **train** bombing.
The **Brisby** suspect you threw out a **window.** The harmless old **vet** that you drowned in his own **garden.**
I'm going to **find** you.
I just don't know **how** quite yet.
NO, NO, NO. SEE, THAT'S THE ***BEAUTY*** OF THIS.
YOU KNOW HUGO, RIGHT? HE MADE AN ***APP.***
WHEN SOMEONE SPOTS THE BAT, THEY JUST HIT A CODE ON THEIR PHONE, RIGHT?
SEE?
TINO'S GOT HIM SPOTTED STOPPING A ROBBERY AT CAPE CARMINE-- THAT'S ***MILES*** FROM HERE, YEAH?

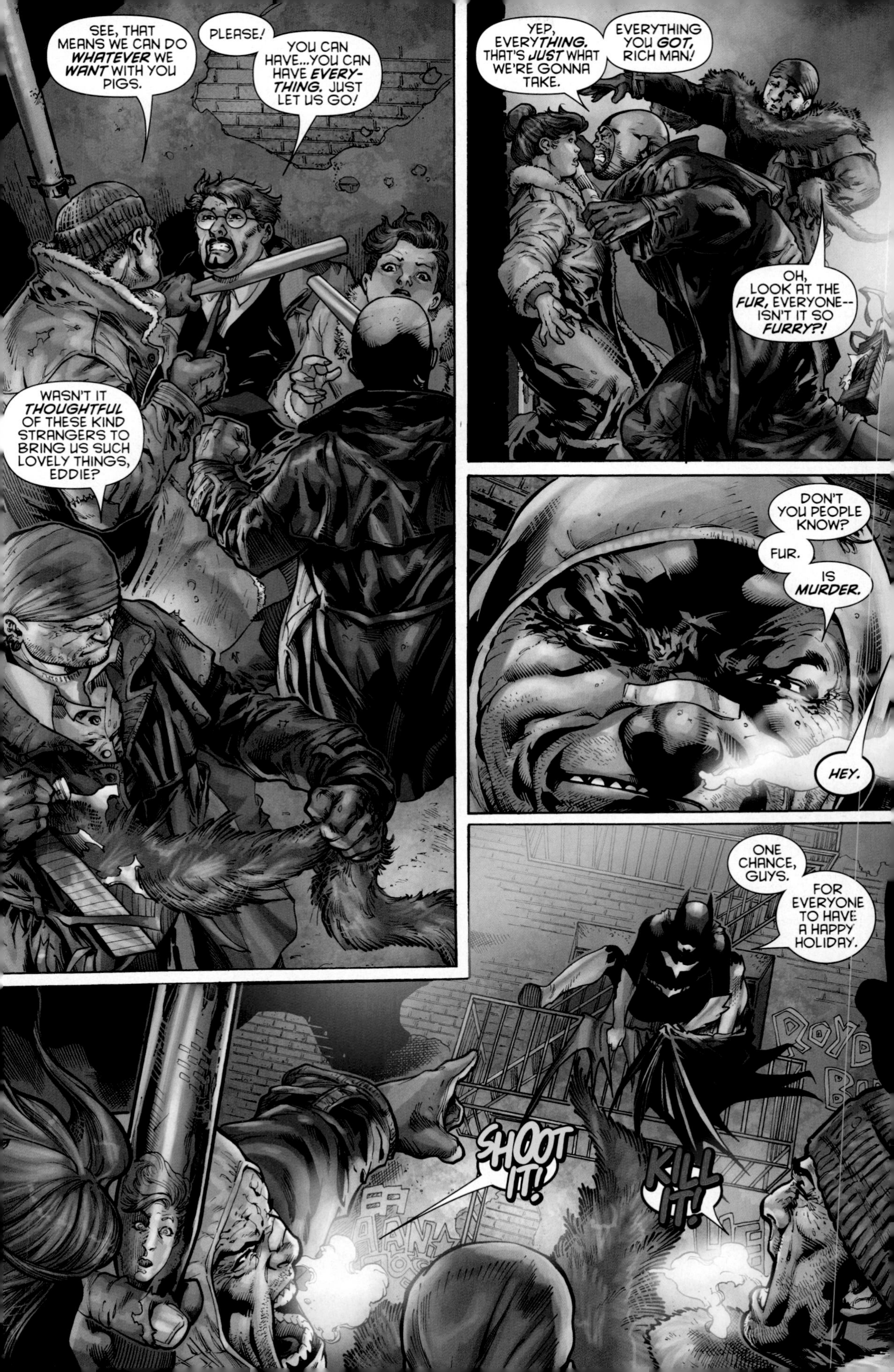
SEE, THAT MEANS WE CAN DO *WHATEVER* WE *WANT* WITH YOU PIGS.
PLEASE!
YOU CAN HAVE...YOU CAN HAVE *EVERY-THING.* JUST LET US GO!
WASN'T IT *THOUGHTFUL* OF THESE KIND STRANGERS TO BRING US SUCH LOVELY THINGS, EDDIE?
YEP, EVERY*THING.* THAT'S *JUST* WHAT WE'RE GONNA TAKE.
EVERYTHING YOU *GOT,* RICH MAN!
OH, LOOK AT THE *FUR,* EVERYONE-- ISN'T IT SO *FURRY?!*
DON'T YOU PEOPLE KNOW?
FUR.
IS *MURDER.*
HEY.
ONE CHANCE, GUYS.
FOR EVERYONE TO HAVE A HAPPY HOLIDAY.
SHOOT IT!
KILL IT!

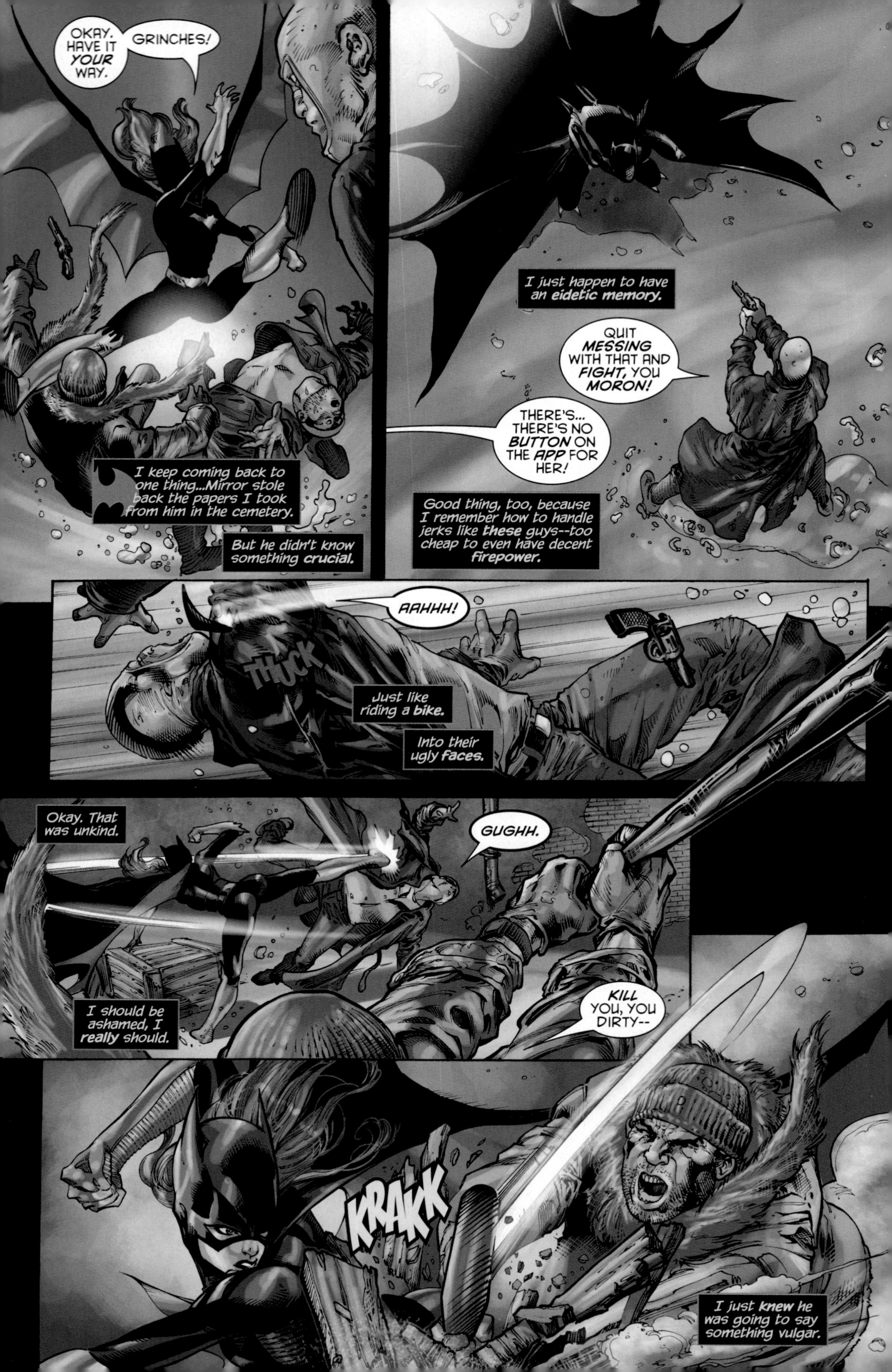

OKAY. HAVE IT YOUR WAY.
GRINCHES!
I keep coming back to one thing...Mirror stole back the papers I took from him in the cemetery.
But he didn't know something crucial.
I just happen to have an eidetic memory.
QUIT MESSING WITH THAT AND FIGHT, YOU MORON!
THERE'S... THERE'S NO BUTTON ON THE APP FOR HER!
Good thing, too, because I remember how to handle jerks like these guys--too cheap to even have decent firepower.
AAHHH!
THUCK
Just like riding a bike.
Into their ugly faces.
Okay. That was unkind.
GUGHH.
I should be ashamed, I really should.
KILL YOU, YOU DIRTY--
KRAKK
I just knew he was going to say something vulgar.

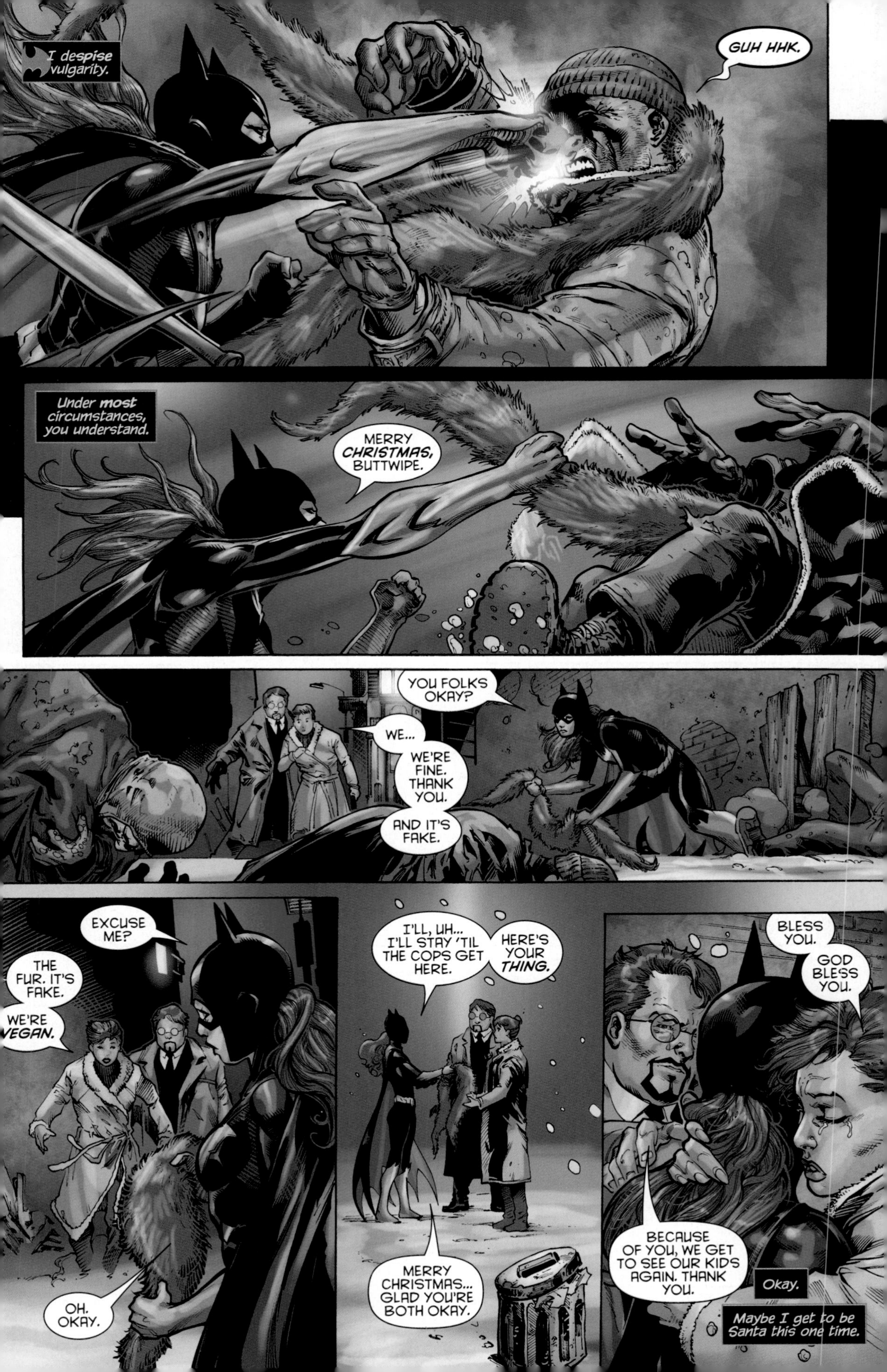
I despise vulgarity.
GUH HHK.
Under most circumstances, you understand.
MERRY CHRISTMAS, BUTTWIPE.
YOU FOLKS OKAY?
WE...
WE'RE FINE. THANK YOU.
AND IT'S FAKE.
EXCUSE ME?
THE FUR. IT'S FAKE.
WE'RE VEGAN.
OH. OKAY.
I'LL, UH... I'LL STAY 'TIL THE COPS GET HERE.
HERE'S YOUR THING.
MERRY CHRISTMAS... GLAD YOU'RE BOTH OKAY.
BLESS YOU.
GOD BLESS YOU.
BECAUSE OF YOU, WE GET TO SEE OUR KIDS AGAIN. THANK YOU.
Okay.
Maybe I get to be Santa this one time.

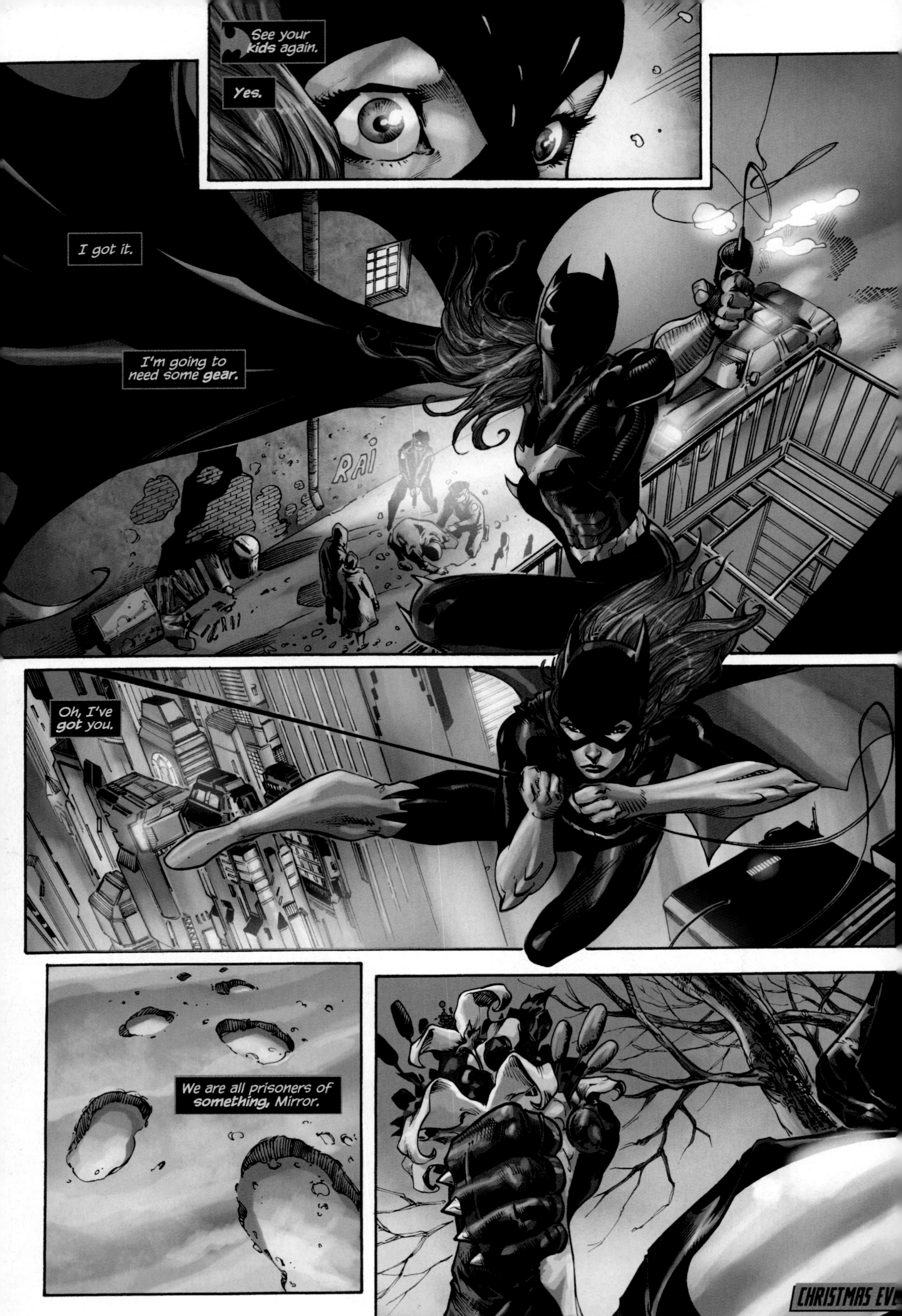

See your kids again.
Yes.
I got it.
I'm going to need some gear.
RAI
Oh, I've got you.
We are all prisoners of something, Mirror.
CHRISTMAS EVE

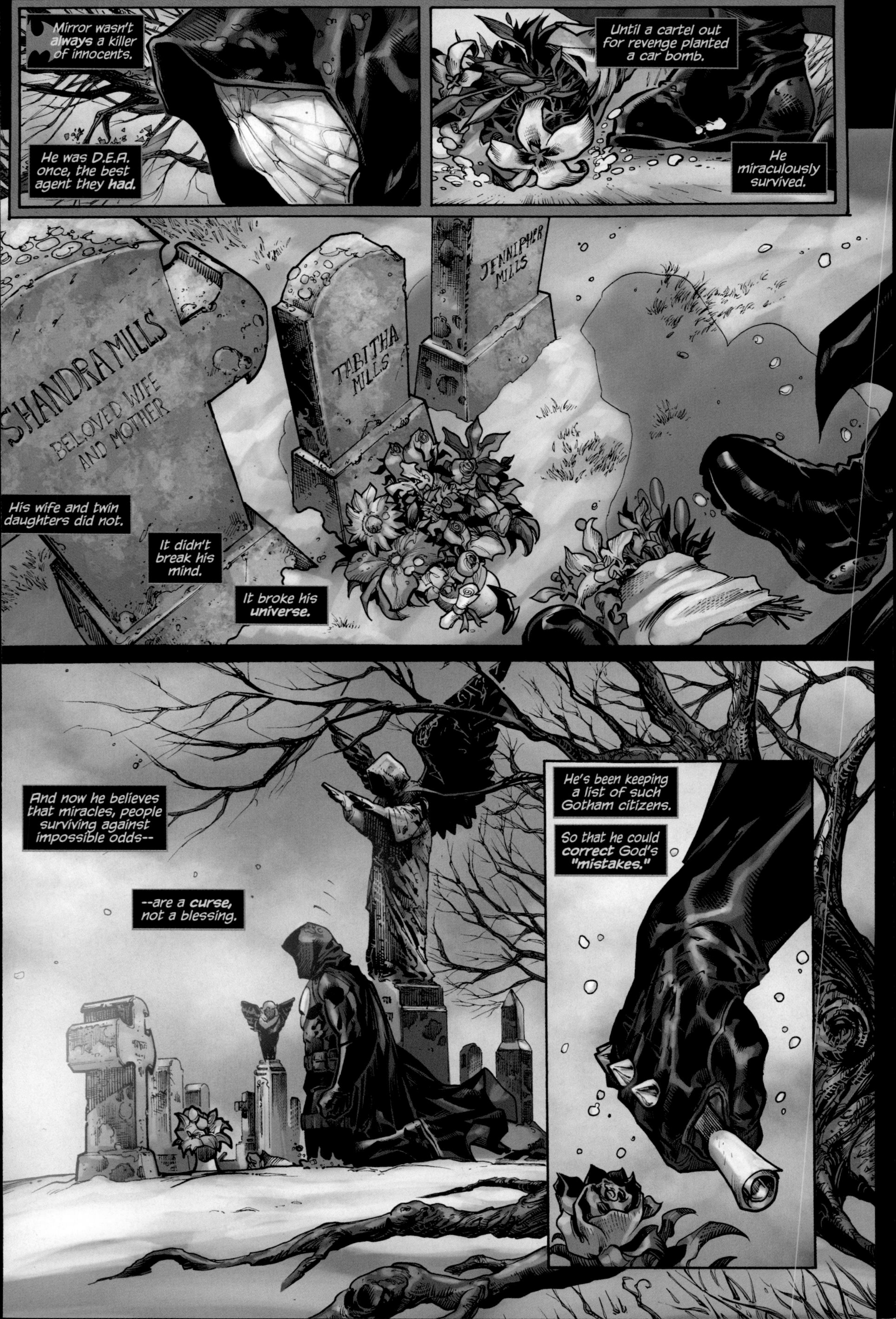

Mirror wasn't always a killer of innocents.
He was D.E.A. once, the best agent they had.
Until a cartel out for revenge planted a car bomb.
He miraculously survived.
JENNIPHER MILLS
TABITHA MILLS
SHANDRA MILLS BELOVED WIFE AND MOTHER
His wife and twin daughters did not.
It didn't break his mind.
It broke his universe.
And now he believes that miracles, people surviving against impossible odds--
--are a curse, not a blessing.
He's been keeping a list of such Gotham citizens.
So that he could correct God's "mistakes."

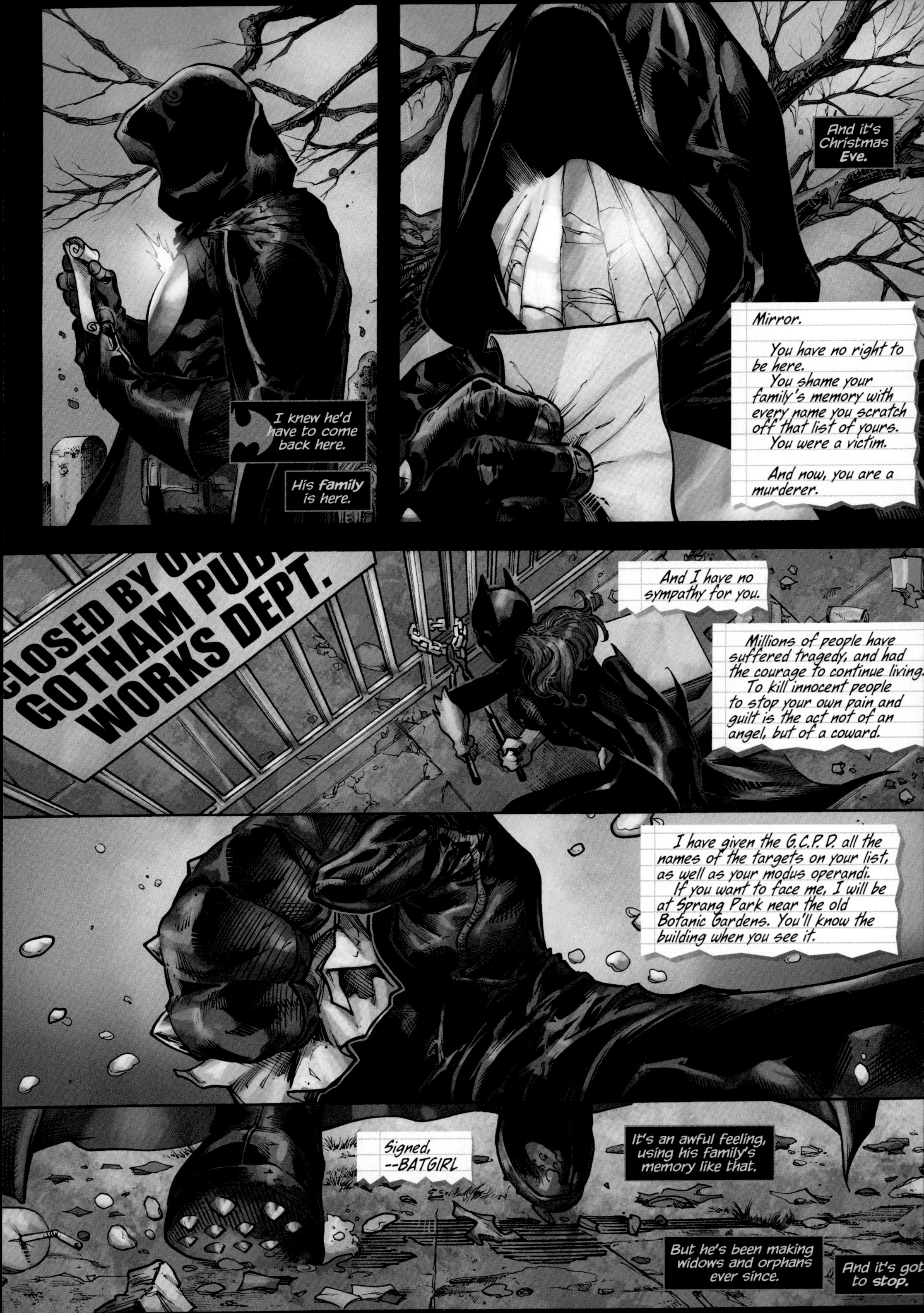
I knew he'd have to come back here.
His family is here.
And it's Christmas Eve.
Mirror.
You have no right to be here.
You shame your family's memory with every name you scratch off that list of yours.
You were a victim.
And now, you are a murderer.
CLOSED BY O
GOTHAM PUB
WORKS DEPT.
And I have no sympathy for you.
Millions of people have suffered tragedy, and had the courage to continue living.
To kill innocent people to stop your own pain and guilt is the act not of an angel, but of a coward.
I have given the G.C.P.D. all the names of the targets on your list, as well as your modus operandi.
If you want to face me, I will be at Sprang Park near the old Botanic Gardens. You'll know the building when you see it.
Signed,
--BATGIRL
It's an awful feeling, using his family's memory like that.
But he's been making widows and orphans ever since.
And it's go
to stop.

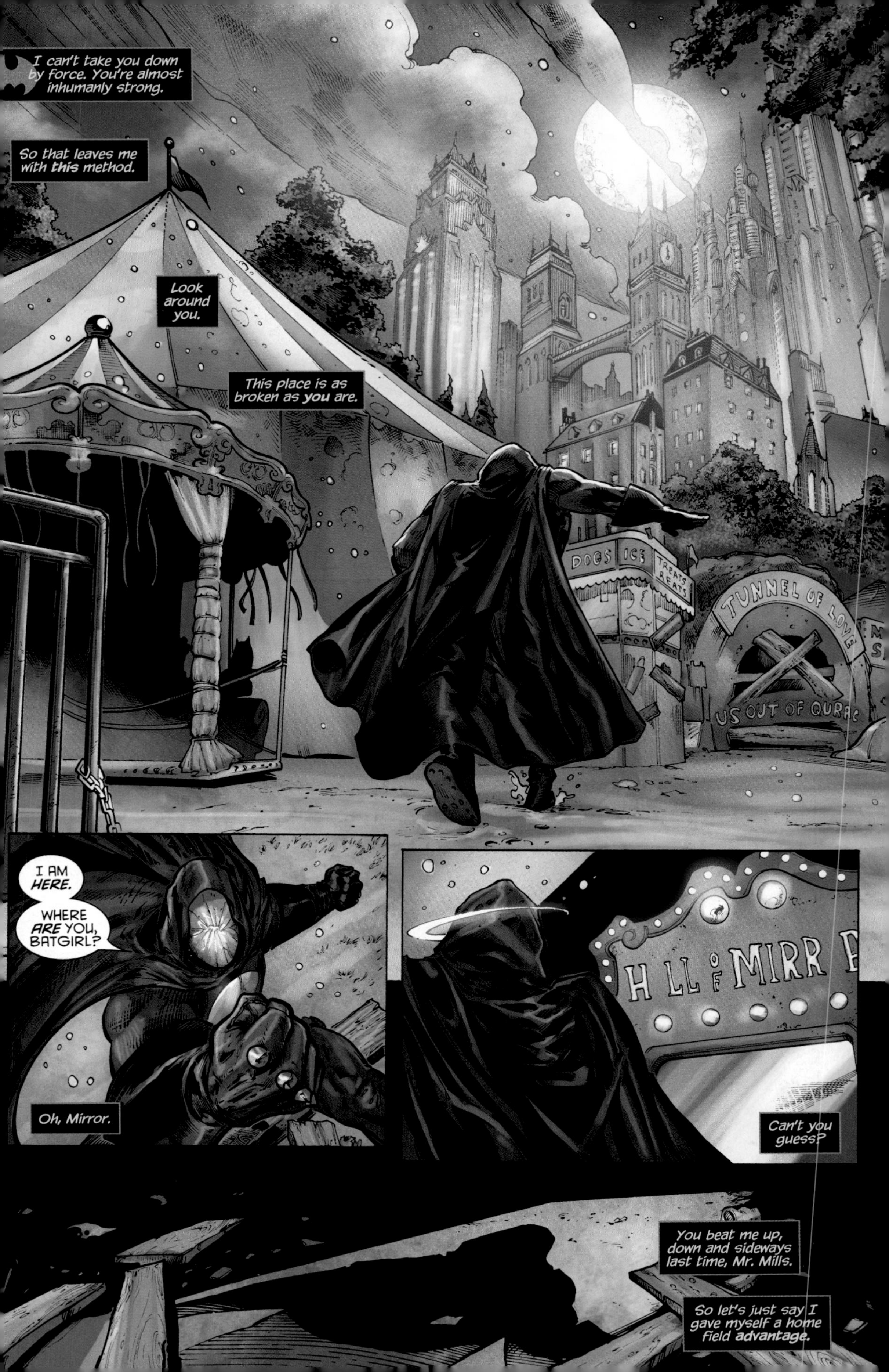

I can't take you down by force. You're almost inhumanly strong.
So that leaves me with **this** method.
Look around you.
This place is as broken as **you** are.
DOGS
ICE
TREATS
TUNNEL OF LOVE
US OUT OF QURAC
I AM ***HERE.***
WHERE ***ARE*** YOU, BATGIRL?
Oh, Mirror.
H LL OF MIRR
Can't you guess?
You beat me up, down and sideways last time, Mr. Mills.
So let's just say I gave myself a home field **advantage.**

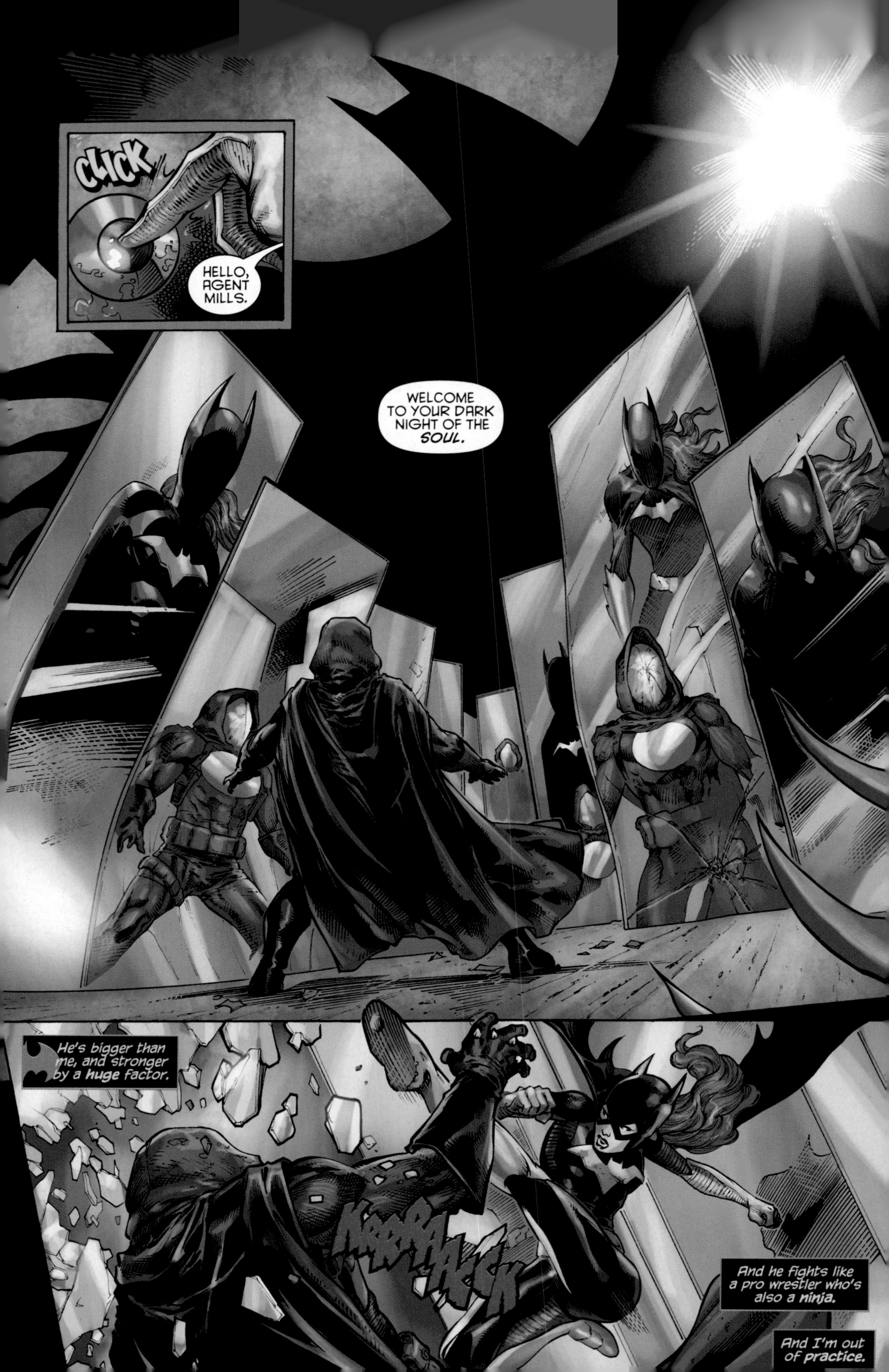
CLICK
HELLO, AGENT MILLS.
WELCOME TO YOUR DARK NIGHT OF THE SOUL.
He's bigger than me, and stronger by a huge factor.
KRRRAACK
And he fights like a pro wrestler who's also a ninja.
And I'm out of practice.

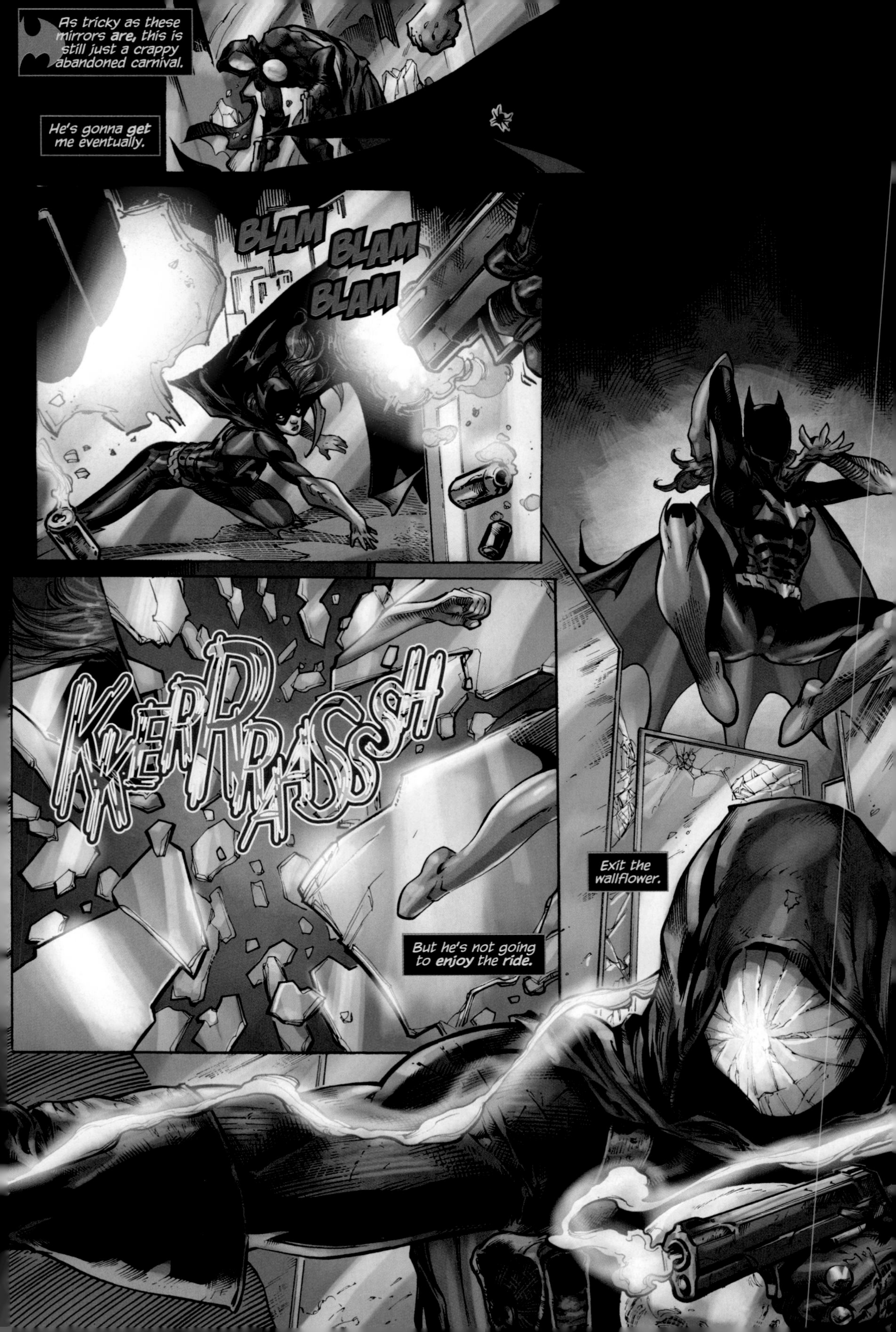
As tricky as these mirrors are, this is still just a crappy abandoned carnival.
He's gonna get me eventually.
BLAM BLAM BLAM
KKERRRASSSH
But he's not going to enjoy the ride.
Exit the wallflower.

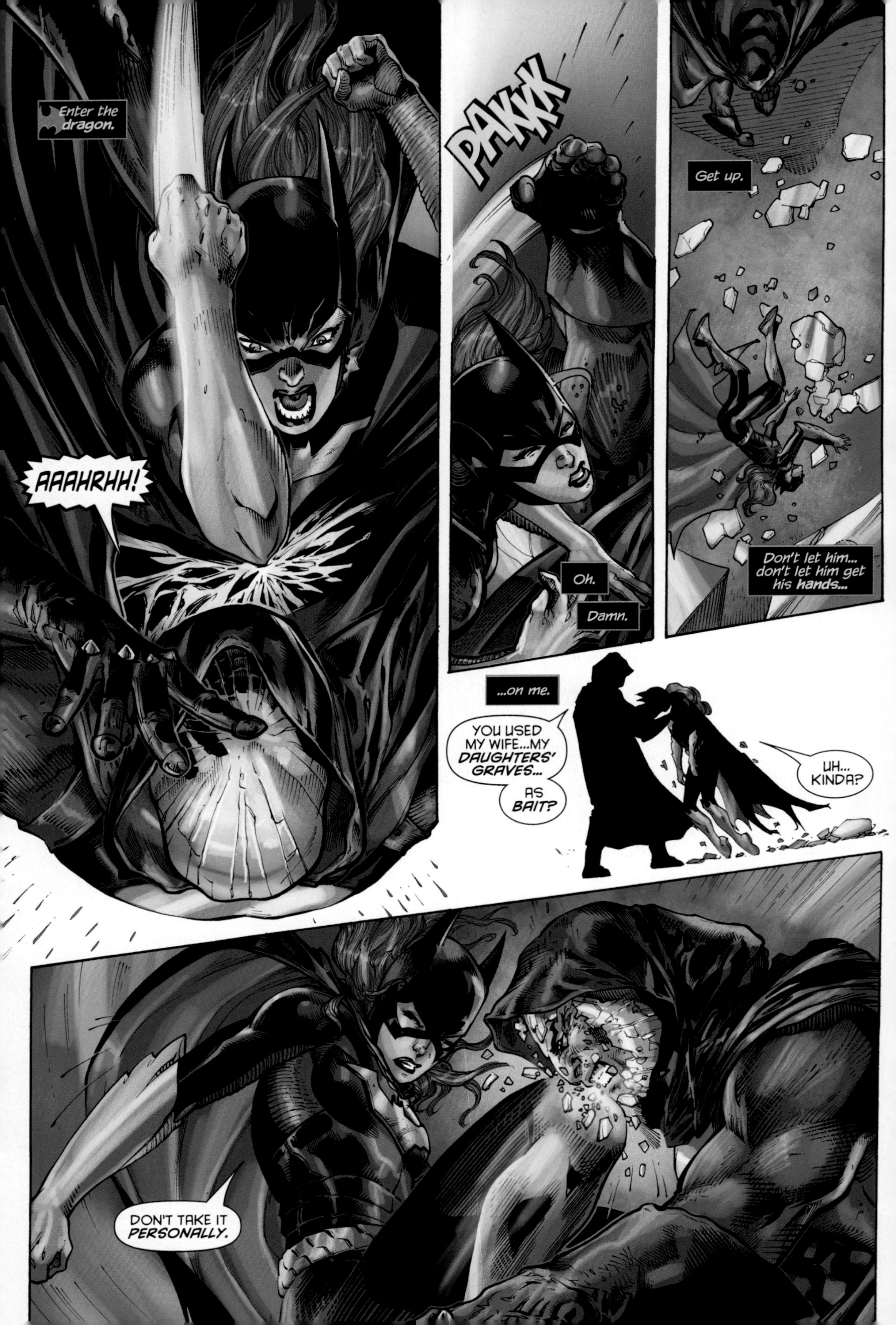

Enter the dragon.
AAAHRHH!
PAKKK
Oh.
Damn.
Get up.
Don't let him... don't let him get his hands...
...on me.
YOU USED MY WIFE...MY DAUGHTERS' GRAVES...
AS BAIT?
UH... KINDA?
DON'T TAKE IT PERSONALLY.

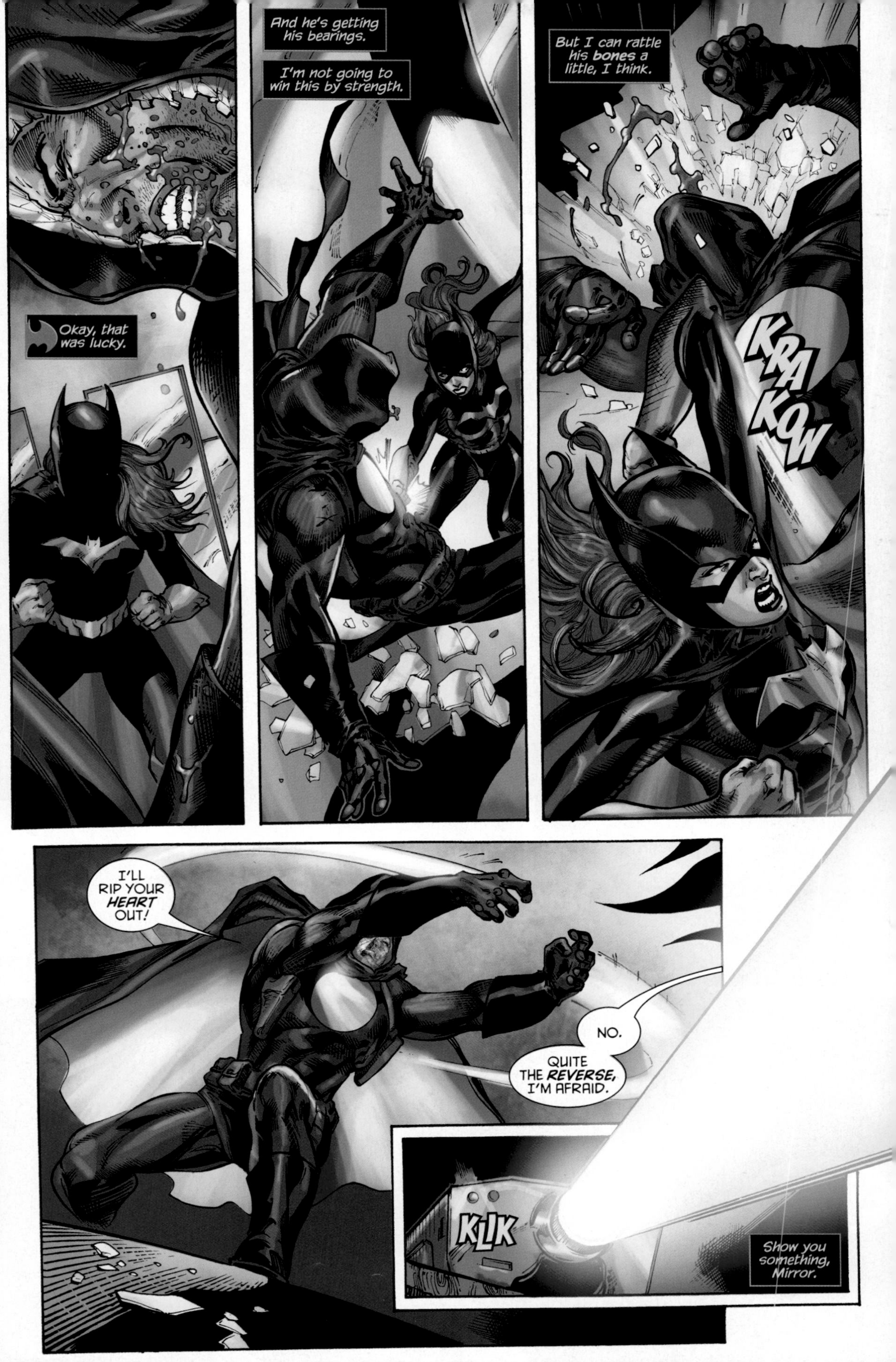
Okay, that was lucky.
And he's getting his bearings.
I'm not going to win this by strength.
But I can rattle his bones a little, I think.
KRAKOW
I'LL RIP YOUR HEART OUT!
NO.
QUITE THE REVERSE, I'M AFRAID.
KLIK
Show you something, Mirror.

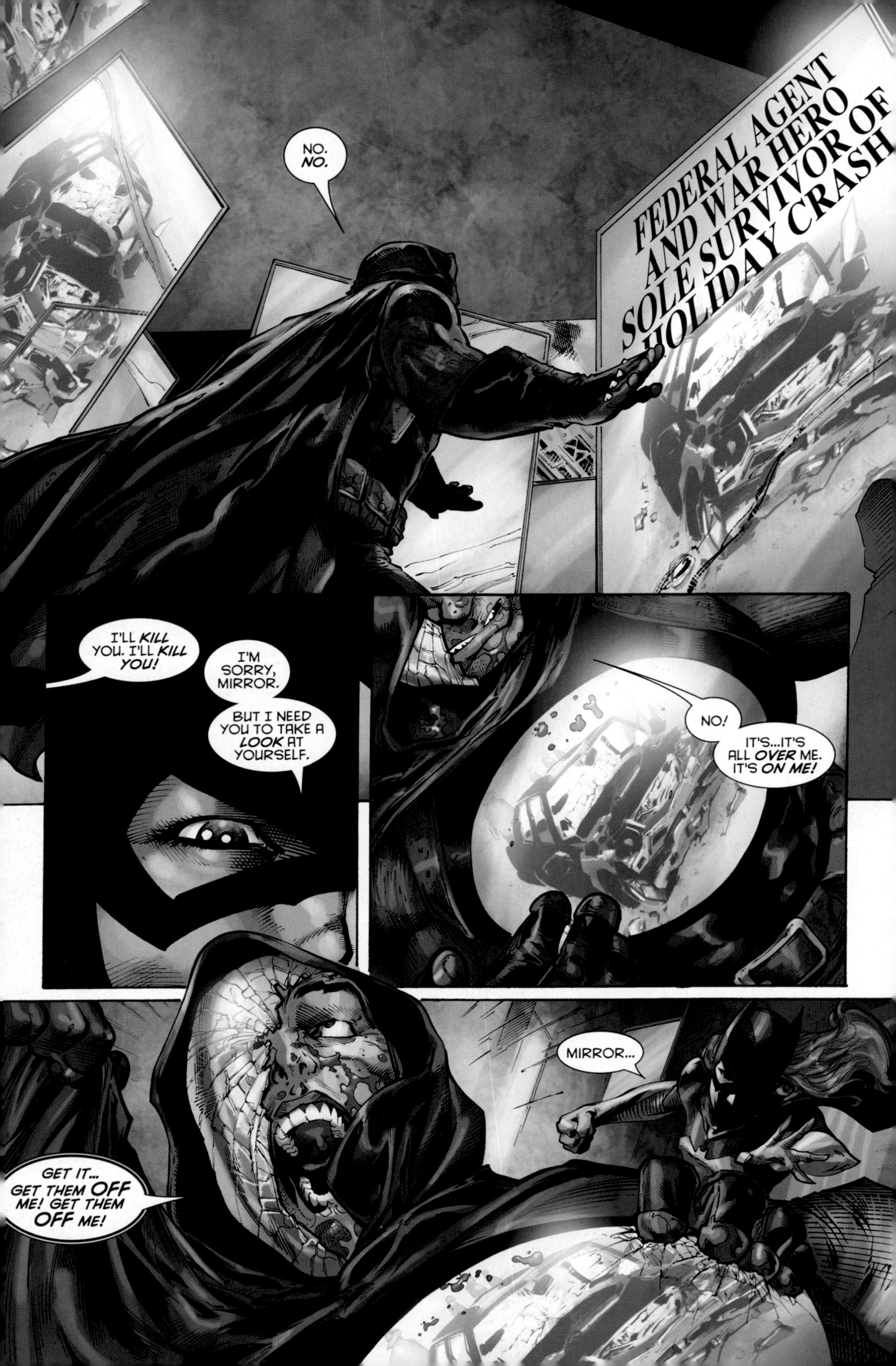
NO. NO.
FEDERAL AGENT AND WAR HERO SOLE SURVIVOR OF HOLIDAY CRASH
I'LL KILL YOU. I'LL KILL YOU!
I'M SORRY, MIRROR.
BUT I NEED YOU TO TAKE A LOOK AT YOURSELF.
NO!
IT'S...IT'S ALL OVER ME. IT'S ON ME!
MIRROR...
GET IT... GET THEM OFF ME! GET THEM OFF ME!

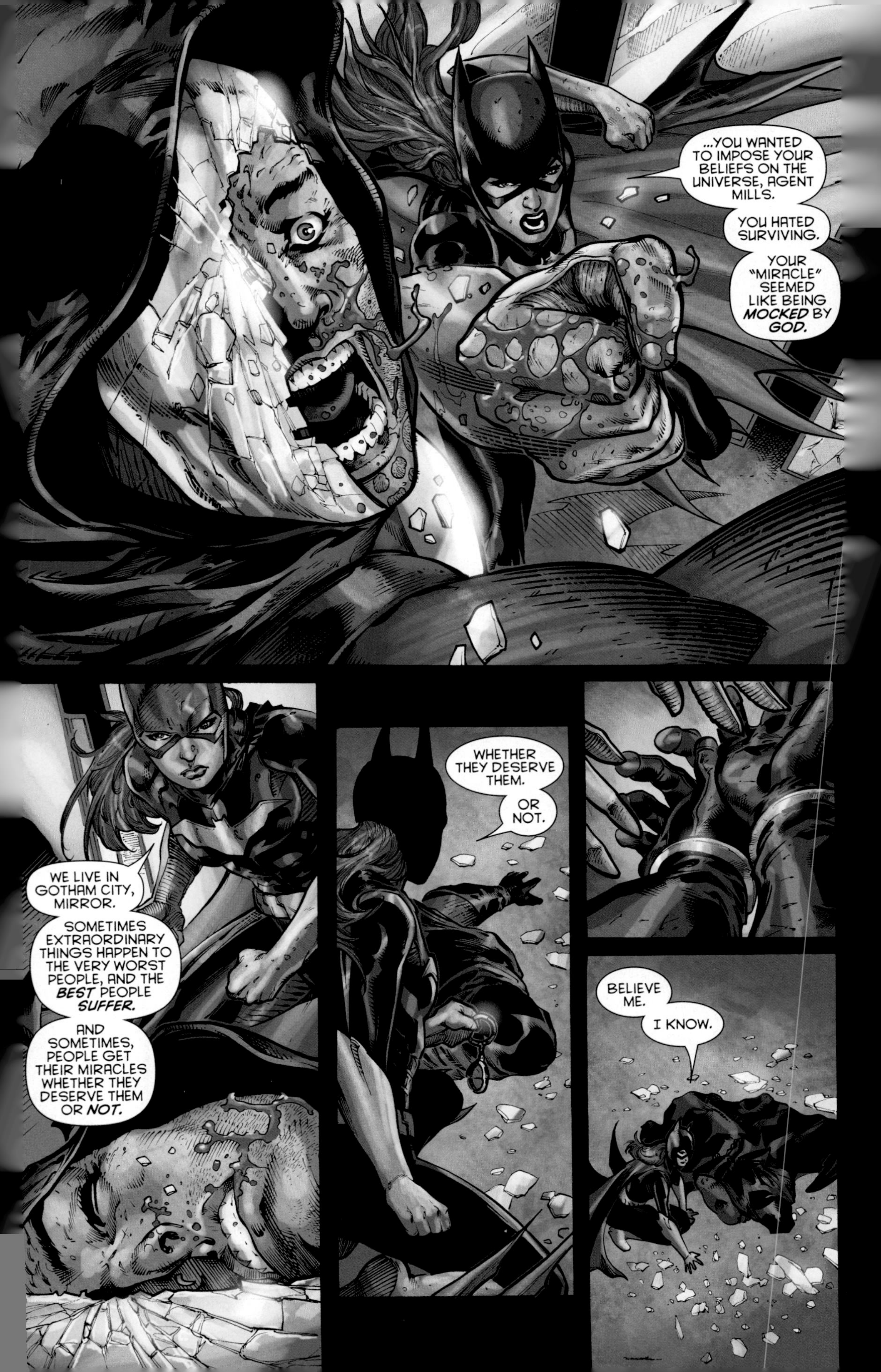
...YOU WANTED TO IMPOSE YOUR BELIEFS ON THE UNIVERSE, AGENT MILLS.
YOU HATED SURVIVING.
YOUR "MIRACLE" SEEMED LIKE BEING *MOCKED* BY *GOD.*
WE LIVE IN GOTHAM CITY, MIRROR.
SOMETIMES EXTRAORDINARY THINGS HAPPEN TO THE VERY WORST PEOPLE, AND THE *BEST* PEOPLE *SUFFER.*
AND SOMETIMES, PEOPLE GET THEIR MIRACLES WHETHER THEY DESERVE THEM OR *NOT.*
WHETHER THEY DESERVE THEM.
OR NOT.
BELIEVE ME.
I KNOW.

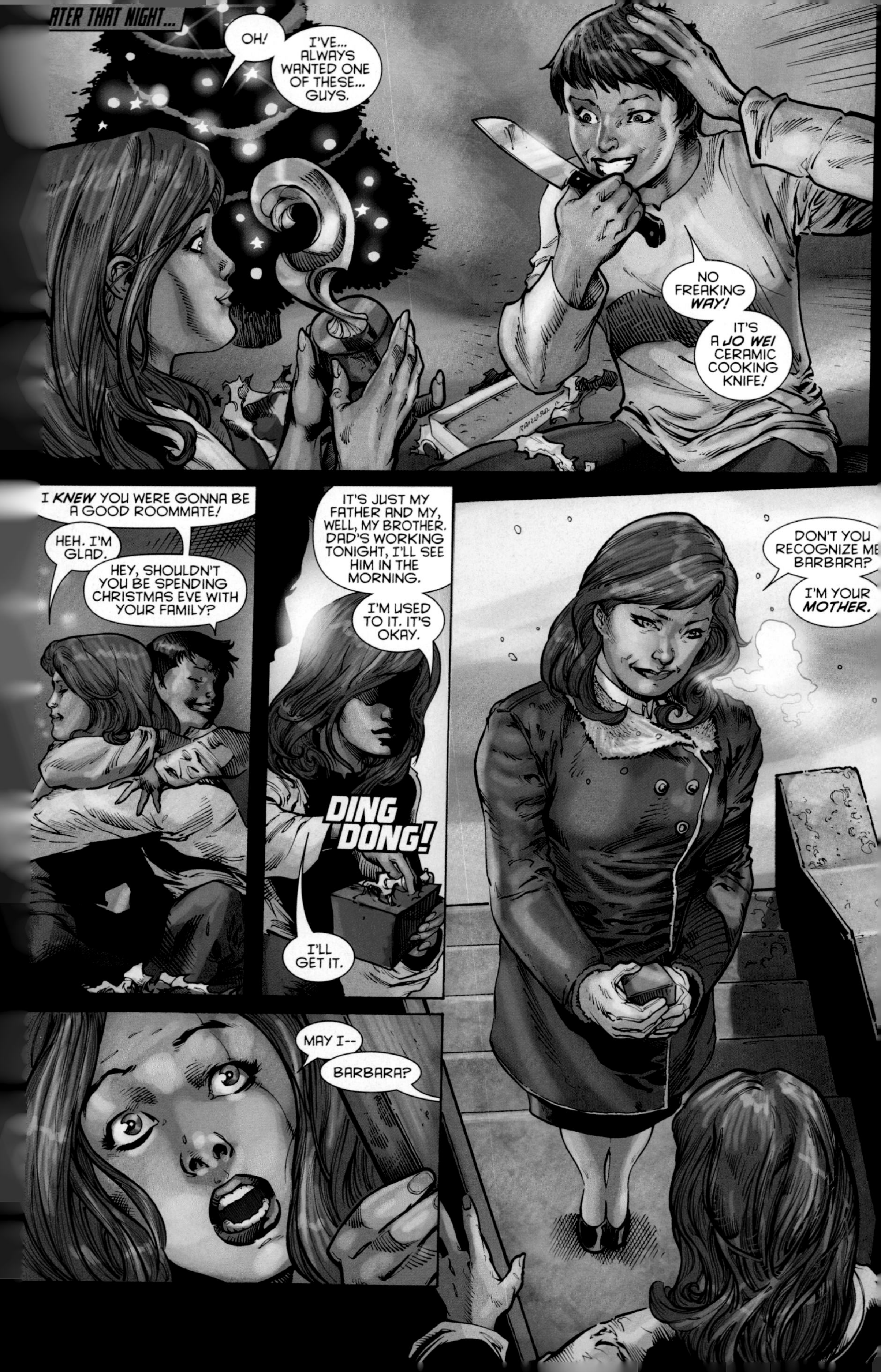
LATER THAT NIGHT...
OH!
I'VE... ALWAYS WANTED ONE OF THESE... GUYS.
NO FREAKING WAY!
IT'S A JO WEI CERAMIC COOKING KNIFE!
I KNEW YOU WERE GONNA BE A GOOD ROOMMATE!
HEH. I'M GLAD.
HEY, SHOULDN'T YOU BE SPENDING CHRISTMAS EVE WITH YOUR FAMILY?
IT'S JUST MY FATHER AND MY, WELL, MY BROTHER. DAD'S WORKING TONIGHT, I'LL SEE HIM IN THE MORNING.
I'M USED TO IT. IT'S OKAY.
DING DONG!
I'LL GET IT.
DON'T YOU RECOGNIZE ME, BARBARA?
I'M YOUR MOTHER.
MAY I--
BARBARA?

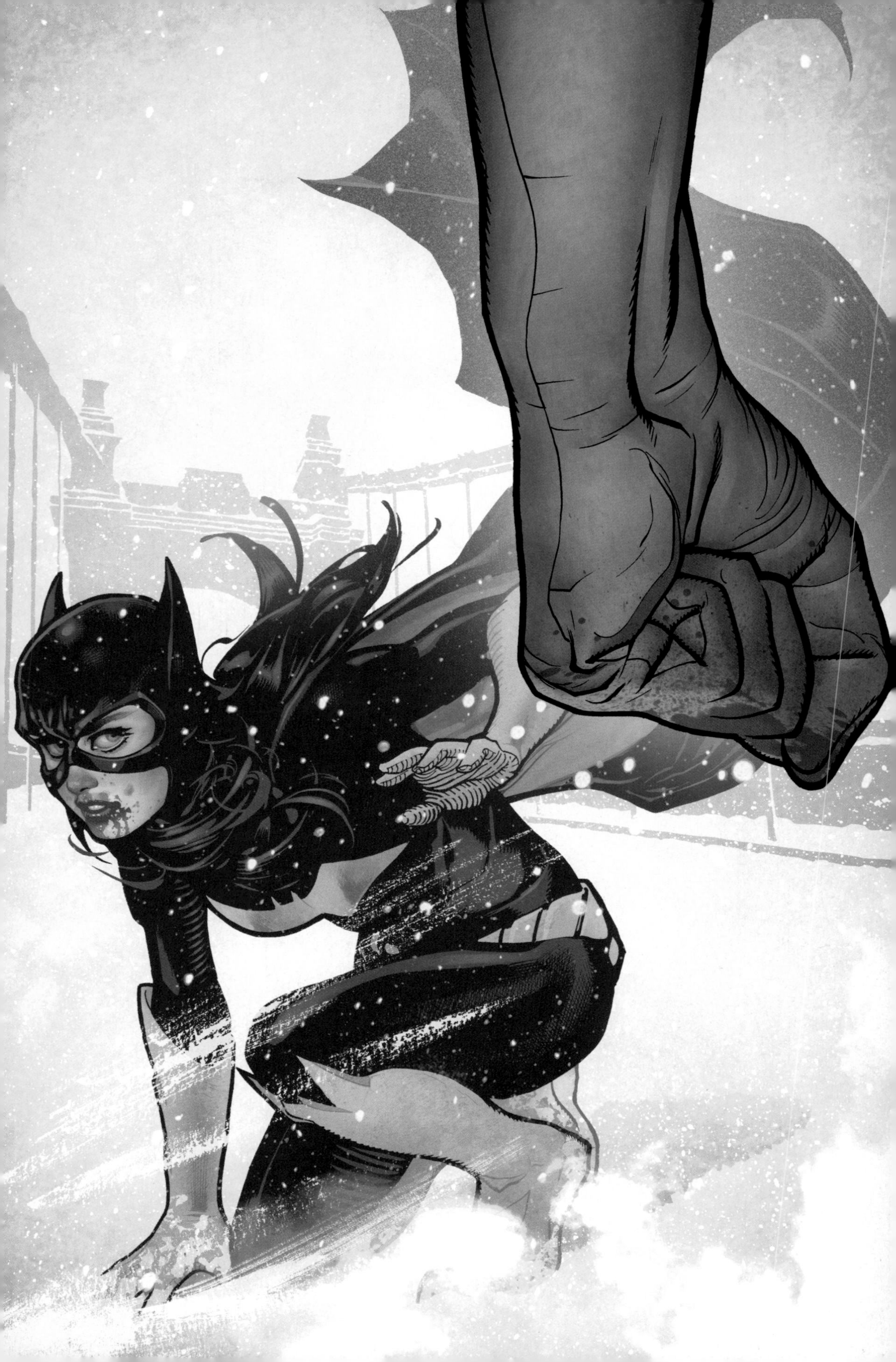

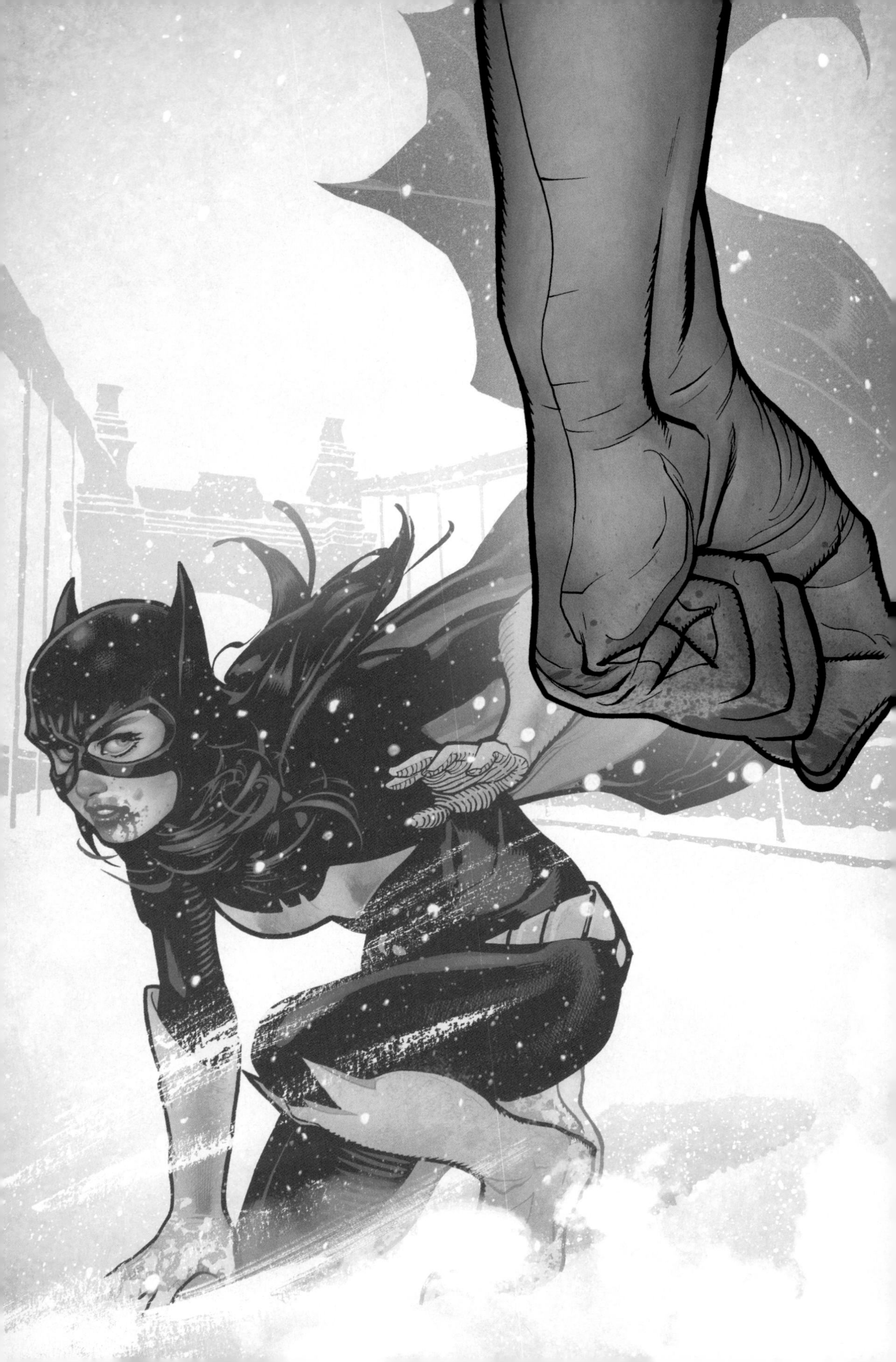

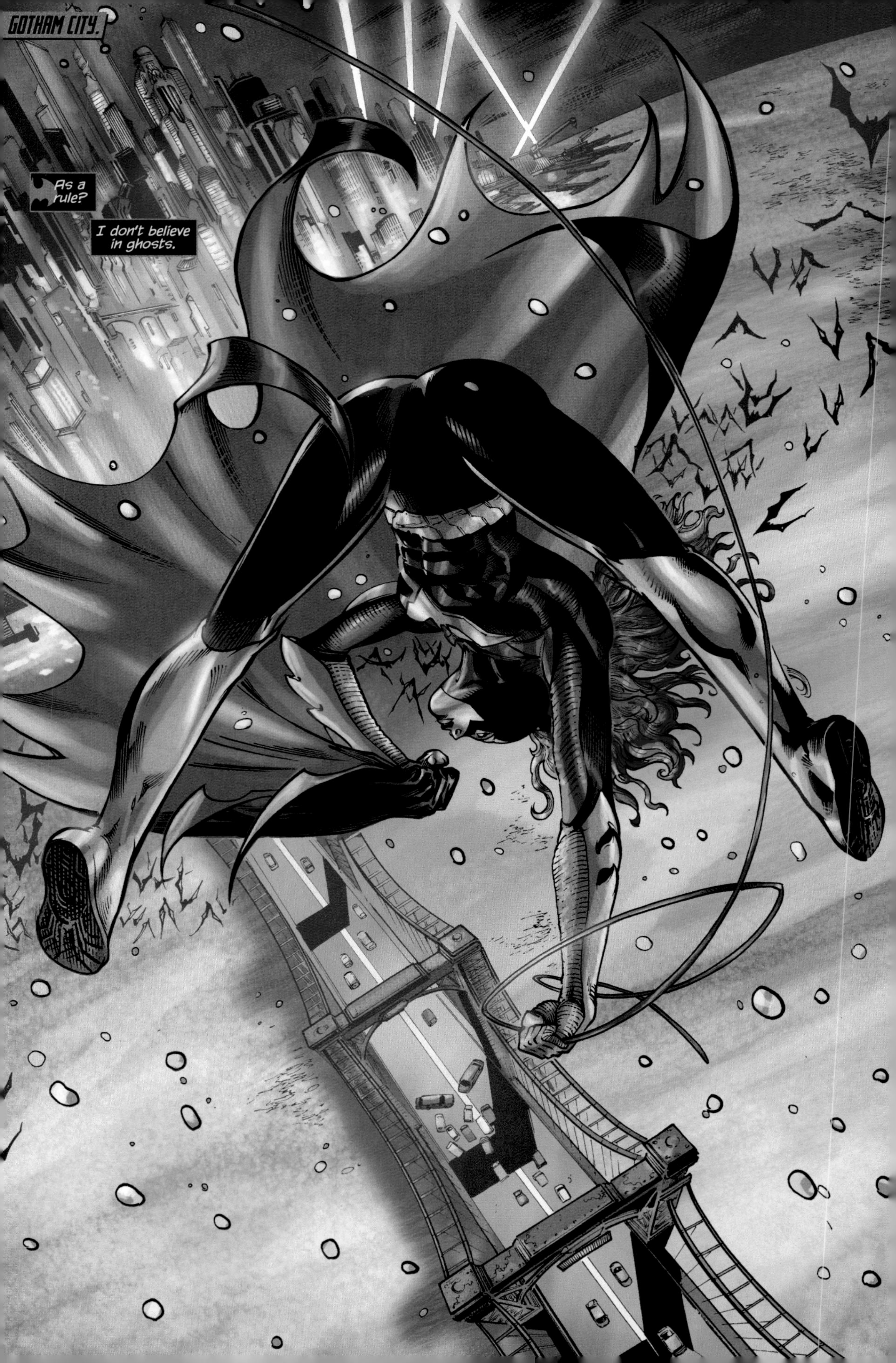
GOTHAM CITY.
As a rule?
I don't believe in ghosts.

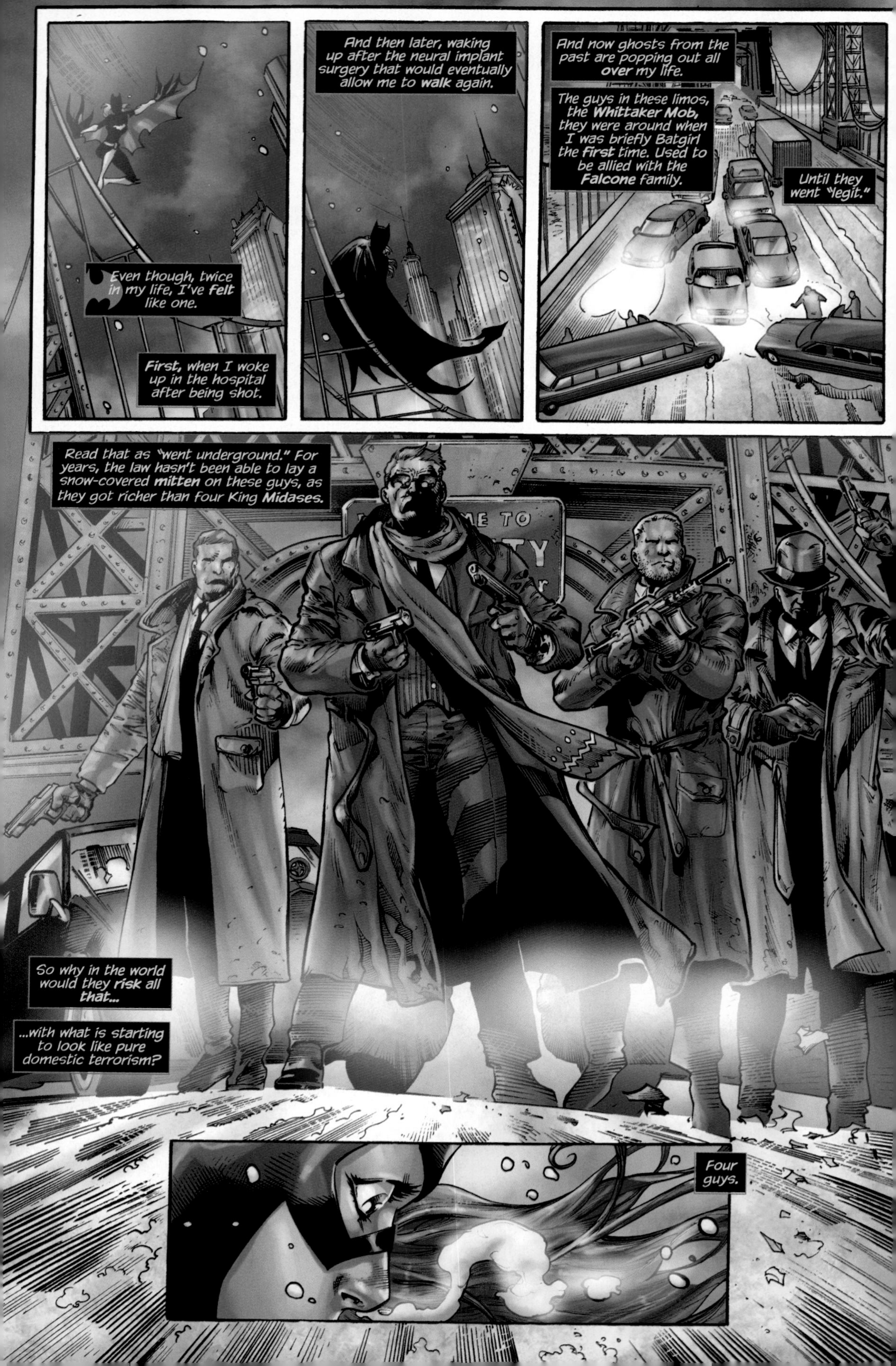
Even though, twice in my life, I've felt like one.
First, when I woke up in the hospital after being shot.
And then later, waking up after the neural implant surgery that would eventually allow me to walk again.
And now ghosts from the past are popping out all over my life.
The guys in these limos, the Whittaker Mob, they were around when I was briefly Batgirl the first time. Used to be allied with the Falcone family.
Until they went "legit."
Read that as "went underground." For years, the law hasn't been able to lay a snow-covered mitten on these guys, as they got richer than four King Midases.
So why in the world would they risk all that...
...with what is starting to look like pure domestic terrorism?
Four guys.

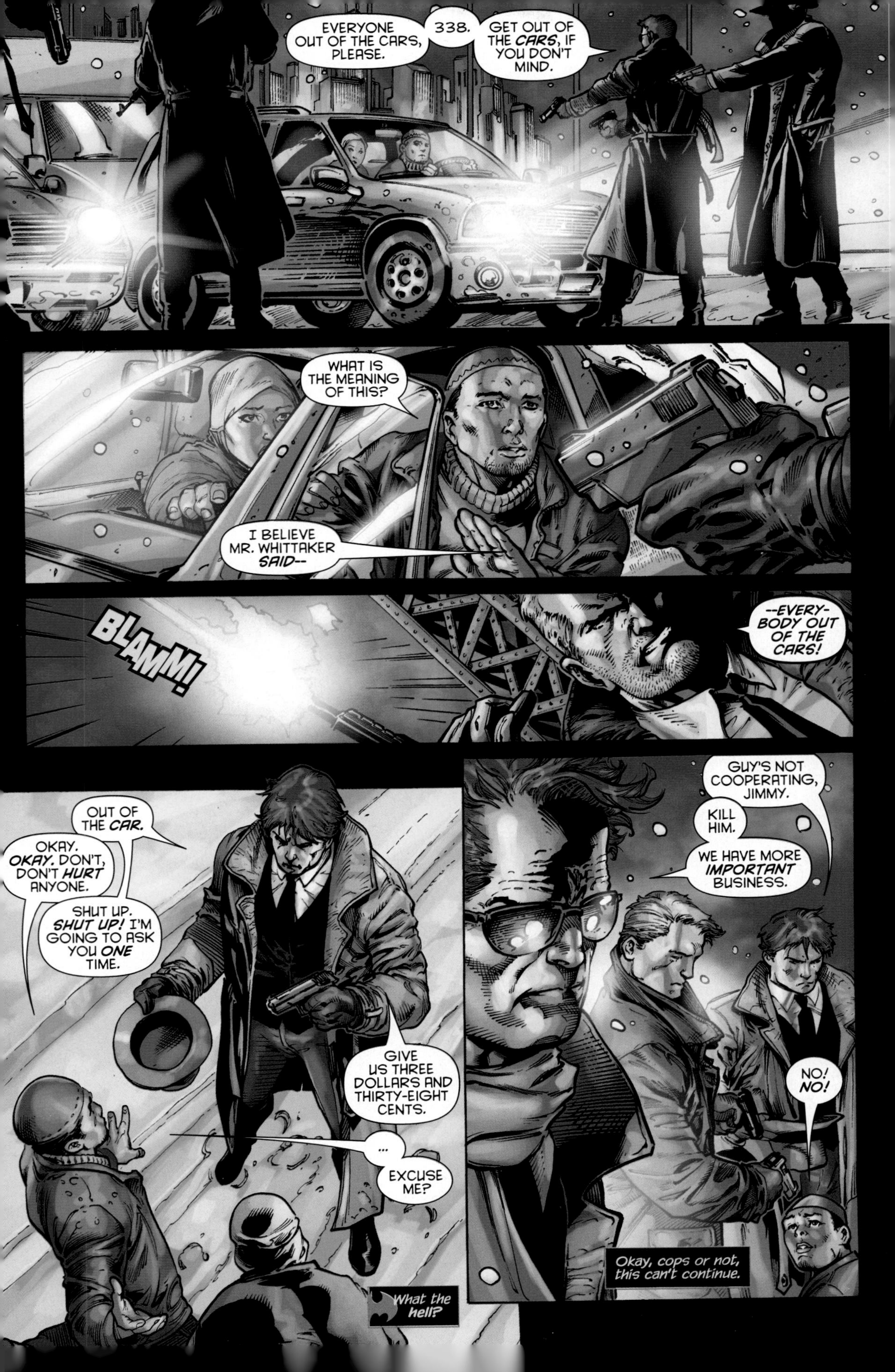
EVERYONE OUT OF THE CARS, PLEASE.
338.
GET OUT OF THE CARS, IF YOU DON'T MIND.
WHAT IS THE MEANING OF THIS?
I BELIEVE MR. WHITTAKER SAID--
BLAMM!
--EVERY-BODY OUT OF THE CARS!
OUT OF THE CAR.
OKAY. OKAY. DON'T, DON'T HURT ANYONE.
SHUT UP. SHUT UP! I'M GOING TO ASK YOU ONE TIME.
GIVE US THREE DOLLARS AND THIRTY-EIGHT CENTS.
...
EXCUSE ME?
What the hell?
GUY'S NOT COOPERATING, JIMMY.
KILL HIM.
WE HAVE MORE IMPORTANT BUSINESS.
NO! NO!
Okay, cops or not, this can't continue.

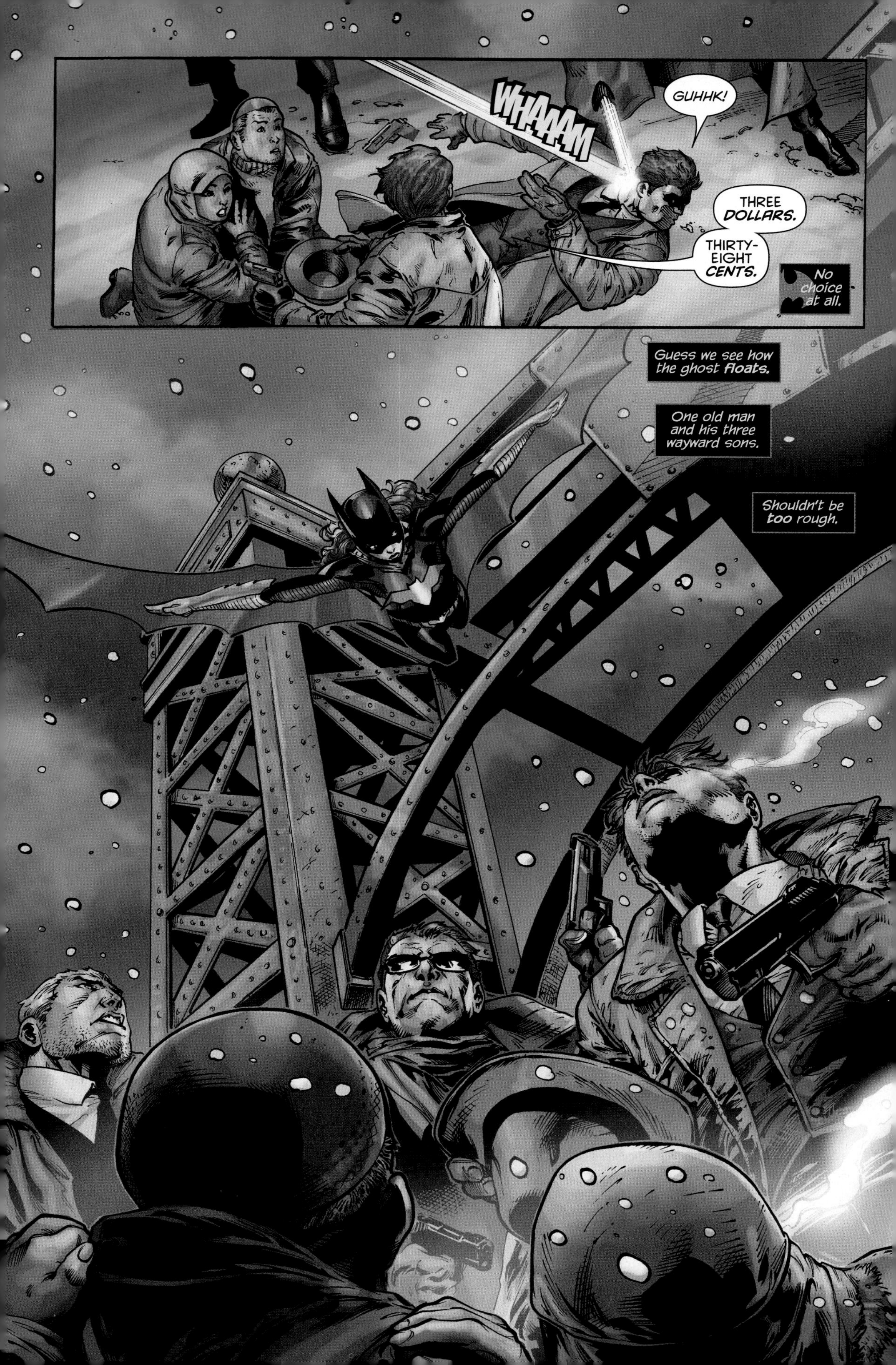
WHAAAAM
GUHHK!
THREE DOLLARS.
THIRTY-EIGHT CENTS.
No choice at all.
Guess we see how the ghost floats.
One old man and his three wayward sons.
Shouldn't be too rough.

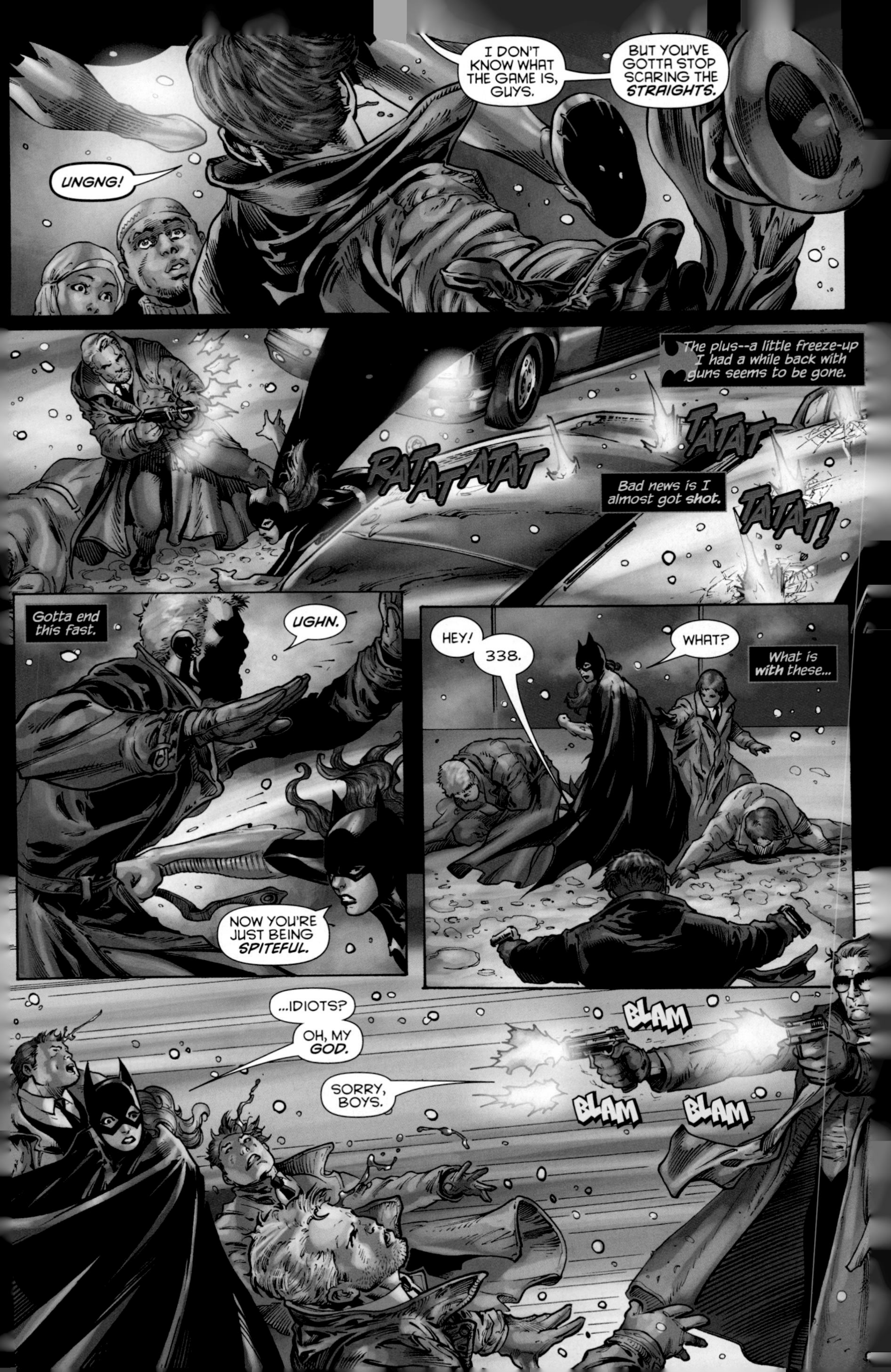

I DON'T KNOW WHAT THE GAME IS, GUYS.
BUT YOU'VE GOTTA STOP SCARING THE STRAIGHTS.
UNGNG!
The plus--a little freeze-up I had a while back with guns seems to be gone.
RAT AT AT AT AT
TATAT
Bad news is I almost got shot.
TATAT!
Gotta end this fast.
UGHN.
NOW YOU'RE JUST BEING SPITEFUL.
HEY!
338.
WHAT?
What is with these...
...IDIOTS?
OH, MY GOD.
SORRY, BOYS.
BLAM
BLAM
BLAM

His family. His *sons.*

These were his *sons.*

I FEEL ALL DIRTY. I COULD USE A COLD BATH.

Okay. It's *Gotham.*

Crazy lives here on a long-term *lease.*

That's Gotham.

But this... I don't know *what* this is.

I think I'm gonna be *sick.*

NO. WAIT.

MR. WHITTAKER.

STOP!

FORGOT MY SHOWER CAP.

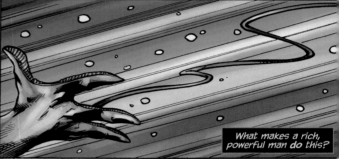

What makes a rich, powerful man *do* this?

FWIP FWIP

Oh, man.

I *lucked* out with that throw. I *so* lucked out.

Guy might have a sprain...but he'll *live.*

Maybe.

If my *arms* hold out.

BURNS, DOESN'T IT?

FEEL LIKE YOUR JOINTS'LL POP, MUSCLES'LL TEAR RIGHT OUT OF YOUR SKIN?

Oh, God, what *now?*

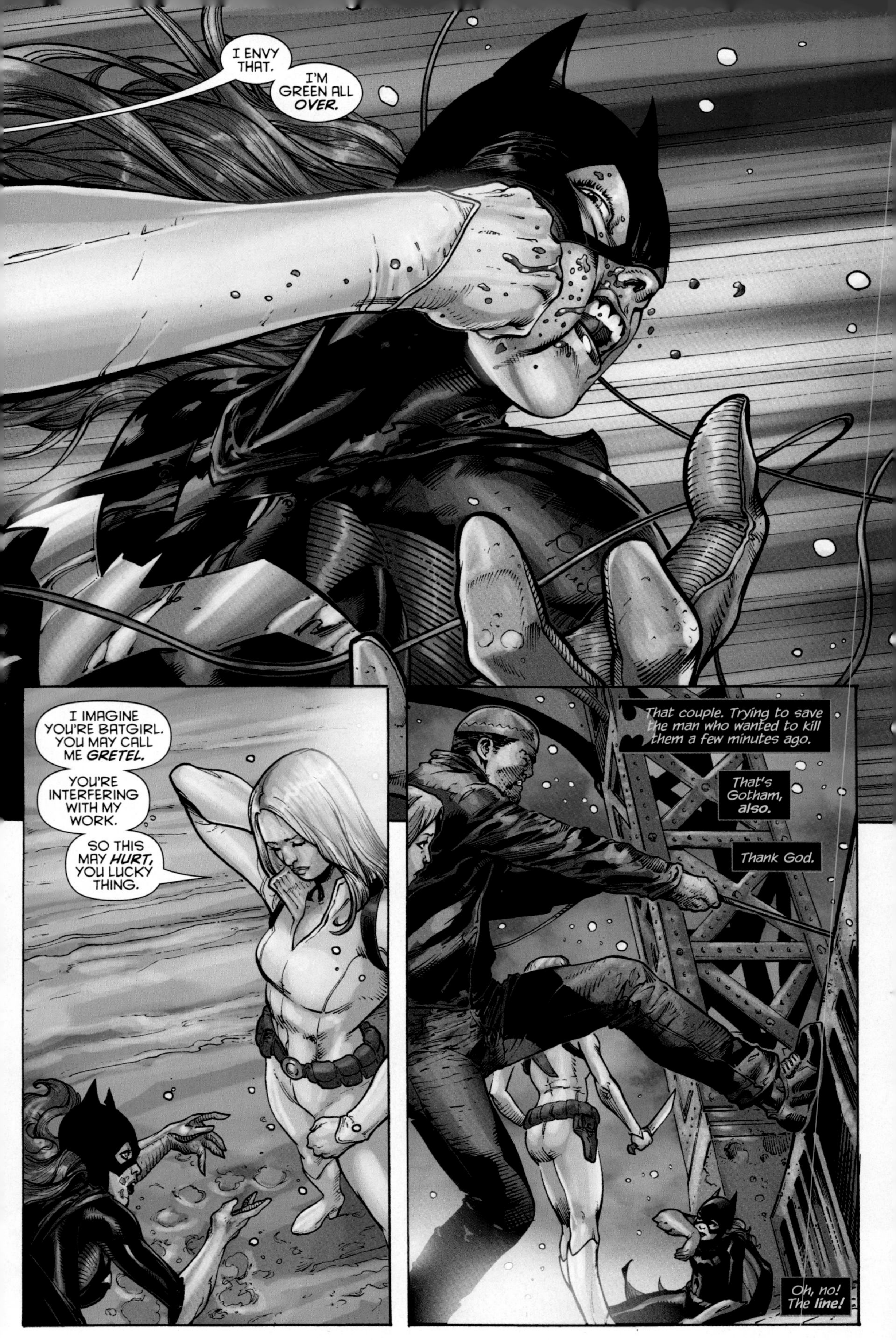
I ENVY THAT.
I'M GREEN ALL OVER.
I IMAGINE YOU'RE BATGIRL. YOU MAY CALL ME GRETEL.
YOU'RE INTERFERING WITH MY WORK.
SO THIS MAY HURT, YOU LUCKY THING.
That couple. Trying to save the man who wanted to kill them a few minutes ago.
That's Gotham, also.
Thank God.
Oh, no! The line!

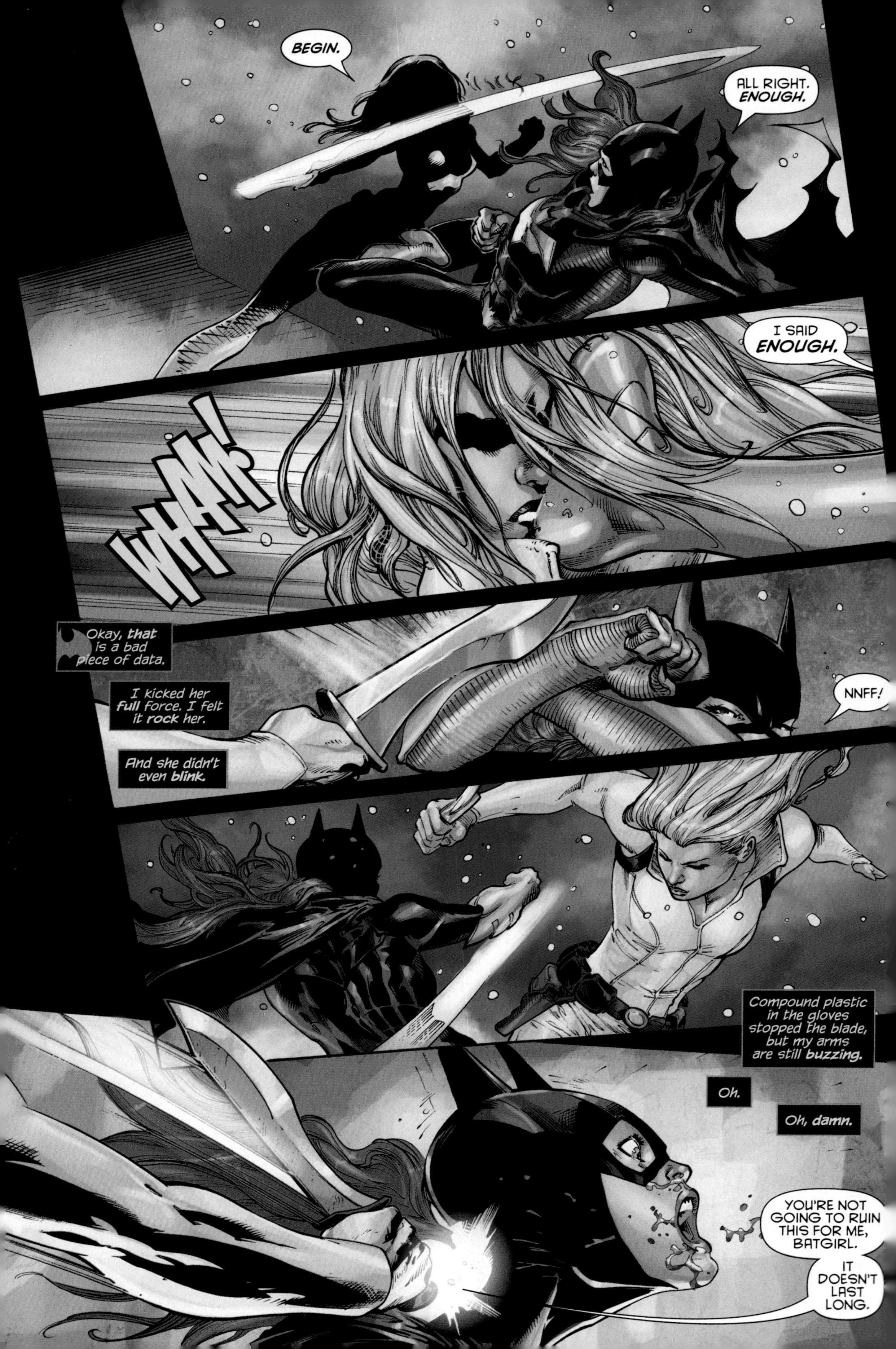
BEGIN.
ALL RIGHT. ENOUGH.
I SAID ENOUGH.
WHAM!
Okay, that is a bad piece of data.
I kicked her full force. I felt it rock her.
And she didn't even blink.
NNFF!
Compound plastic in the gloves stopped the blade, but my arms are still buzzing.
Oh.
Oh, damn.
YOU'RE NOT GOING TO RUIN THIS FOR ME, BATGIRL.
IT DOESN'T LAST LONG.

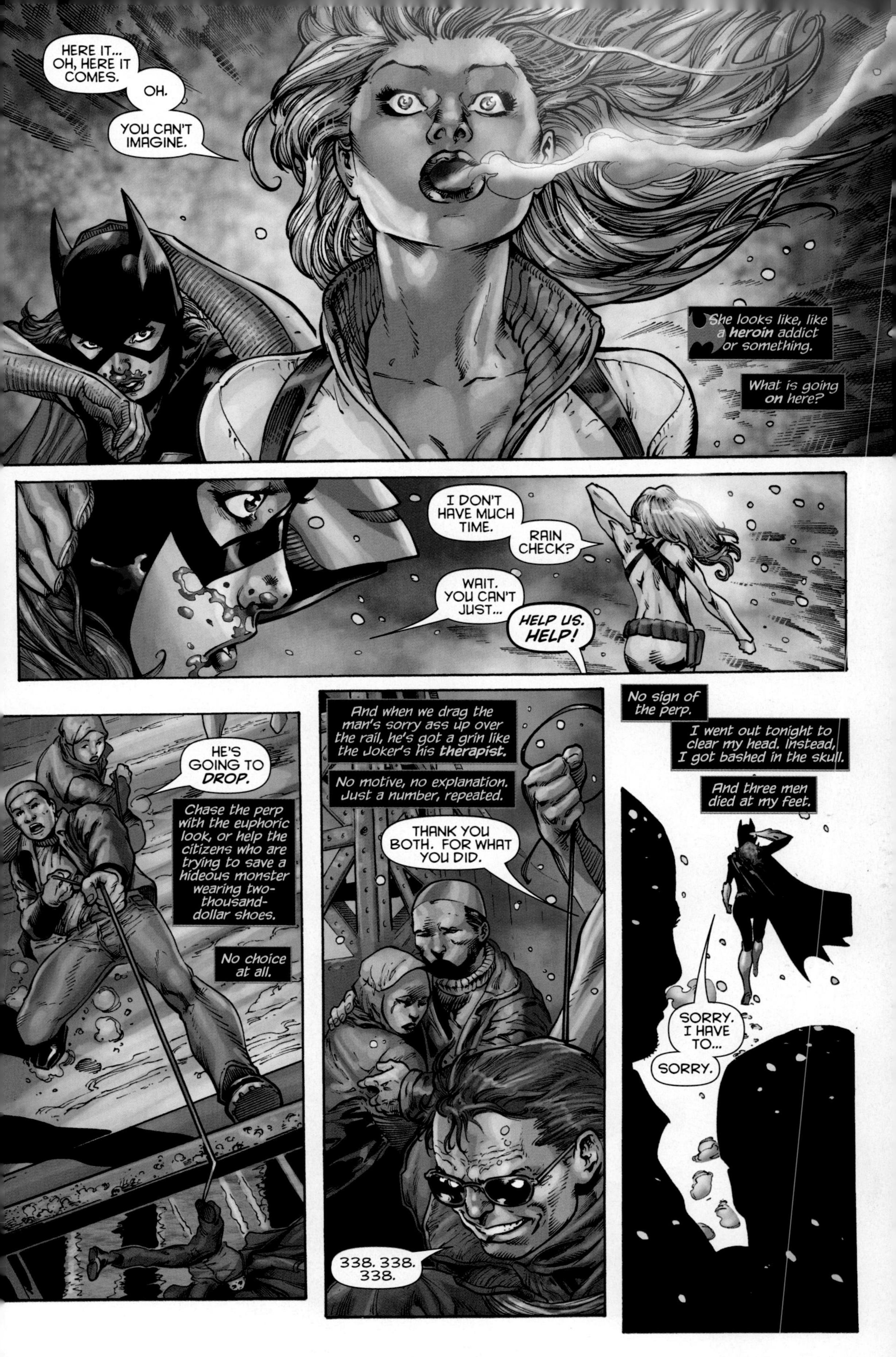
HERE IT... OH, HERE IT COMES.
OH.
YOU CAN'T IMAGINE.
She looks like, like a heroin addict or something.
What is going on here?
I DON'T HAVE MUCH TIME.
RAIN CHECK?
WAIT. YOU CAN'T JUST...
HELP US. HELP!
HE'S GOING TO DROP.
Chase the perp with the euphoric look, or help the citizens who are trying to save a hideous monster wearing two-thousand-dollar shoes.
No choice at all.
And when we drag the man's sorry ass up over the rail, he's got a grin like the Joker's his therapist.
No motive, no explanation. Just a number, repeated.
THANK YOU BOTH. FOR WHAT YOU DID.
338. 338. 338.
No sign of the perp.
I went out tonight to clear my head. Instead, I got bashed in the skull.
And three men died at my feet.
SORRY. I HAVE TO...
SORRY.

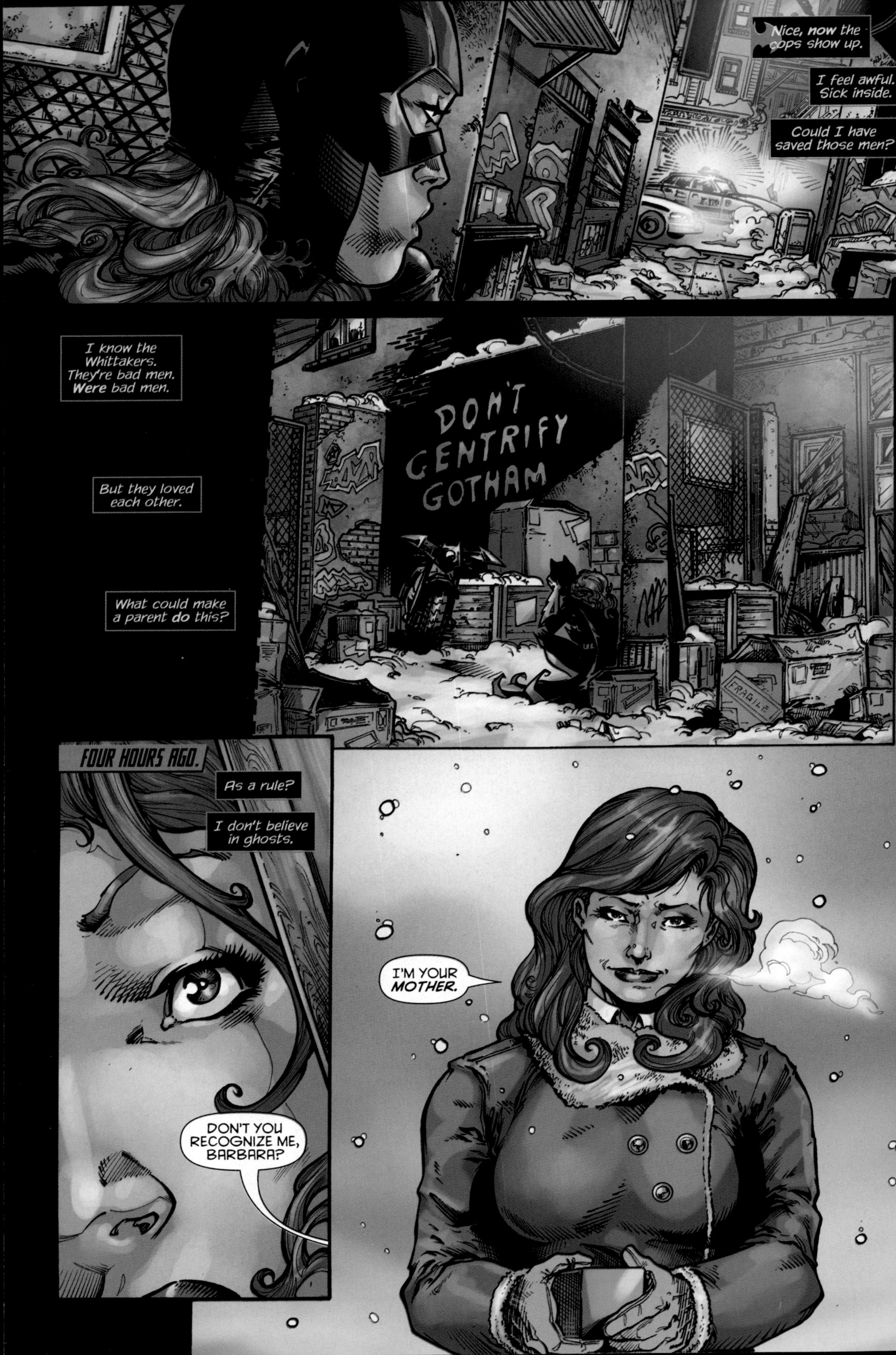
Nice, now the cops show up.
I feel awful. Sick inside.
Could I have saved those men?
I know the Whittakers. They're bad men. Were bad men.
DON'T GENTRIFY GOTHAM
But they loved each other.
What could make a parent do this?
FRAGILE
FOUR HOURS AGO.
As a rule?
I don't believe in ghosts.
DON'T YOU RECOGNIZE ME, BARBARA?
I'M YOUR MOTHER.

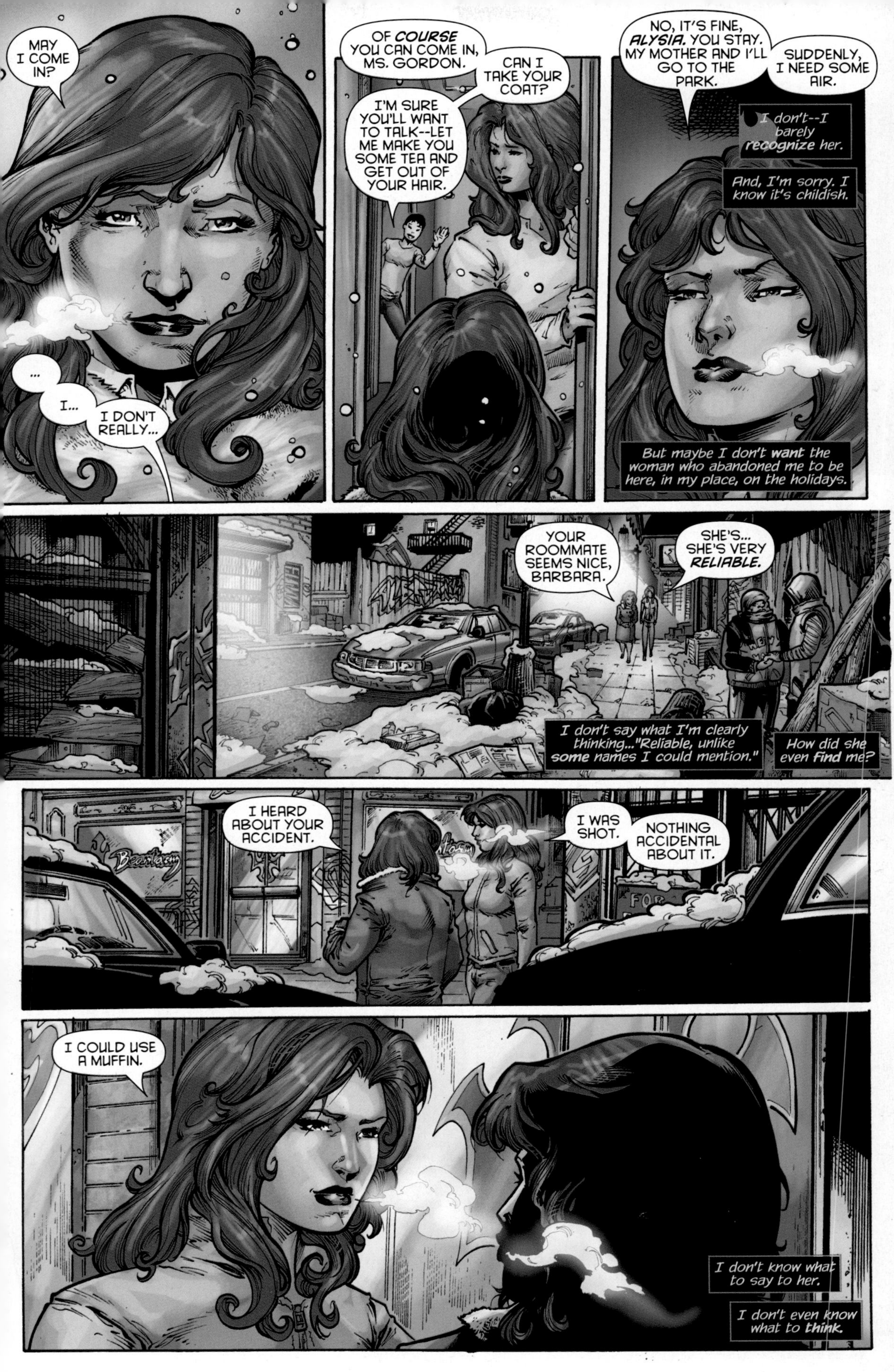

MAY I COME IN?
...
I...
I DON'T REALLY...
OF COURSE YOU CAN COME IN, MS. GORDON.
CAN I TAKE YOUR COAT?
I'M SURE YOU'LL WANT TO TALK--LET ME MAKE YOU SOME TEA AND GET OUT OF YOUR HAIR.
NO, IT'S FINE, ALYSIA. YOU STAY. MY MOTHER AND I'LL GO TO THE PARK.
SUDDENLY, I NEED SOME AIR.
I don't--I barely recognize her.
And, I'm sorry. I know it's childish.
But maybe I don't want the woman who abandoned me to be here, in my place, on the holidays.
YOUR ROOMMATE SEEMS NICE, BARBARA.
SHE'S... SHE'S VERY RELIABLE.
I don't say what I'm clearly thinking..."Reliable, unlike some names I could mention."
How did she even find me?
I HEARD ABOUT YOUR ACCIDENT.
I WAS SHOT.
NOTHING ACCIDENTAL ABOUT IT.
I COULD USE A MUFFIN.
I don't know what to say to her.
I don't even know what to think.

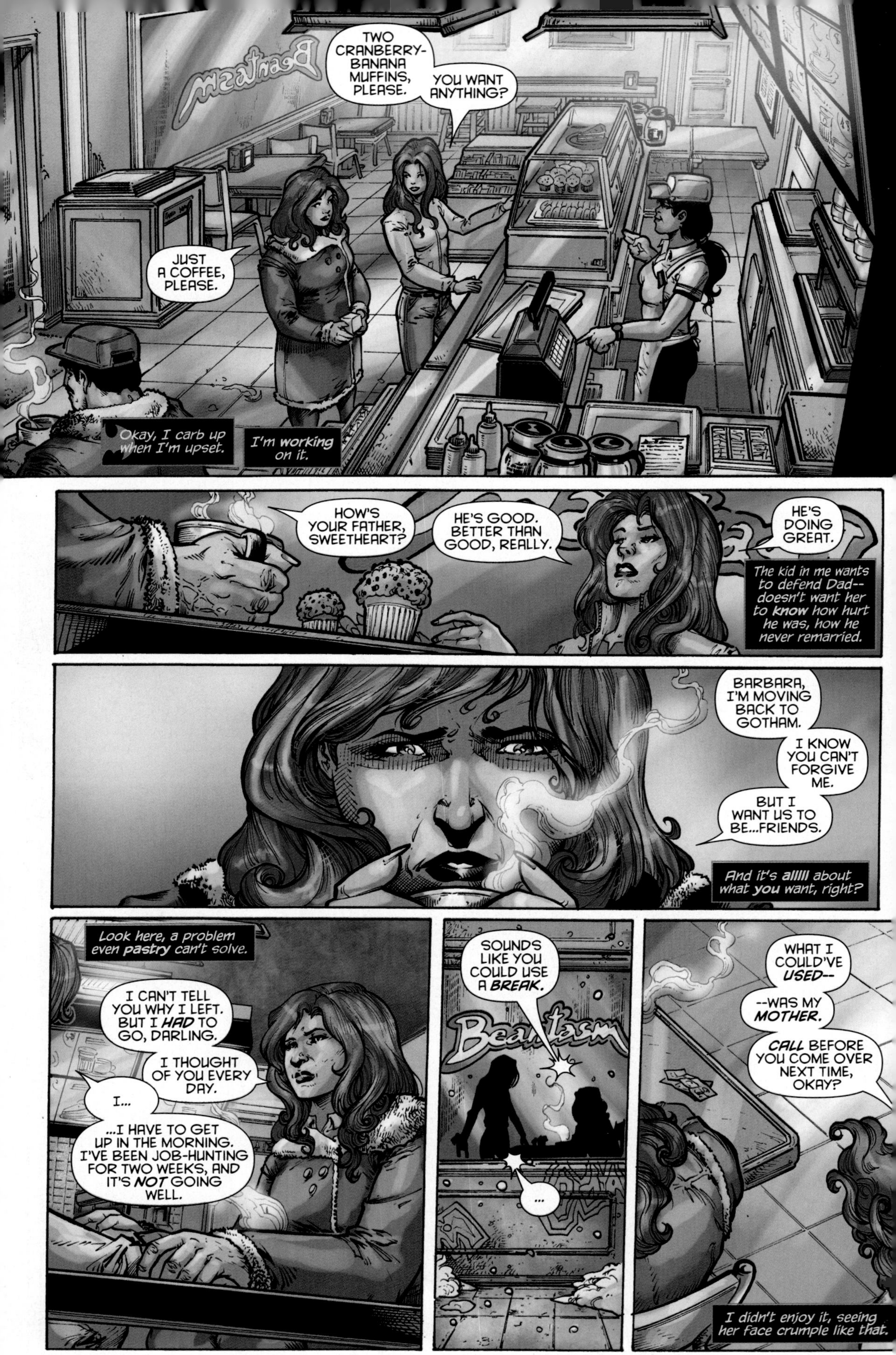
Beantasm
TWO CRANBERRY-BANANA MUFFINS, PLEASE.
YOU WANT ANYTHING?
JUST A COFFEE, PLEASE.
Okay, I carb up when I'm upset.
I'm working on it.
HOW'S YOUR FATHER, SWEETHEART?
HE'S GOOD. BETTER THAN GOOD, REALLY.
HE'S DOING GREAT.
The kid in me wants to defend Dad--doesn't want her to know how hurt he was, how he never remarried.
BARBARA, I'M MOVING BACK TO GOTHAM.
I KNOW YOU CAN'T FORGIVE ME.
BUT I WANT US TO BE...FRIENDS.
And it's allll about what you want, right?
Look here, a problem even pastry can't solve.
I CAN'T TELL YOU WHY I LEFT. BUT I HAD TO GO, DARLING.
I THOUGHT OF YOU EVERY DAY.
I...
...I HAVE TO GET UP IN THE MORNING. I'VE BEEN JOB-HUNTING FOR TWO WEEKS, AND IT'S NOT GOING WELL.
SOUNDS LIKE YOU COULD USE A BREAK.
Beantasm
...
WHAT I COULD'VE USED--
--WAS MY MOTHER.
CALL BEFORE YOU COME OVER NEXT TIME, OKAY?
I didn't enjoy it, seeing her face crumple like that.

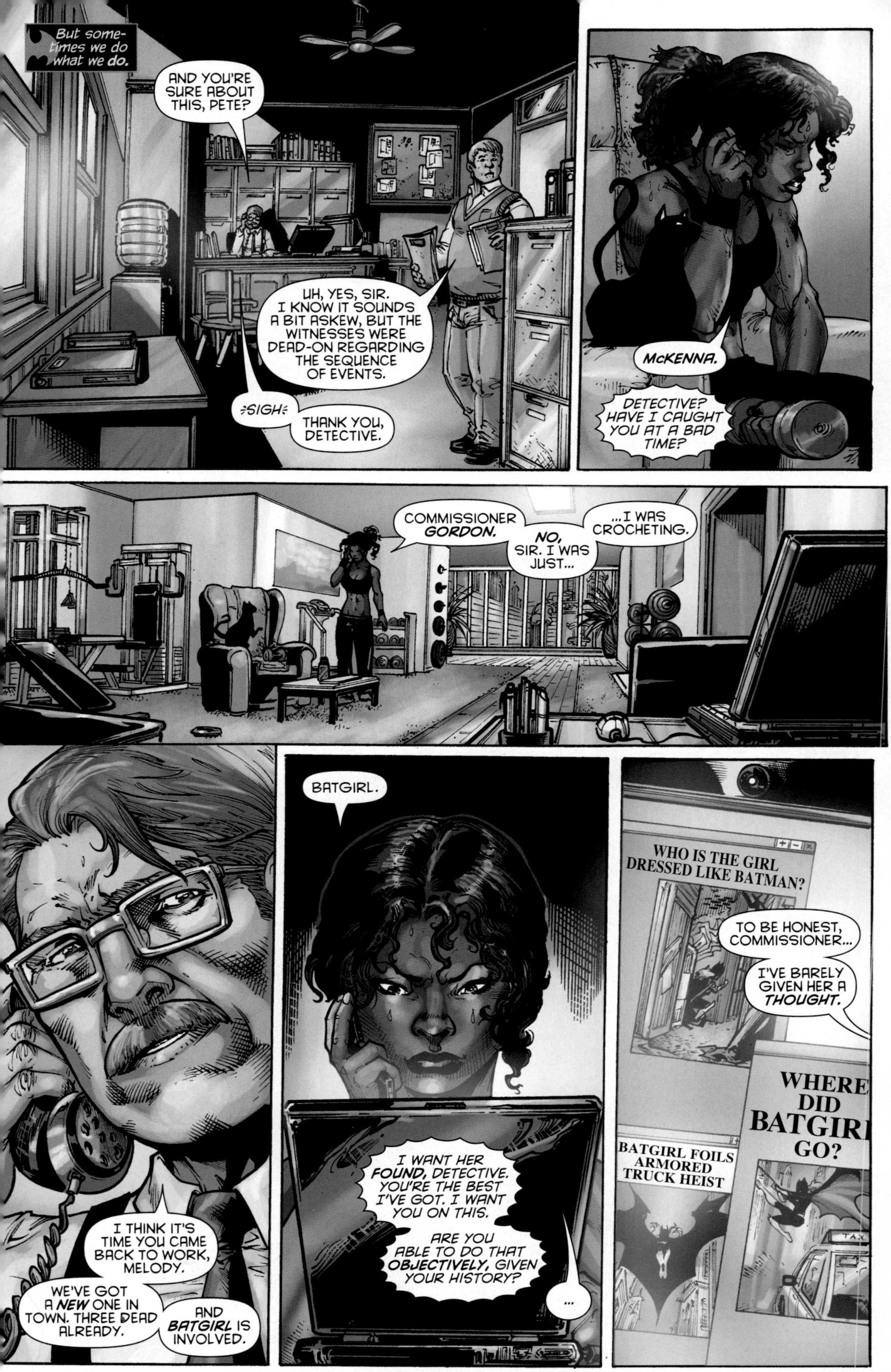
But sometimes we do what we do.
AND YOU'RE SURE ABOUT THIS, PETE?
UH, YES, SIR. I KNOW IT SOUNDS A BIT ASKEW, BUT THE WITNESSES WERE DEAD-ON REGARDING THE SEQUENCE OF EVENTS.
SIGH
THANK YOU, DETECTIVE.
McKENNA.
DETECTIVE? HAVE I CAUGHT YOU AT A BAD TIME?
COMMISSIONER GORDON.
NO, SIR. I WAS JUST...
...I WAS CROCHETING.
I THINK IT'S TIME YOU CAME BACK TO WORK, MELODY.
WE'VE GOT A NEW ONE IN TOWN. THREE DEAD ALREADY.
AND BATGIRL IS INVOLVED.
BATGIRL.
I WANT HER FOUND, DETECTIVE. YOU'RE THE BEST I'VE GOT. I WANT YOU ON THIS.
ARE YOU ABLE TO DO THAT OBJECTIVELY, GIVEN YOUR HISTORY?
...
WHO IS THE GIRL DRESSED LIKE BATMAN?
TO BE HONEST, COMMISSIONER...
I'VE BARELY GIVEN HER A THOUGHT.
WHERE DID BATGIRL GO?
BATGIRL FOILS ARMORED TRUCK HEIST

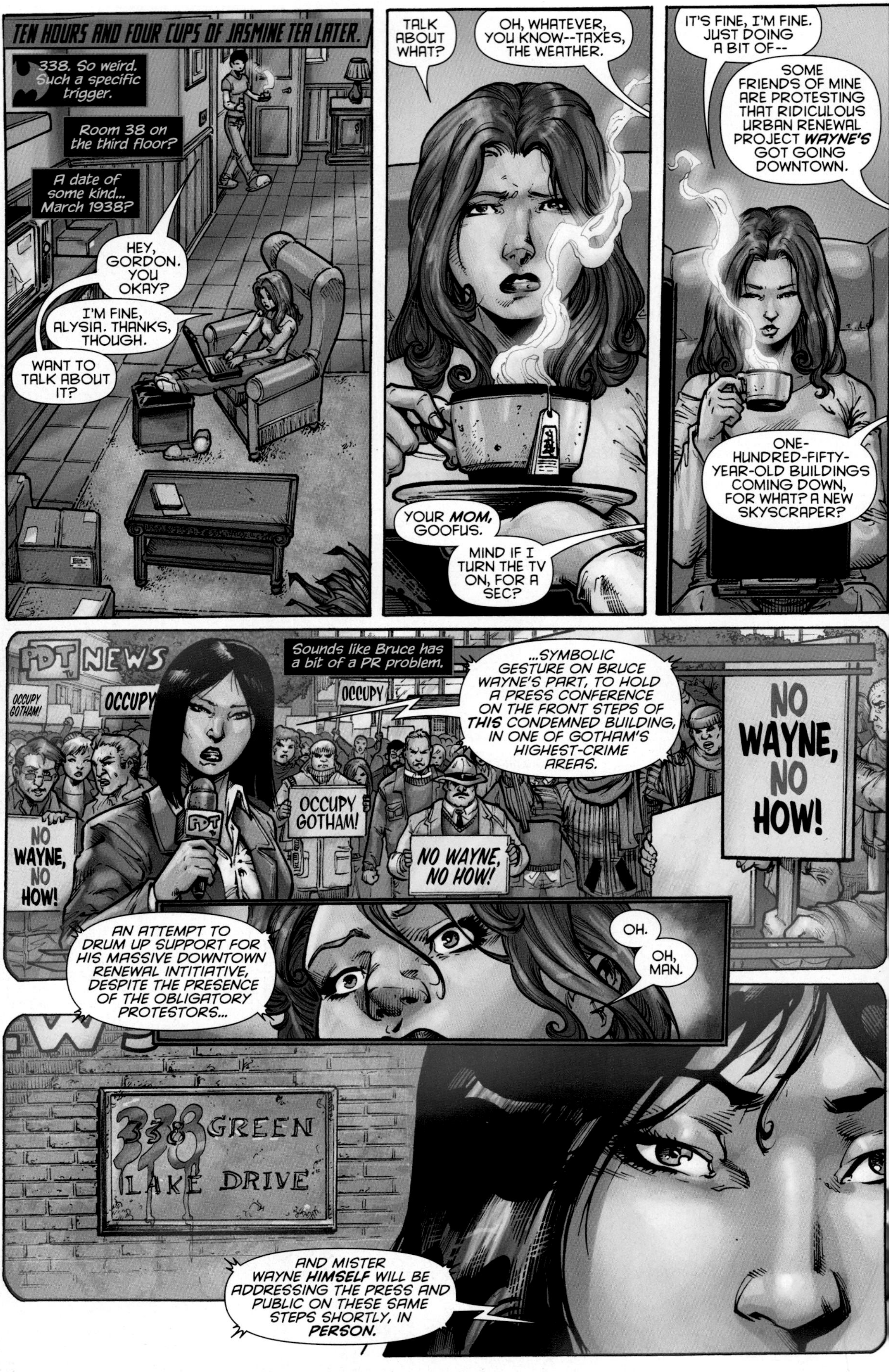

TEN HOURS AND FOUR CUPS OF JASMINE TEA LATER.
338. So weird. Such a specific trigger.
Room 38 on the third floor?
A date of some kind... March 1938?
HEY, GORDON. YOU OKAY?
I'M FINE, ALYSIA. THANKS, THOUGH.
WANT TO TALK ABOUT IT?
TALK ABOUT WHAT?
OH, WHATEVER, YOU KNOW--TAXES, THE WEATHER.
YOUR MOM, GOOFUS.
MIND IF I TURN THE TV ON, FOR A SEC?
IT'S FINE, I'M FINE. JUST DOING A BIT OF--
SOME FRIENDS OF MINE ARE PROTESTING THAT RIDICULOUS URBAN RENEWAL PROJECT WAYNE'S GOT GOING DOWNTOWN.
ONE-HUNDRED-FIFTY-YEAR-OLD BUILDINGS COMING DOWN, FOR WHAT? A NEW SKYSCRAPER?
PDT NEWS
Sounds like Bruce has a bit of a PR problem.
...SYMBOLIC GESTURE ON BRUCE WAYNE'S PART, TO HOLD A PRESS CONFERENCE ON THE FRONT STEPS OF THIS CONDEMNED BUILDING, IN ONE OF GOTHAM'S HIGHEST-CRIME AREAS.
OCCUPY GOTHAM!
OCCUPY
OCCUPY
OCCUPY GOTHAM!
NO WAYNE, NO HOW!
NO WAYNE, NO HOW!
NO WAYNE, NO HOW!
AN ATTEMPT TO DRUM UP SUPPORT FOR HIS MASSIVE DOWNTOWN RENEWAL INTITIATIVE, DESPITE THE PRESENCE OF THE OBLIGATORY PROTESTORS...
OH.
OH, MAN.
338 GREEN LAKE DRIVE
AND MISTER WAYNE HIMSELF WILL BE ADDRESSING THE PRESS AND PUBLIC ON THESE SAME STEPS SHORTLY, IN PERSON.

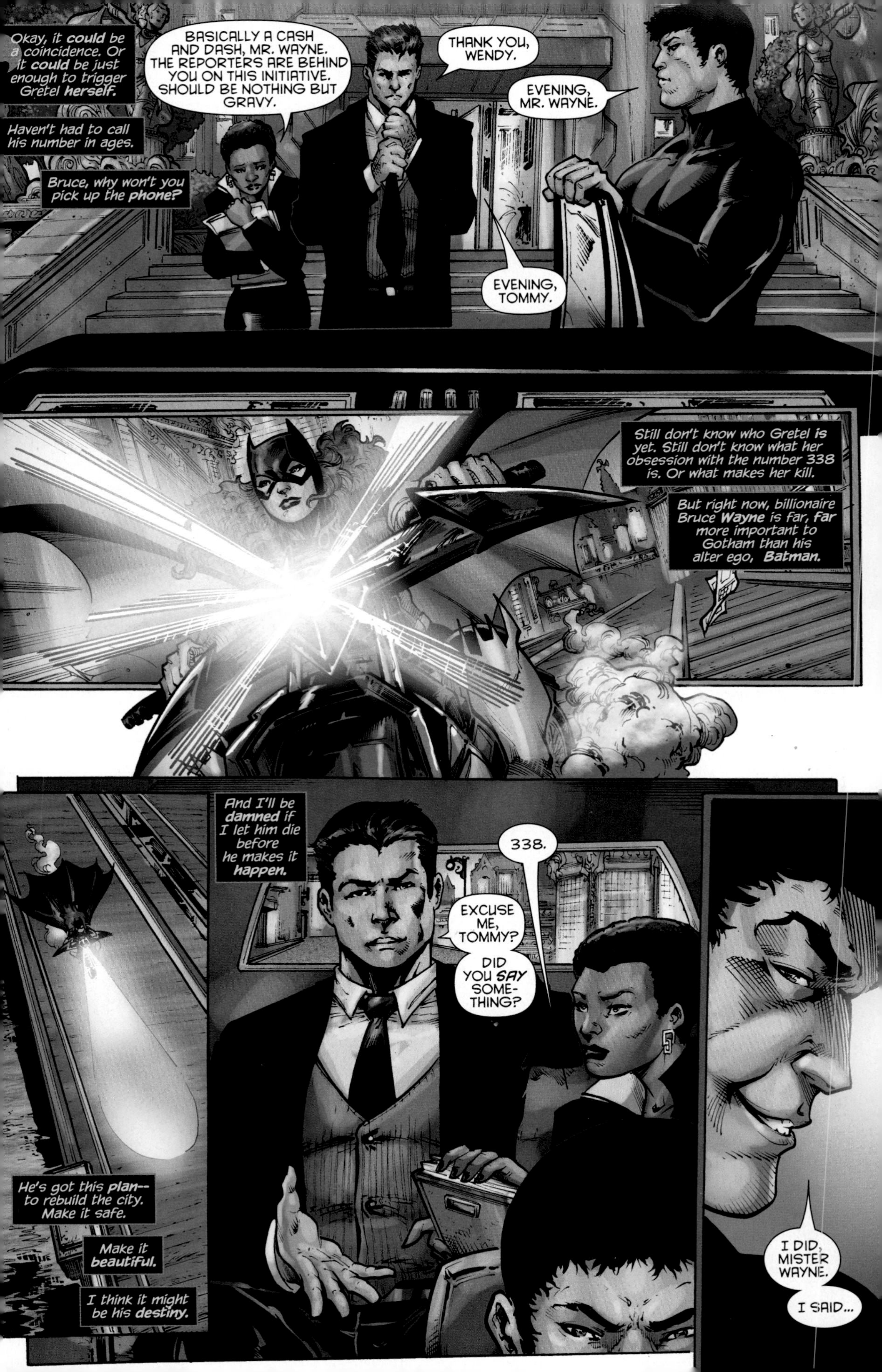

Okay, it could be a coincidence. Or it could be just enough to trigger Gretel herself.
Haven't had to call his number in ages.
Bruce, why won't you pick up the phone?
BASICALLY A CASH AND DASH, MR. WAYNE. THE REPORTERS ARE BEHIND YOU ON THIS INITIATIVE. SHOULD BE NOTHING BUT GRAVY.
THANK YOU, WENDY.
EVENING, MR. WAYNE.
EVENING, TOMMY.
Still don't know who Gretel is yet. Still don't know what her obsession with the number 338 is. Or what makes her kill.
But right now, billionaire Bruce Wayne is far, far more important to Gotham than his alter ego, Batman.
He's got this plan--to rebuild the city. Make it safe.
Make it beautiful.
I think it might be his destiny.
And I'll be damned if I let him die before he makes it happen.
338.
EXCUSE ME, TOMMY?
DID YOU SAY SOME-THING?
I DID, MISTER WAYNE.
I SAID...

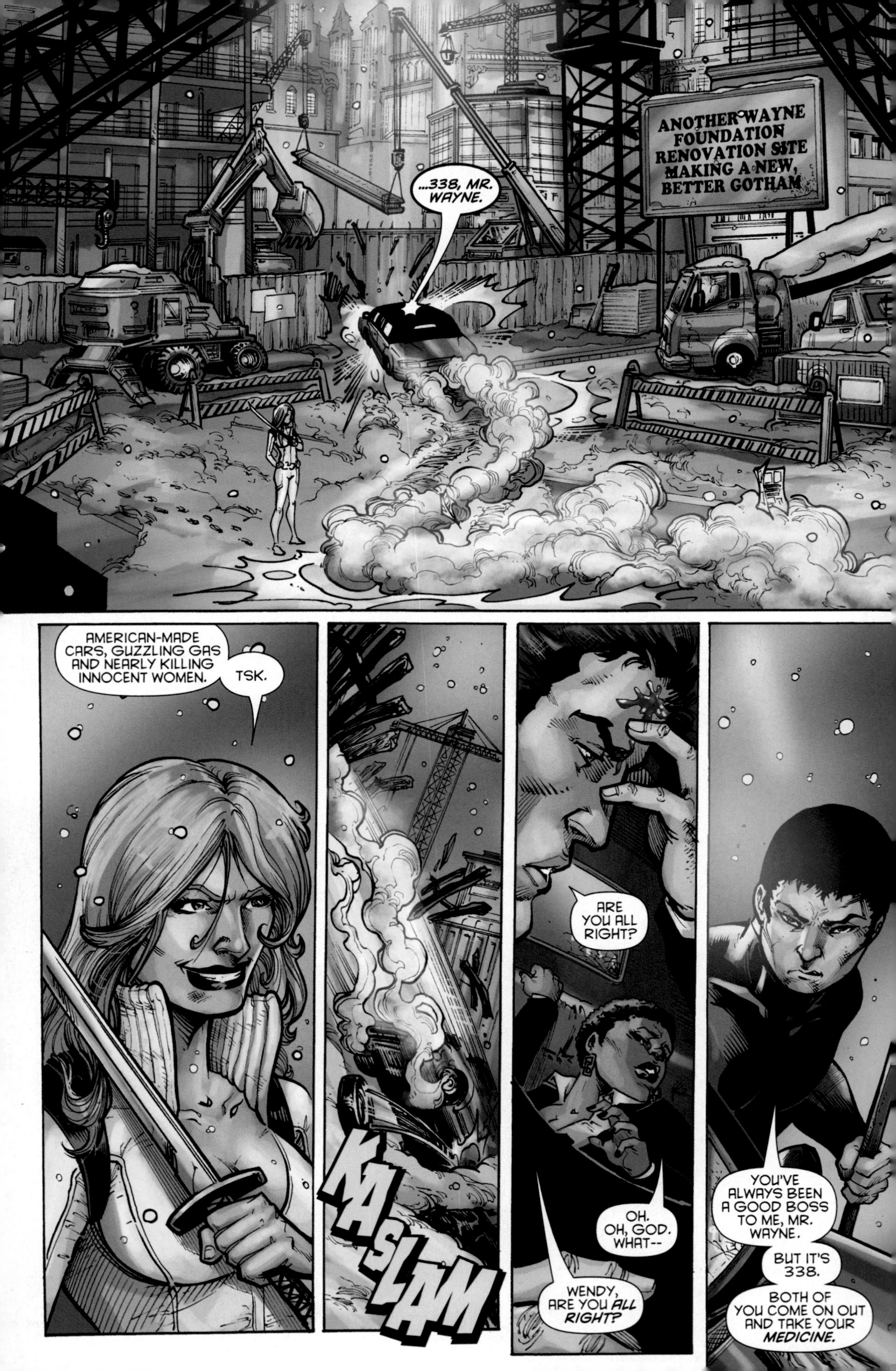

ANOTHER WAYNE FOUNDATION RENOVATION SITE MAKING A NEW, BETTER GOTHAM
...338, MR. WAYNE.
AMERICAN-MADE CARS, GUZZLING GAS AND NEARLY KILLING INNOCENT WOMEN.
TSK.
KASLAM
ARE YOU ALL RIGHT?
OH. OH, GOD. WHAT--
WENDY, ARE YOU *ALL RIGHT?*
YOU'VE ALWAYS BEEN A GOOD BOSS TO ME, MR. WAYNE.
BUT IT'S 338.
BOTH OF YOU COME ON OUT AND TAKE YOUR *MEDICINE.*

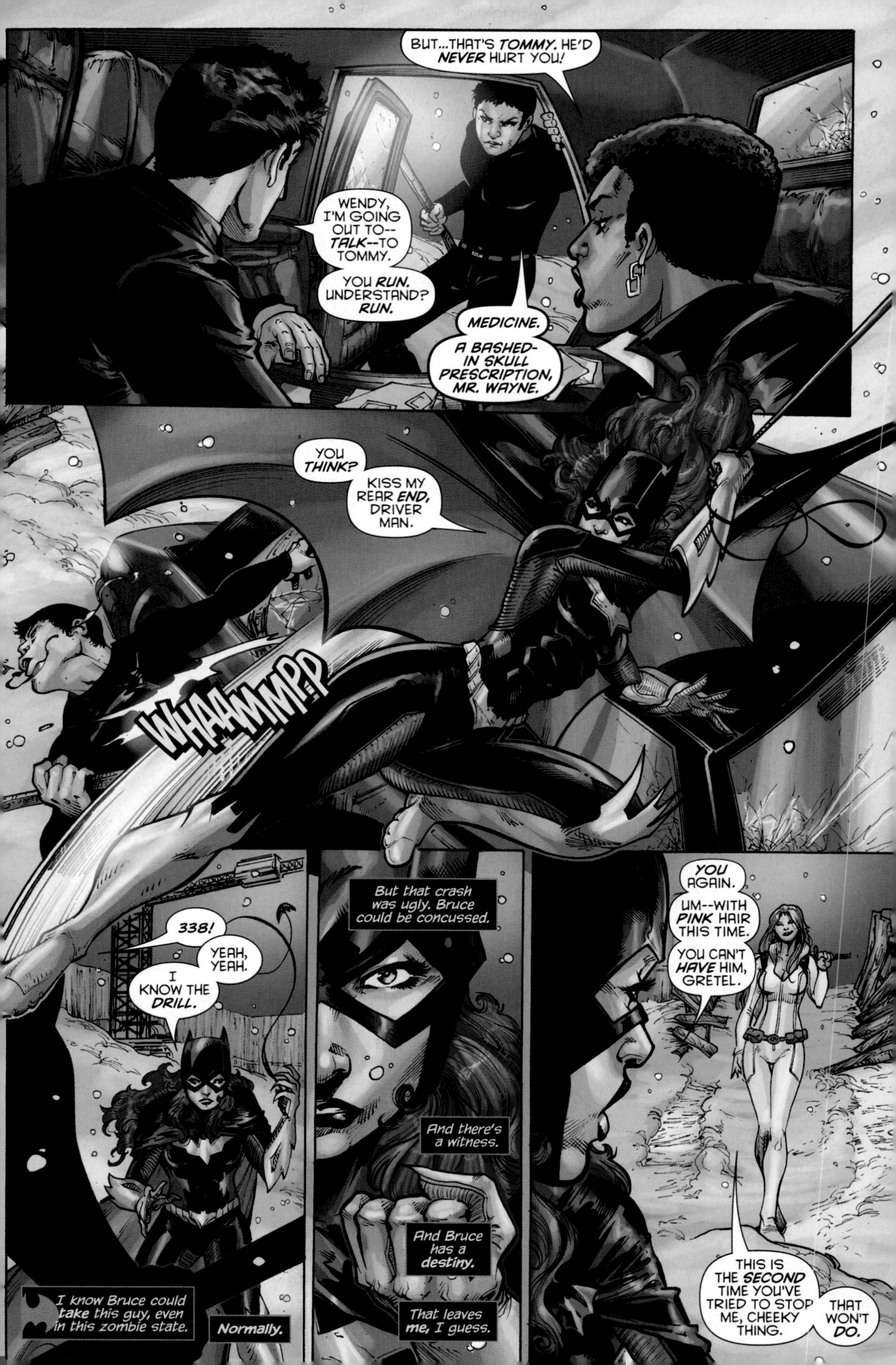

BUT...THAT'S TOMMY. HE'D NEVER HURT YOU!
WENDY, I'M GOING OUT TO--TALK--TO TOMMY.
YOU RUN. UNDERSTAND? RUN.
MEDICINE.
A BASHED-IN SKULL PRESCRIPTION, MR. WAYNE.
YOU THINK?
KISS MY REAR END, DRIVER MAN.
WHAAMMPP
338!
YEAH, YEAH.
I KNOW THE DRILL.
I know Bruce could take this guy, even in this zombie state.
Normally.
But that crash was ugly. Bruce could be concussed.
And there's a witness.
And Bruce has a destiny.
That leaves me, I guess.
YOU AGAIN.
UM--WITH PINK HAIR THIS TIME.
YOU CAN'T HAVE HIM, GRETEL.
THIS IS THE SECOND TIME YOU'VE TRIED TO STOP ME, CHEEKY THING.
THAT WON'T DO.

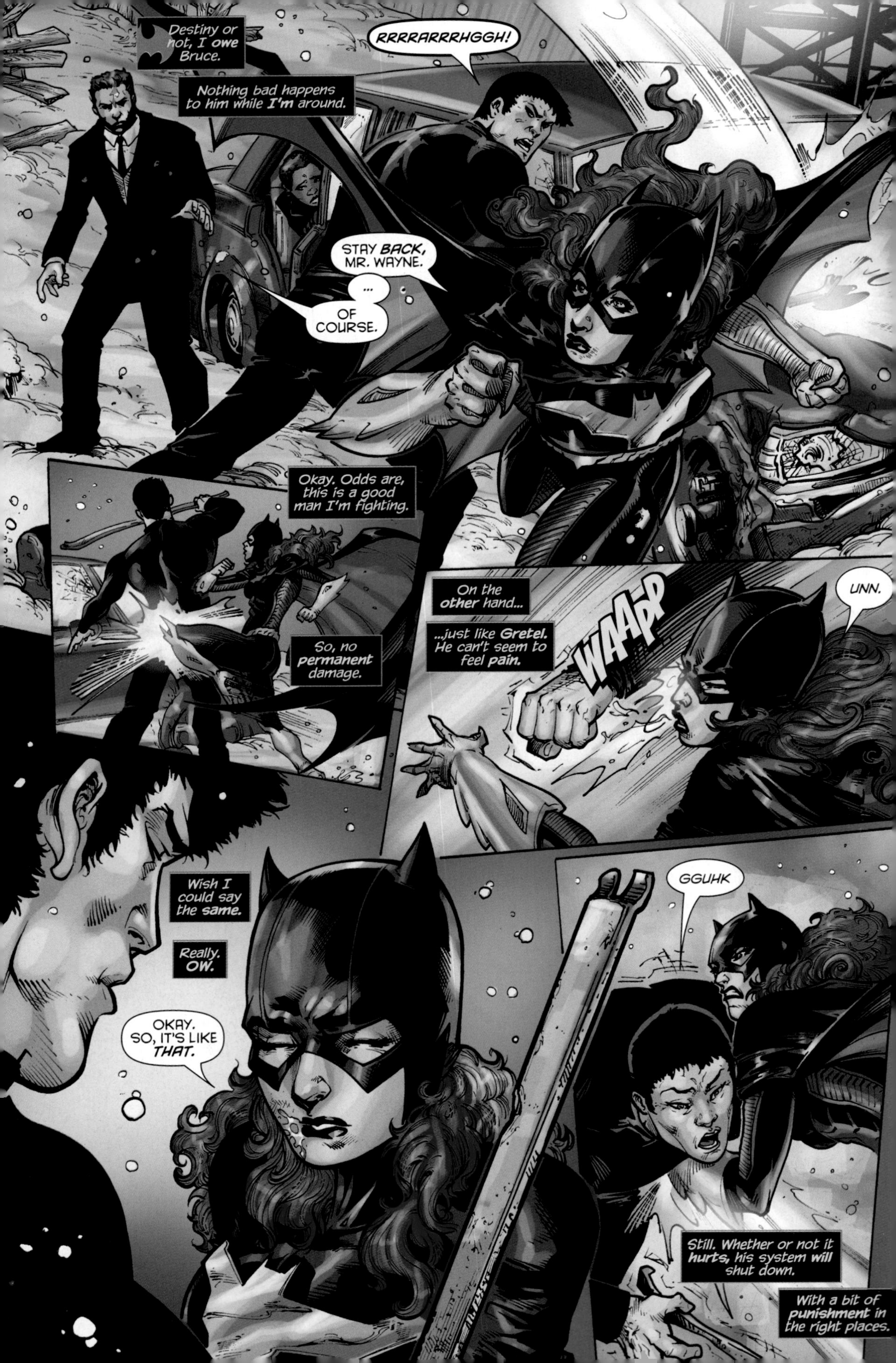
Destiny or not, I owe Bruce.
Nothing bad happens to him while I'm around.
RRRRARRRHGGH!
STAY BACK, MR. WAYNE.
...
OF COURSE.
Okay. Odds are, this is a good man I'm fighting.
So, no permanent damage.
On the other hand...
...just like Gretel. He can't seem to feel pain.
WAAPP
UNN.
Wish I could say the same.
Really. OW.
OKAY. SO, IT'S LIKE THAT.
GGUHK
Still. Whether or not it hurts, his system will shut down.
With a bit of punishment in the right places.

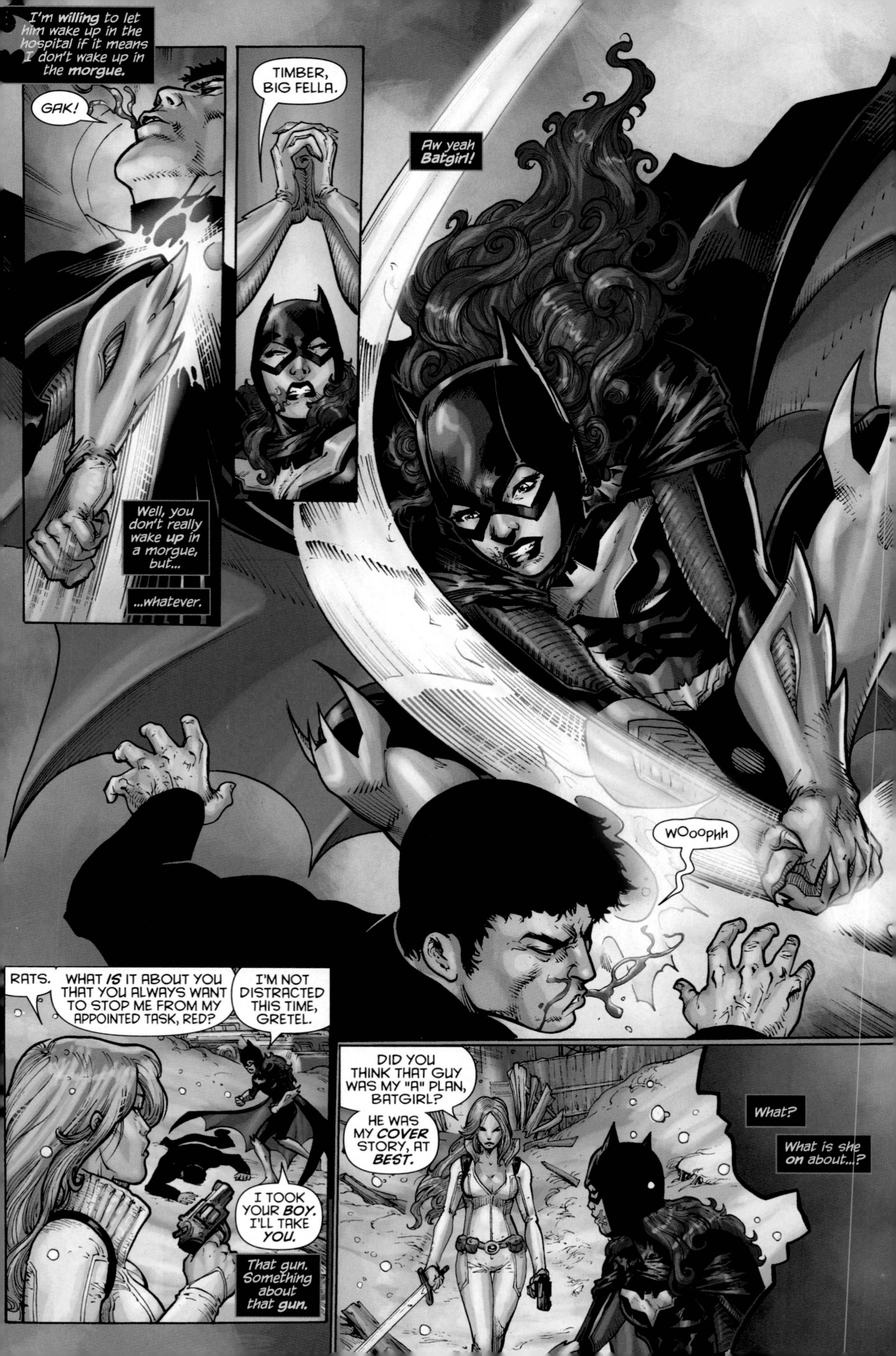
I'm willing to let him wake up in the hospital if it means I don't wake up in the morgue.
GAK!
TIMBER, BIG FELLA.
Aw yeah Batgirl!
Well, you don't really wake up in a morgue, but...
...whatever.
WOoophh
RATS.
WHAT IS IT ABOUT YOU THAT YOU ALWAYS WANT TO STOP ME FROM MY APPOINTED TASK, RED?
I'M NOT DISTRACTED THIS TIME, GRETEL.
I TOOK YOUR BOY. I'LL TAKE YOU.
That gun. Something about that gun.
DID YOU THINK THAT GUY WAS MY "A" PLAN, BATGIRL?
HE WAS MY COVER STORY, AT BEST.
What?
What is she on about...?

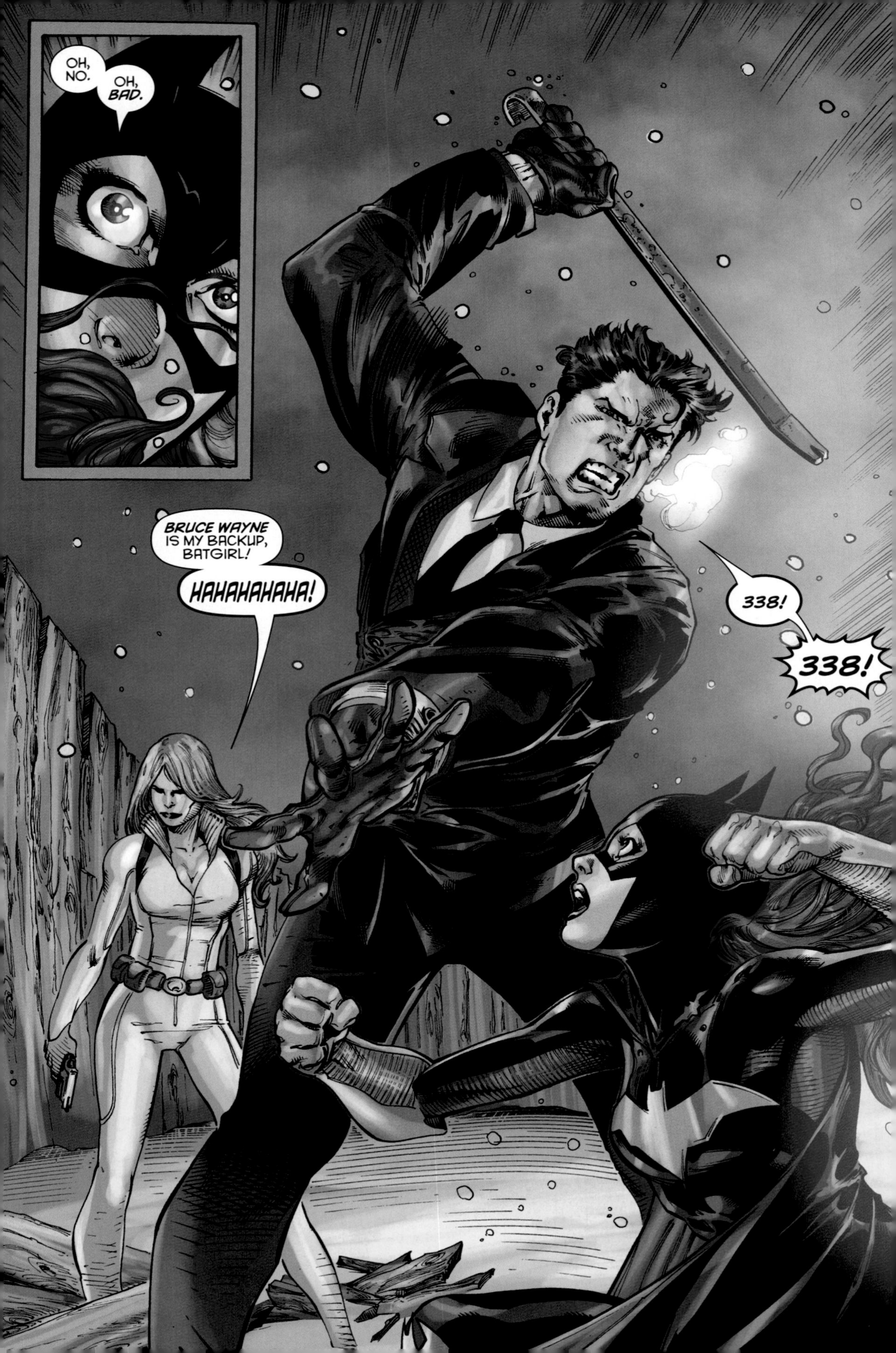
OH, NO.
OH, BAD.
BRUCE WAYNE IS MY BACKUP, BATGIRL!
HAHAHAHAHA!
338!
338!

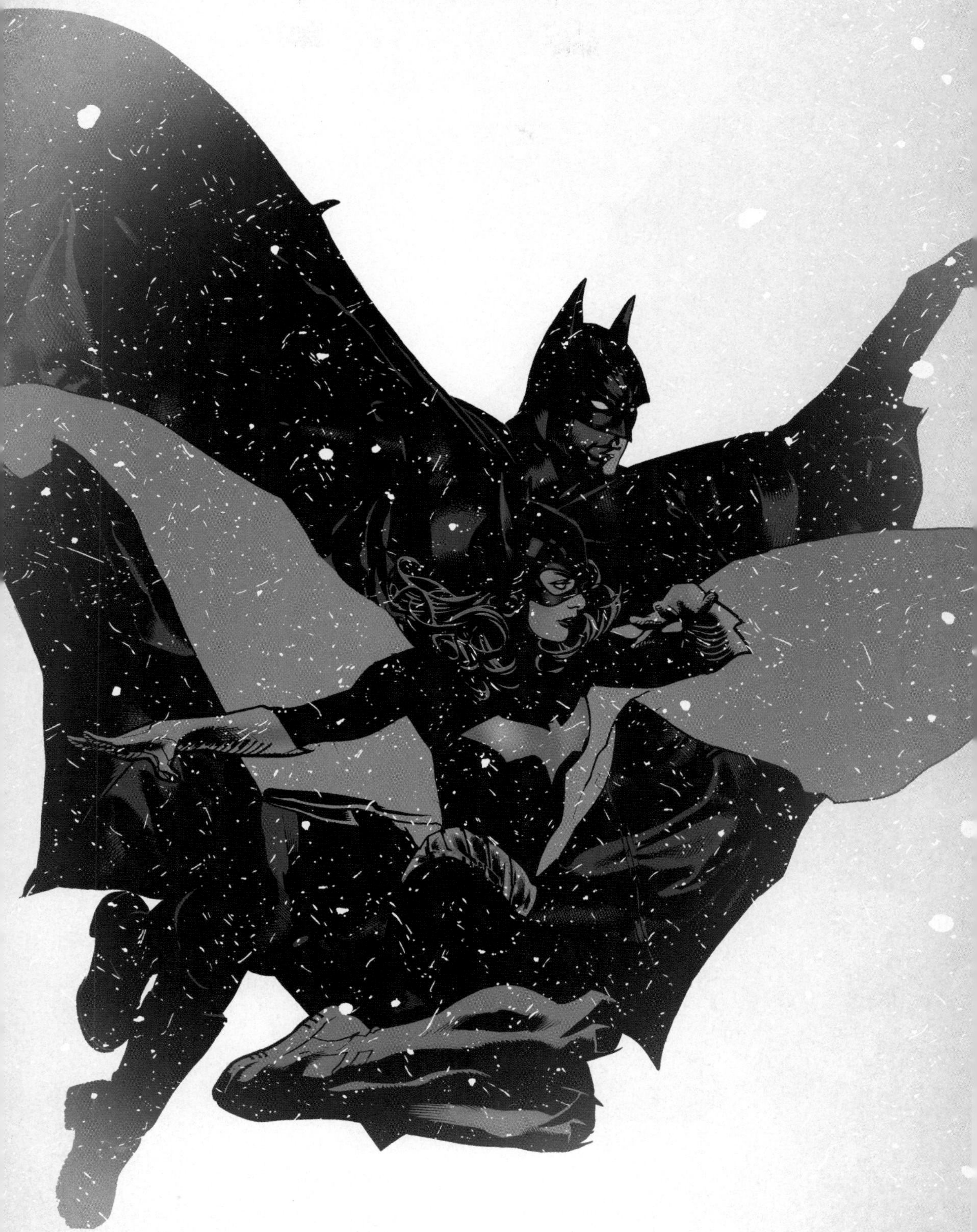

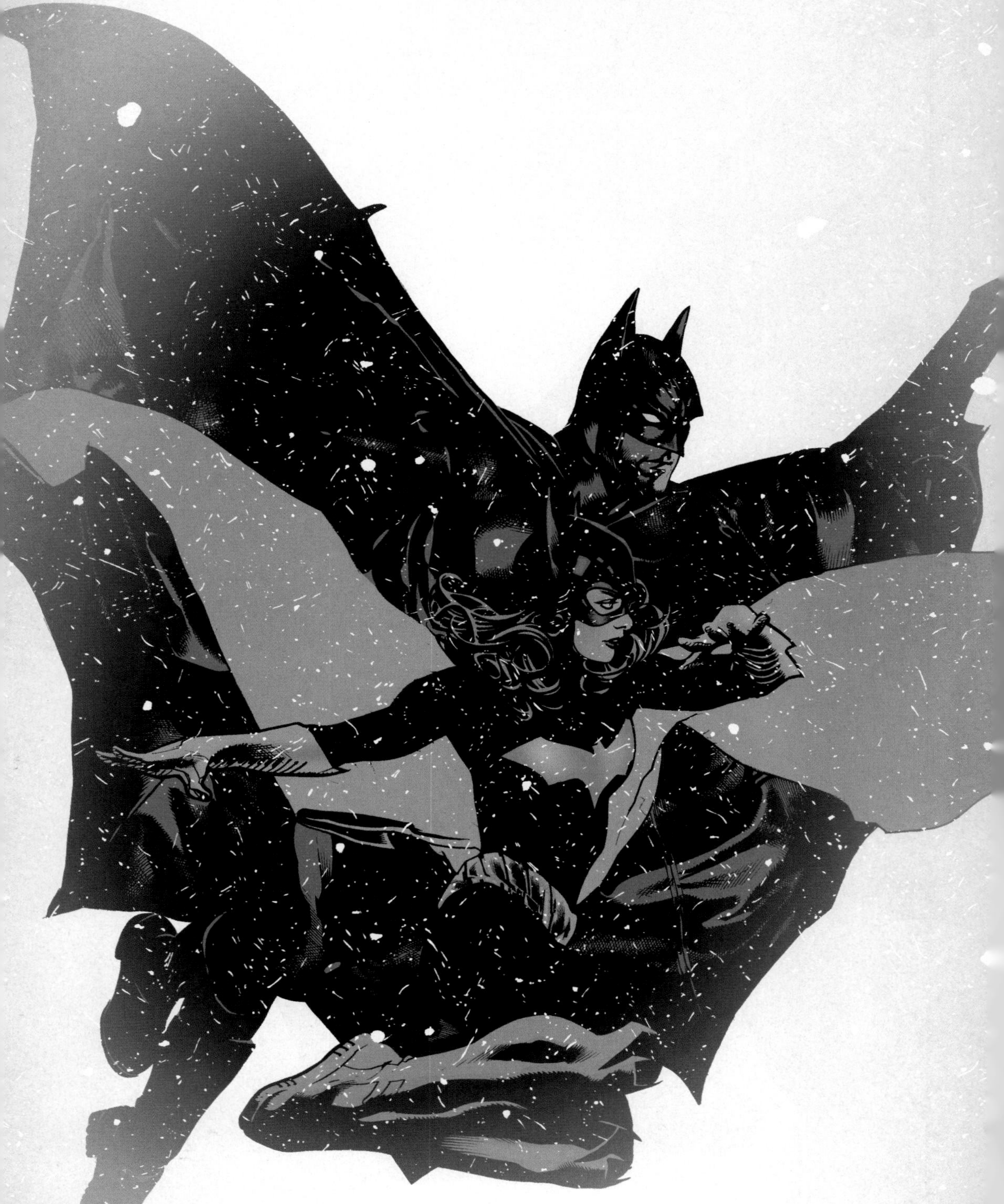

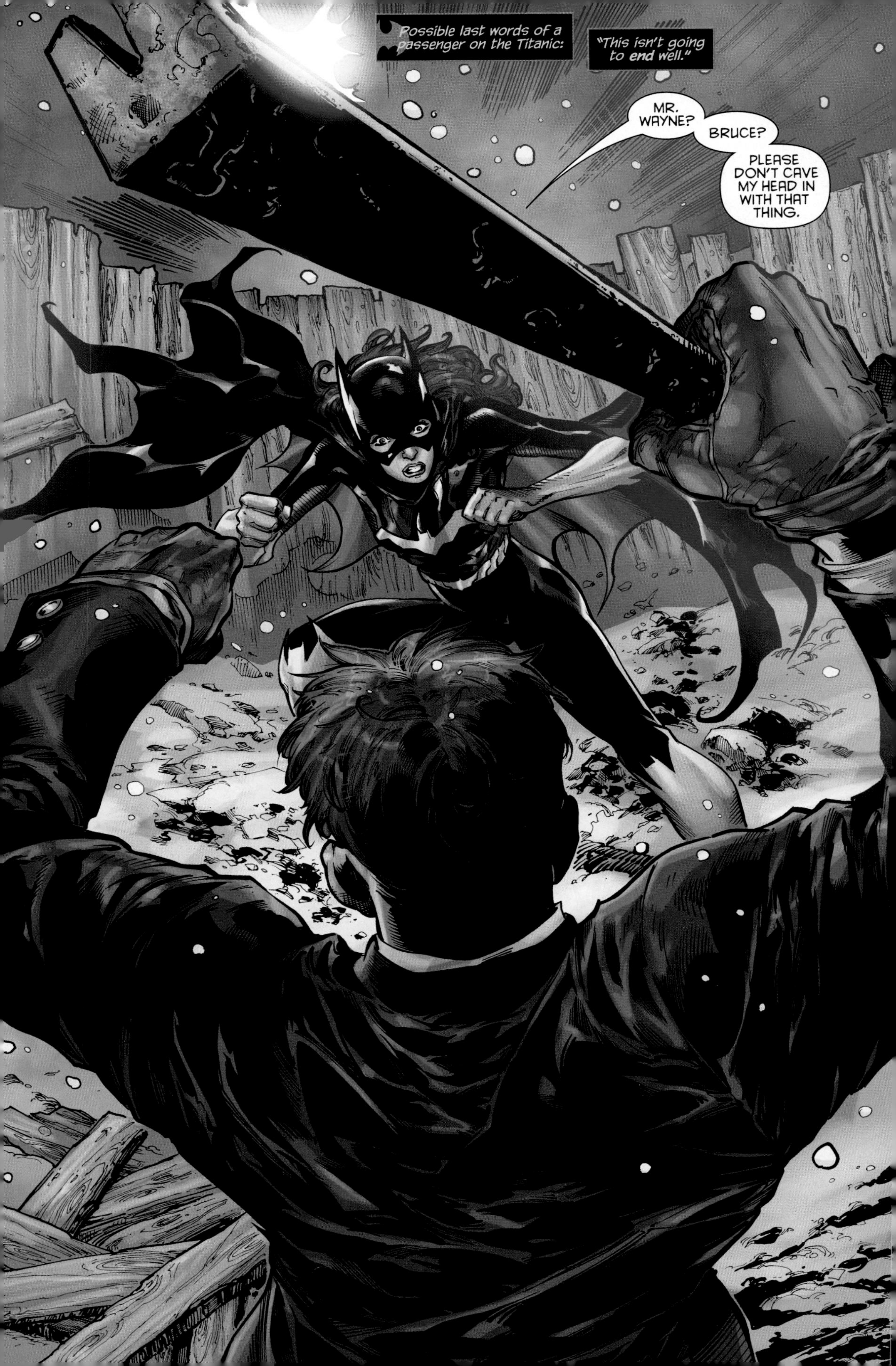
Possible last words of a passenger on the Titanic:
"This isn't going to end well."
MR. WAYNE?
BRUCE?
PLEASE DON'T CAVE MY HEAD IN WITH THAT THING.

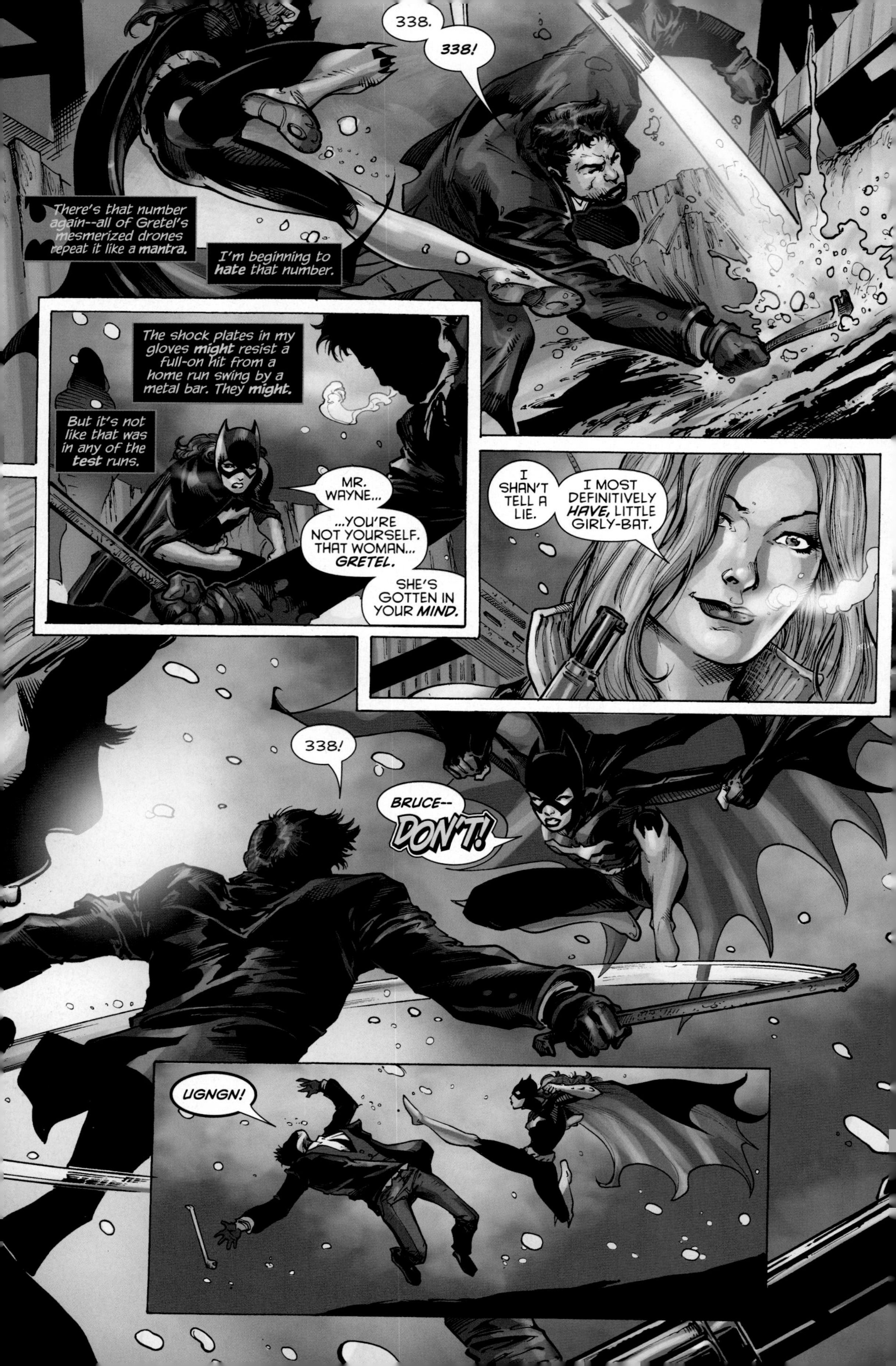
338.
338!
There's that number again--all of Gretel's mesmerized drones repeat it like a mantra.
I'm beginning to hate that number.
The shock plates in my gloves might resist a full-on hit from a home run swing by a metal bar. They might.
But it's not like that was in any of the test runs.
MR. WAYNE...
...YOU'RE NOT YOURSELF. THAT WOMAN... GRETEL.
SHE'S GOTTEN IN YOUR MIND.
I SHAN'T TELL A LIE.
I MOST DEFINITIVELY HAVE, LITTLE GIRLY-BAT.
338!
BRUCE--
DON'T!
UGNGN!

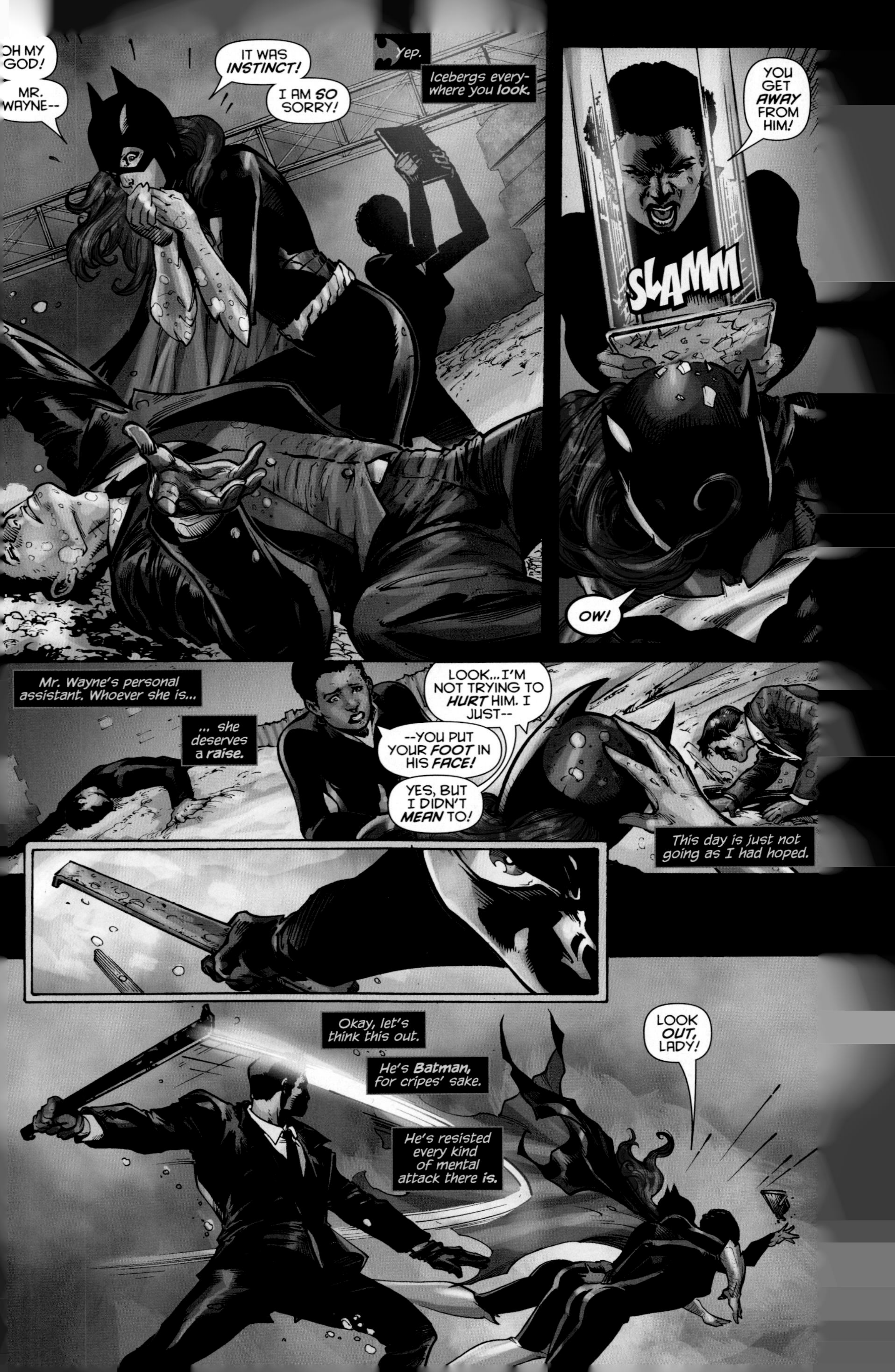
OH MY GOD!
MR. WAYNE--
IT WAS INSTINCT!
I AM SO SORRY!
Yep.
Icebergs everywhere you look.
YOU GET AWAY FROM HIM!
SLAMM
OW!
Mr. Wayne's personal assistant. Whoever she is...
... she deserves a raise.
LOOK...I'M NOT TRYING TO HURT HIM. I JUST--
--YOU PUT YOUR FOOT IN HIS FACE!
YES, BUT I DIDN'T MEAN TO!
This day is just not going as I had hoped.
Okay, let's think this out.
He's Batman, for cripes' sake.
He's resisted every kind of mental attack there is.
LOOK OUT, LADY!

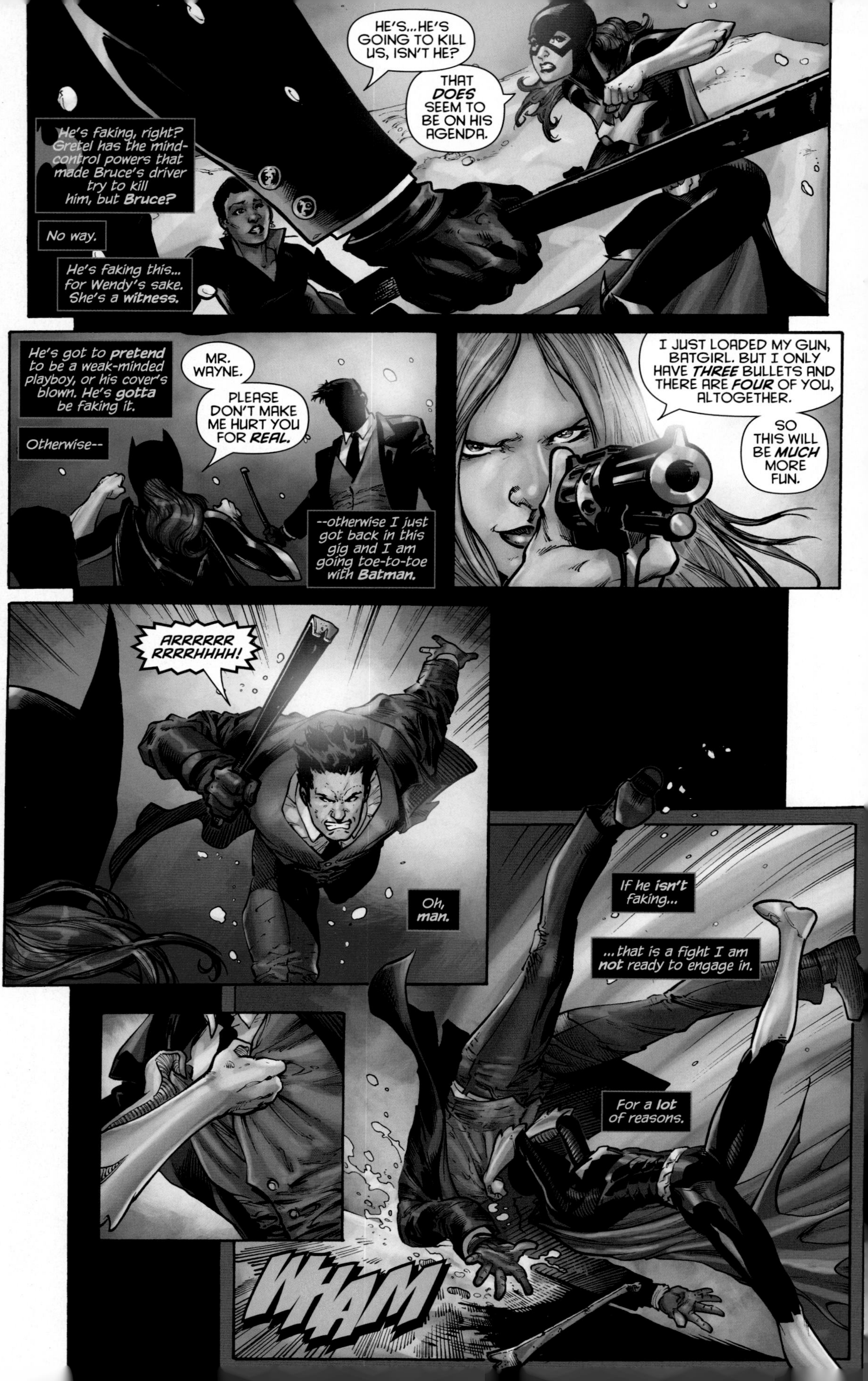
HE'S...HE'S GOING TO KILL US, ISN'T HE?
THAT DOES SEEM TO BE ON HIS AGENDA.
He's faking, right? Gretel has the mind-control powers that made Bruce's driver try to kill him, but Bruce?
No way.
He's faking this... for Wendy's sake. She's a witness.
He's got to pretend to be a weak-minded playboy, or his cover's blown. He's gotta be faking it.
MR. WAYNE.
PLEASE DON'T MAKE ME HURT YOU FOR REAL.
Otherwise--
--otherwise I just got back in this gig and I am going toe-to-toe with Batman.
I JUST LOADED MY GUN, BATGIRL. BUT I ONLY HAVE THREE BULLETS AND THERE ARE FOUR OF YOU, ALTOGETHER.
SO THIS WILL BE MUCH MORE FUN.
ARRRRRR RRRRHHHH!
Oh, man.
If he isn't faking...
...that is a fight I am not ready to engage in.
For a lot of reasons.
WHAM

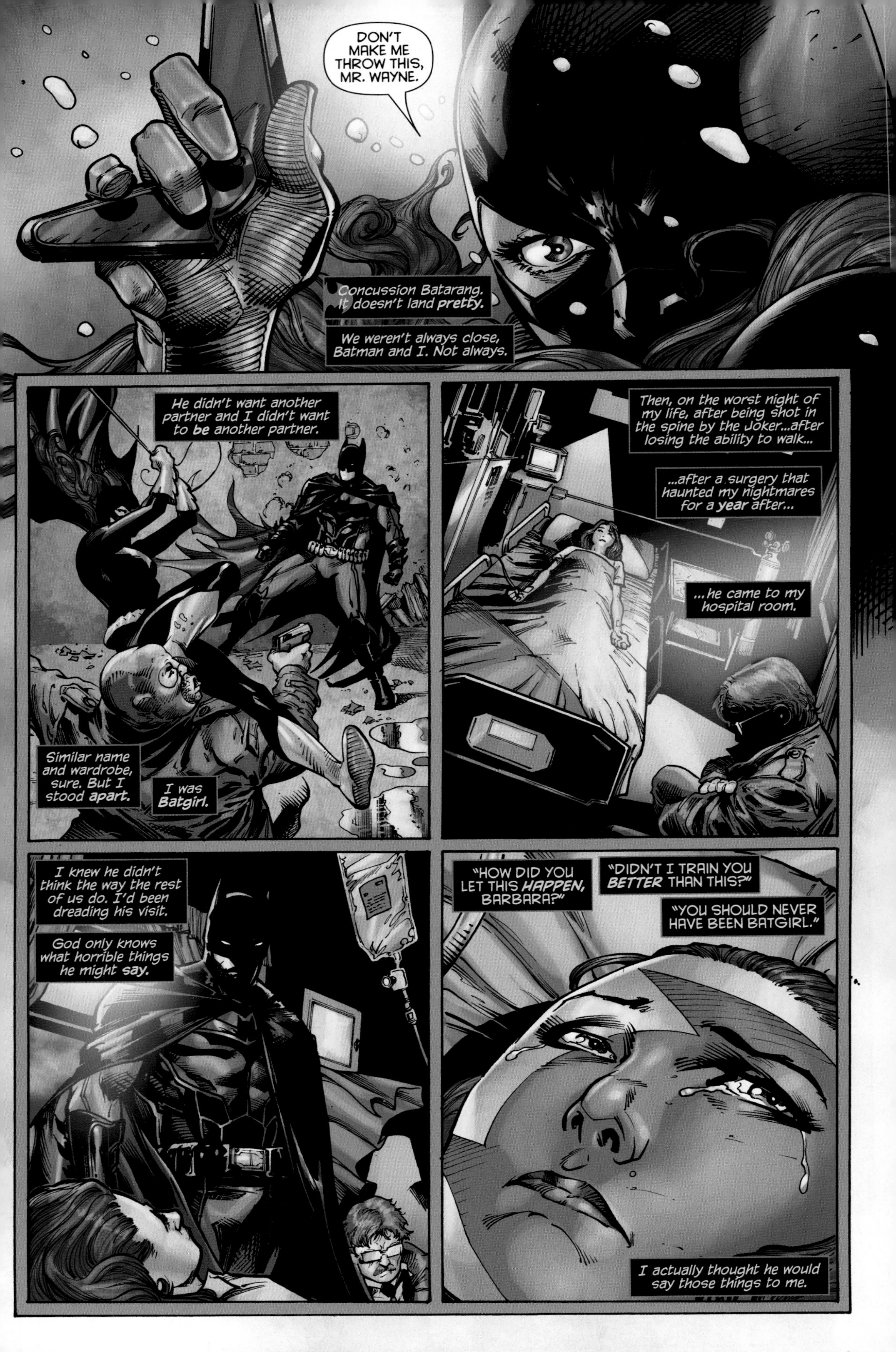
DON'T MAKE ME THROW THIS, MR. WAYNE.
Concussion Batarang. It doesn't land pretty.
We weren't always close, Batman and I. Not always.
He didn't want another partner and I didn't want to be another partner.
Similar name and wardrobe, sure. But I stood apart.
I was Batgirl.
Then, on the worst night of my life, after being shot in the spine by the Joker...after losing the ability to walk...
...after a surgery that haunted my nightmares for a year after...
...he came to my hospital room.
I knew he didn't think the way the rest of us do. I'd been dreading his visit.
God only knows what horrible things he might say.
"HOW DID YOU LET THIS HAPPEN, BARBARA?"
"DIDN'T I TRAIN YOU BETTER THAN THIS?"
"YOU SHOULD NEVER HAVE BEEN BATGIRL."
I actually thought he would say those things to me.

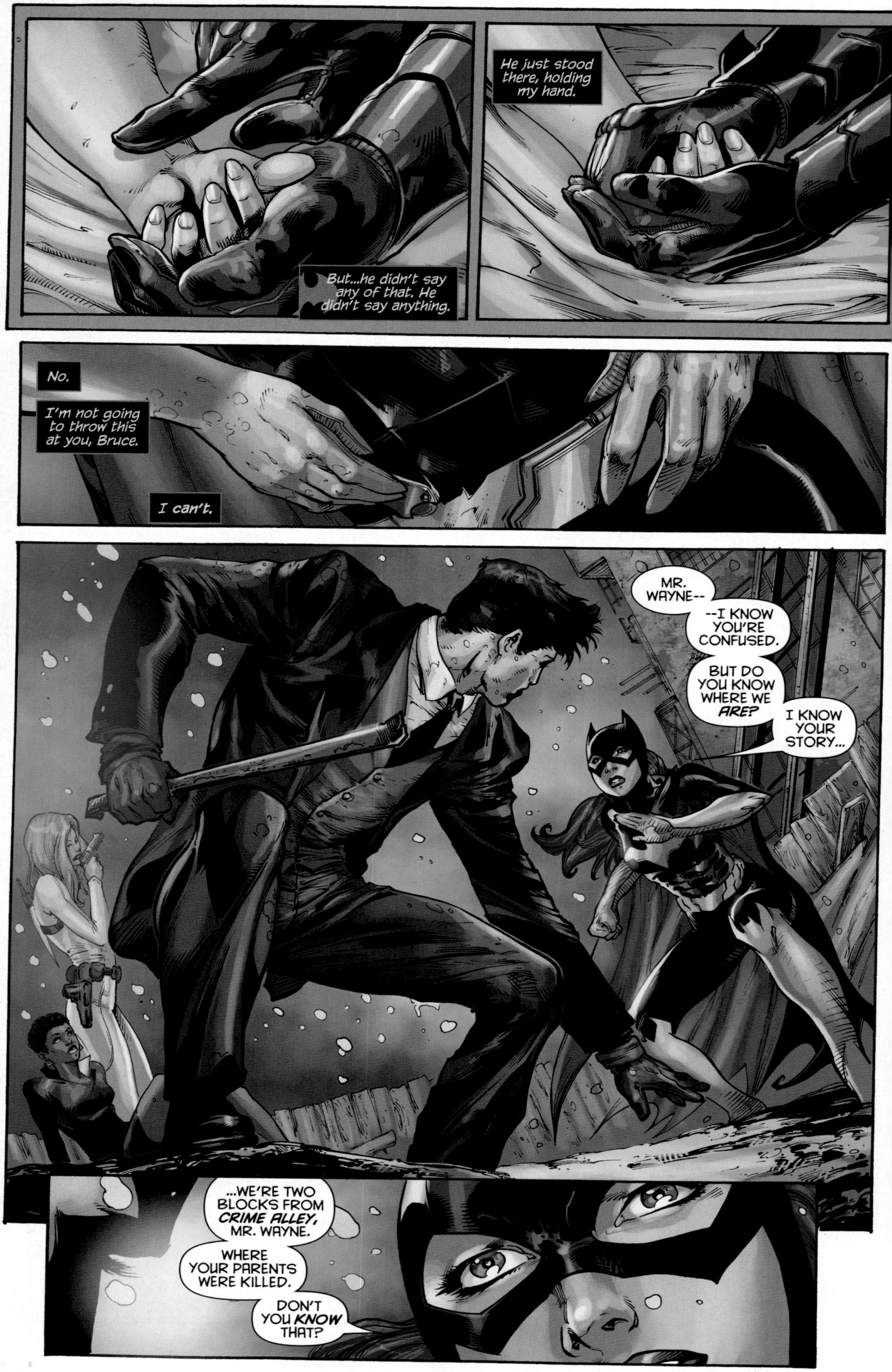
But...he didn't say any of that. He didn't say anything.
He just stood there, holding my hand.
No.
I'm not going to throw this at you, Bruce.
I can't.
MR. WAYNE--
--I KNOW YOU'RE CONFUSED.
BUT DO YOU KNOW WHERE WE ARE?
I KNOW YOUR STORY...
...WE'RE TWO BLOCKS FROM CRIME ALLEY, MR. WAYNE.
WHERE YOUR PARENTS WERE KILLED.
DON'T YOU KNOW THAT?

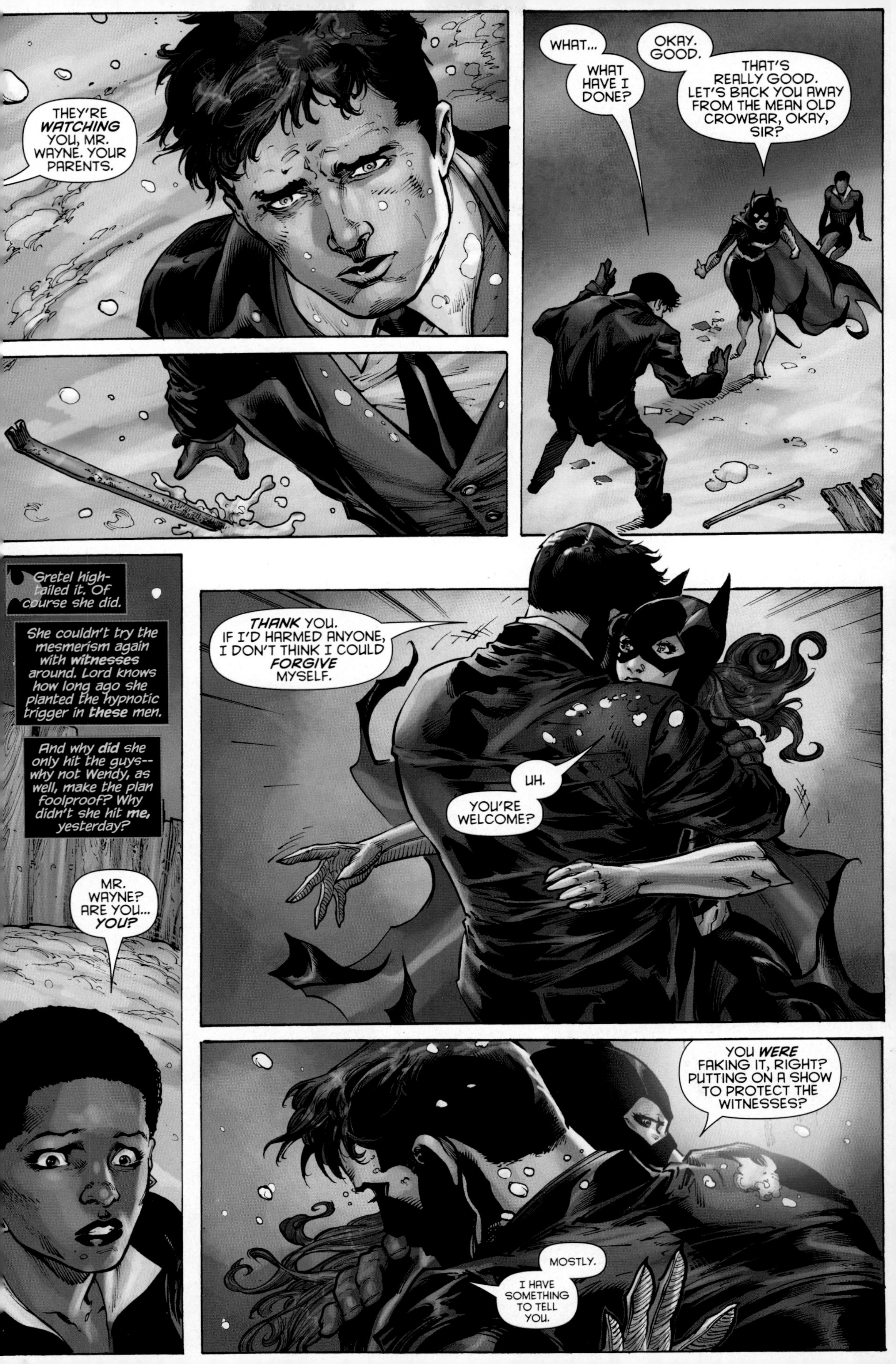
THEY'RE WATCHING YOU, MR. WAYNE. YOUR PARENTS.
WHAT...
WHAT HAVE I DONE?
OKAY. GOOD.
THAT'S REALLY GOOD. LET'S BACK YOU AWAY FROM THE MEAN OLD CROWBAR, OKAY, SIR?
Gretel high-tailed it. Of course she did.
She couldn't try the mesmerism again with witnesses around. Lord knows how long ago she planted the hypnotic trigger in these men.
And why did she only hit the guys--why not Wendy, as well, make the plan foolproof? Why didn't she hit me, yesterday?
MR. WAYNE? ARE YOU... YOU?
THANK YOU. IF I'D HARMED ANYONE, I DON'T THINK I COULD FORGIVE MYSELF.
UH.
YOU'RE WELCOME?
YOU WERE FAKING IT, RIGHT? PUTTING ON A SHOW TO PROTECT THE WITNESSES?
MOSTLY.
I HAVE SOMETHING TO TELL YOU.

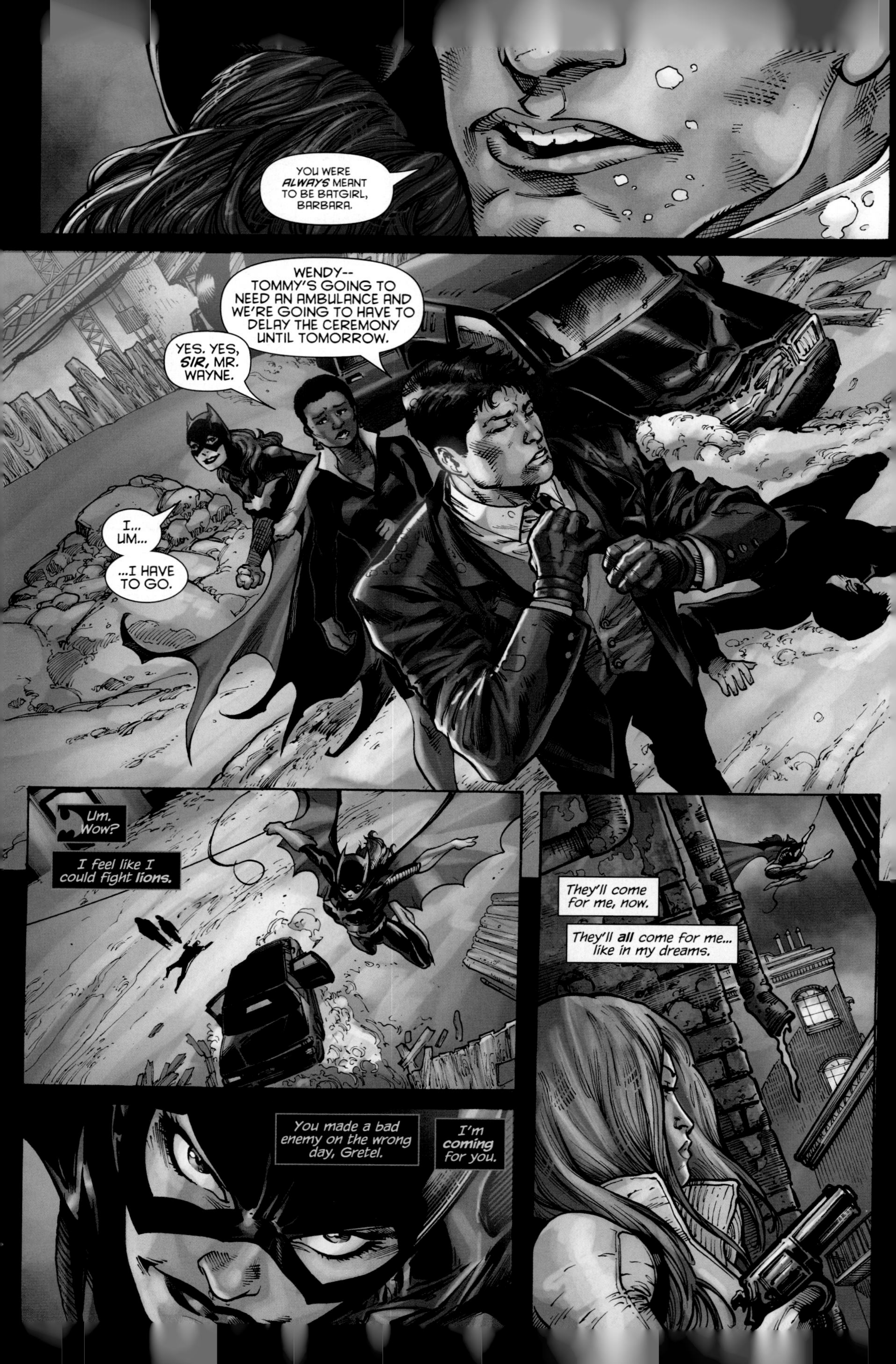
YOU WERE ALWAYS MEANT TO BE BATGIRL, BARBARA.
WENDY-- TOMMY'S GOING TO NEED AN AMBULANCE AND WE'RE GOING TO HAVE TO DELAY THE CEREMONY UNTIL TOMORROW.
YES. YES, SIR, MR. WAYNE.
I... UM...
...I HAVE TO GO.
Um. Wow?
I feel like I could fight lions.
They'll come for me, now.
They'll all come for me... like in my dreams.
You made a bad enemy on the wrong day, Gretel.
I'm coming for you.

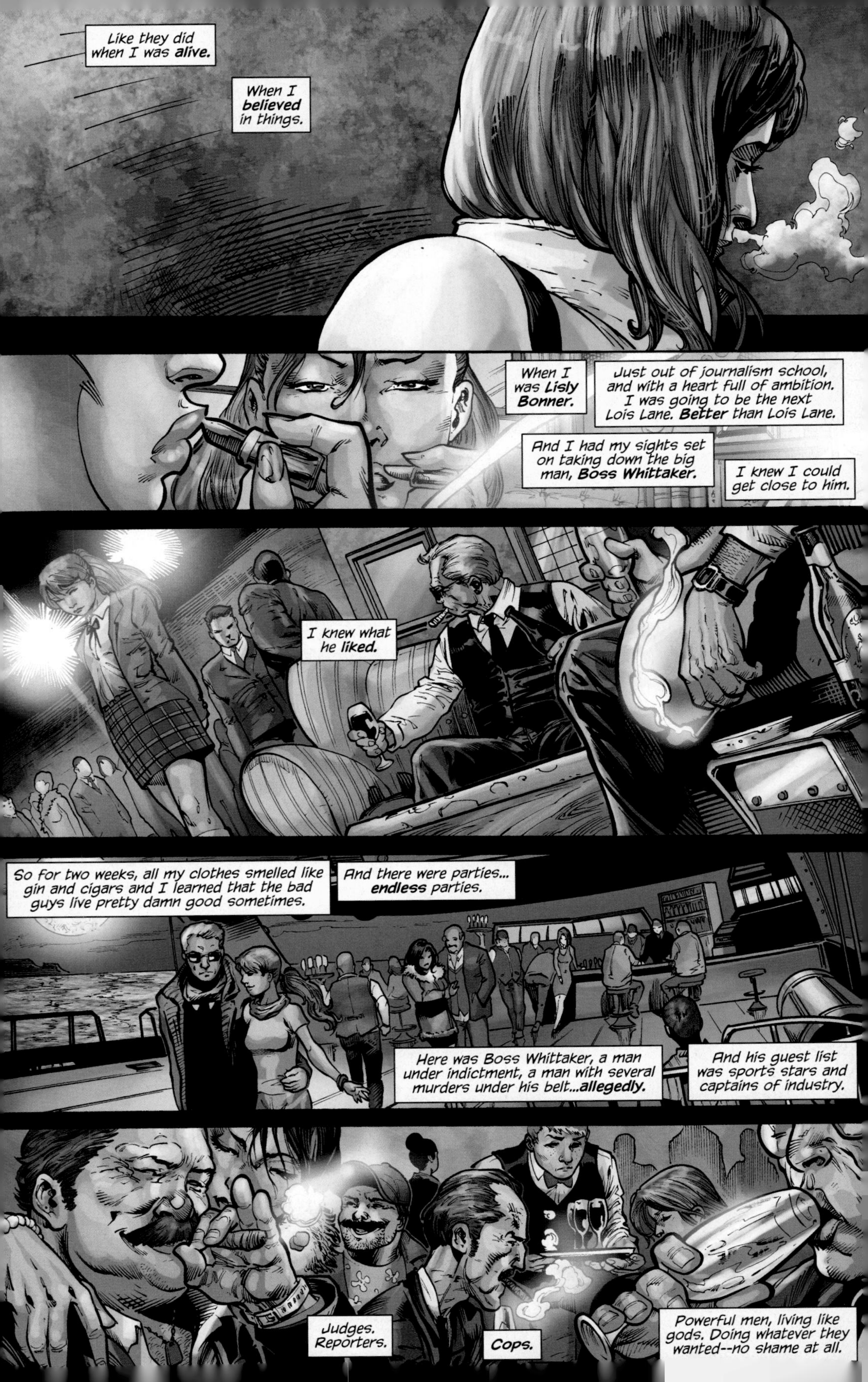

Like they did when I was **alive.**
When I **believed** in things.
When I was **Lisly Bonner.**
Just out of journalism school, and with a heart full of ambition. I was going to be the next Lois Lane. **Better** than Lois Lane.
And I had my sights set on taking down the big man, **Boss Whittaker.**
I knew I could get close to him.
I knew what he **liked.**
So for two weeks, all my clothes smelled like gin and cigars and I learned that the bad guys live pretty damn good sometimes.
And there were parties... **endless** parties.
Here was Boss Whittaker, a man under indictment, a man with several murders under his belt...**allegedly.**
And his guest list was sports stars and captains of industry.
Judges. Reporters.
Cops.
Powerful men, living like gods. Doing whatever they wanted--no shame at all.

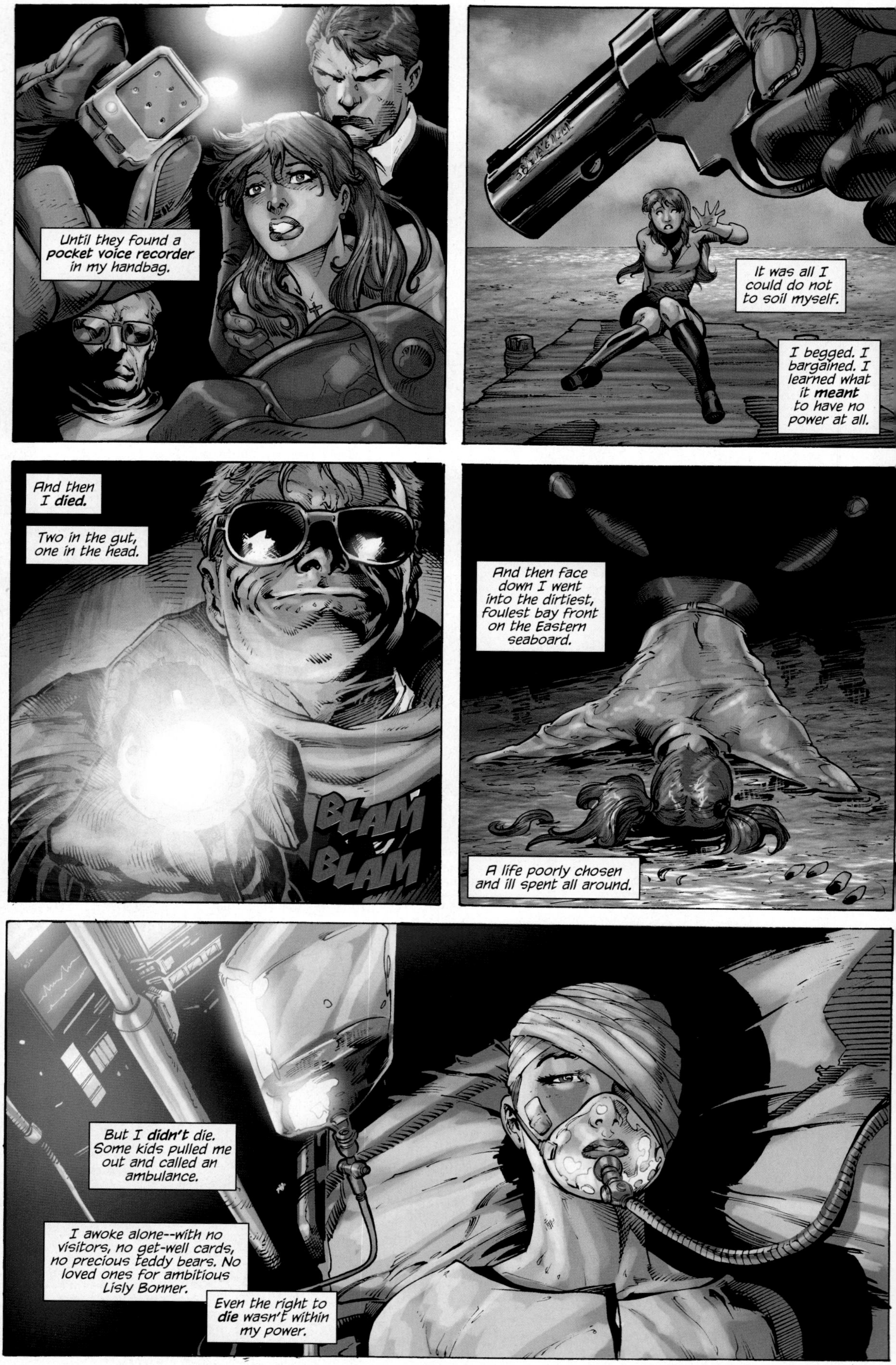

Until they found a **pocket voice recorder** in my handbag.
It was all I could do not to soil myself.
I begged. I bargained. I learned what it **meant** to have no power at all.
And then I **died.**
Two in the gut, one in the head.
BLAM BLAM
And then face down I went into the dirtiest, foulest bay front on the Eastern seaboard.
A life poorly chosen and ill spent all around.
But I **didn't** die. Some kids pulled me out and called an ambulance.
I awoke alone--with no visitors, no get-well cards, no precious teddy bears. No loved ones for ambitious Lisly Bonner.
Even the right to **die** wasn't within my power.

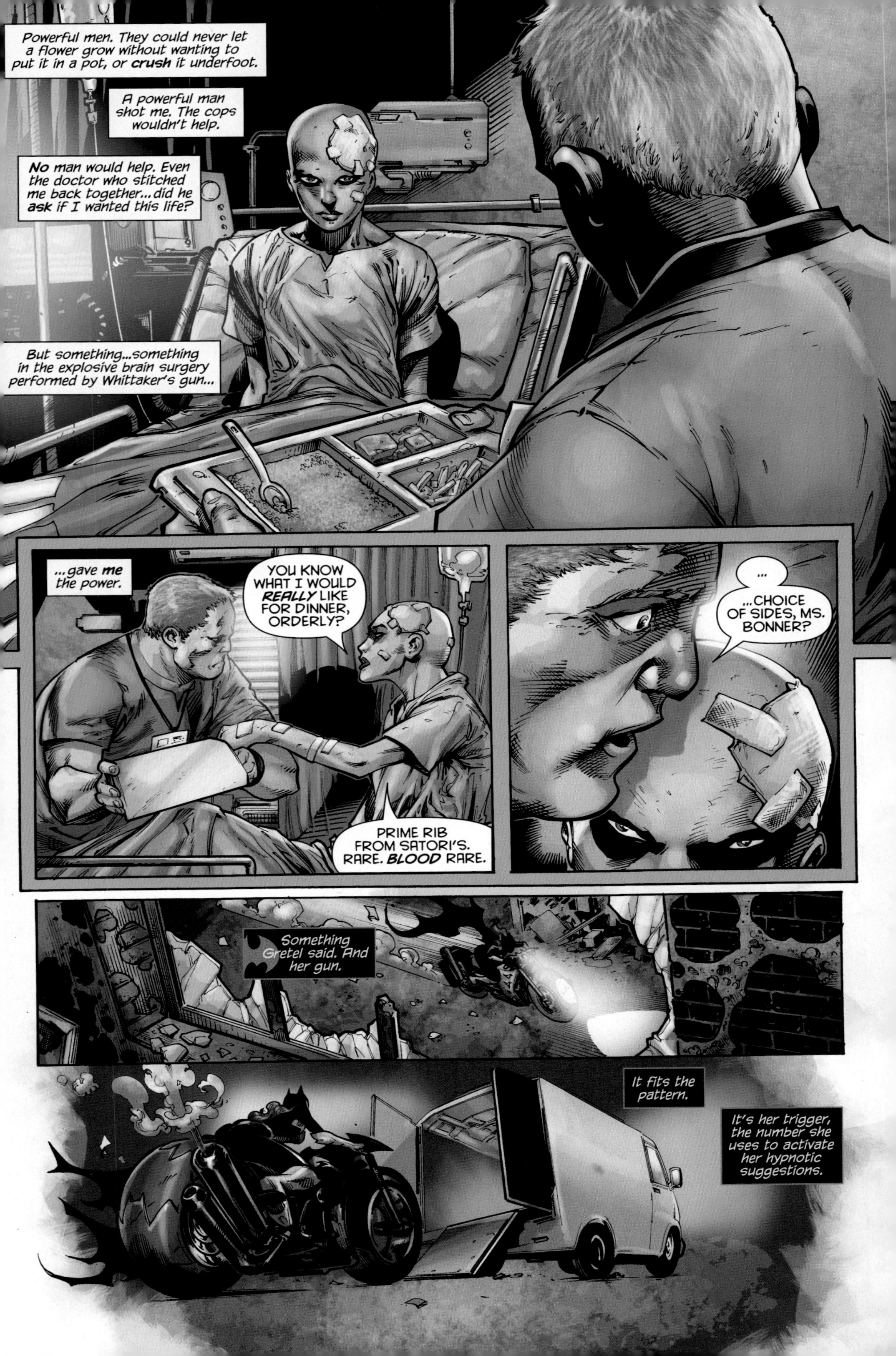

Powerful men. They could never let a flower grow without wanting to put it in a pot, or crush it underfoot.
A powerful man shot me. The cops wouldn't help.
No man would help. Even the doctor who stitched me back together...did he ask if I wanted this life?
But something...something in the explosive brain surgery performed by Whittaker's gun...
...gave me the power.
YOU KNOW WHAT I WOULD REALLY LIKE FOR DINNER, ORDERLY?
PRIME RIB FROM SATORI'S. RARE. BLOOD RARE.
...
...CHOICE OF SIDES, MS. BONNER?
Something Gretel said. And her gun.
It fits the pattern.
It's her trigger, the number she uses to activate her hypnotic suggestions.

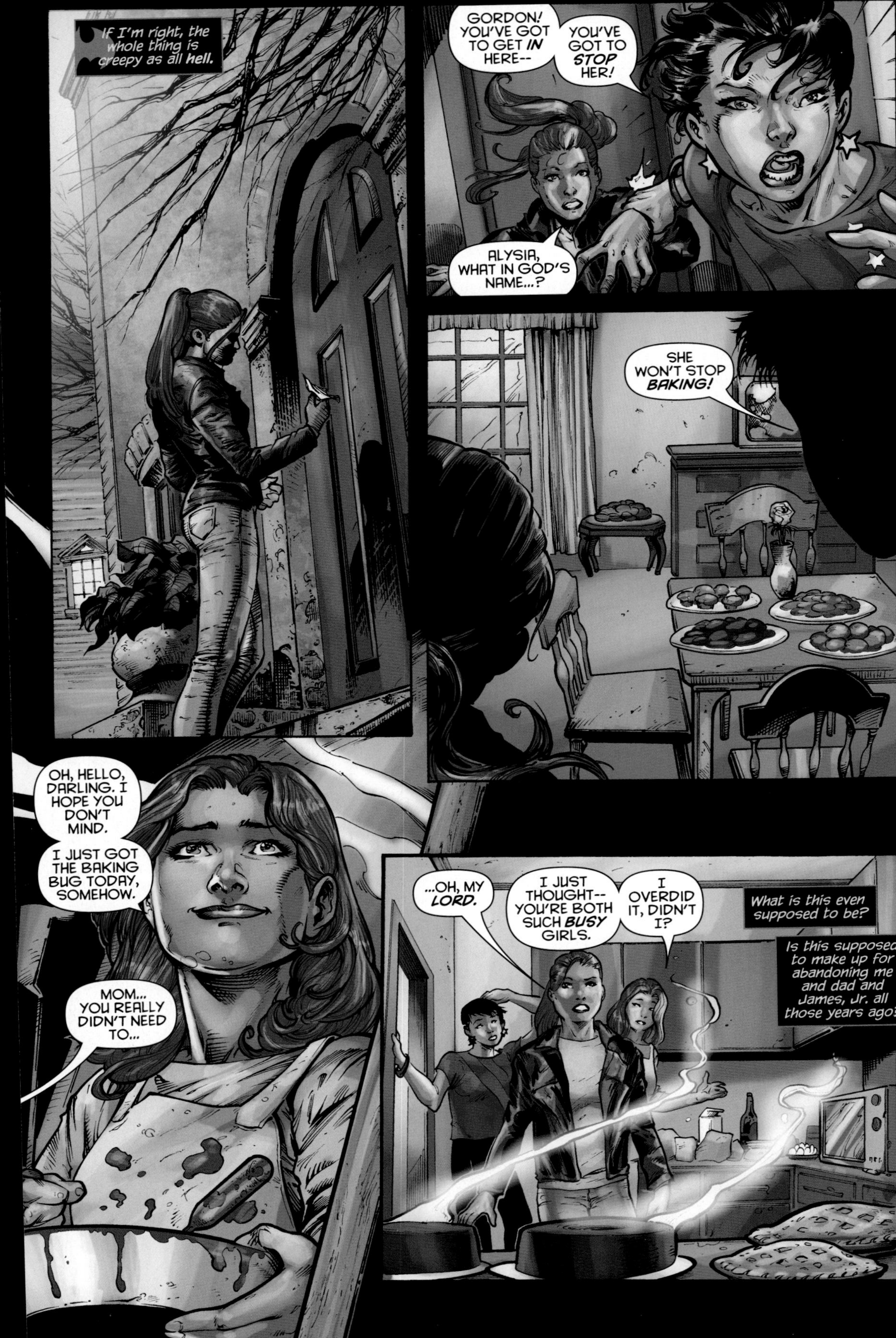

If I'm right, the whole thing is creepy as all hell.
GORDON! YOU'VE GOT TO GET IN HERE--
YOU'VE GOT TO STOP HER!
ALYSIA, WHAT IN GOD'S NAME...?
SHE WON'T STOP BAKING!
OH, HELLO, DARLING. I HOPE YOU DON'T MIND.
I JUST GOT THE BAKING BUG TODAY, SOMEHOW.
MOM... YOU REALLY DIDN'T NEED TO...
...OH, MY LORD.
I JUST THOUGHT-- YOU'RE BOTH SUCH BUSY GIRLS.
I OVERDID IT, DIDN'T I?
What is this even supposed to be?
Is this supposed to make up for abandoning me and dad and James, Jr. all those years ago?

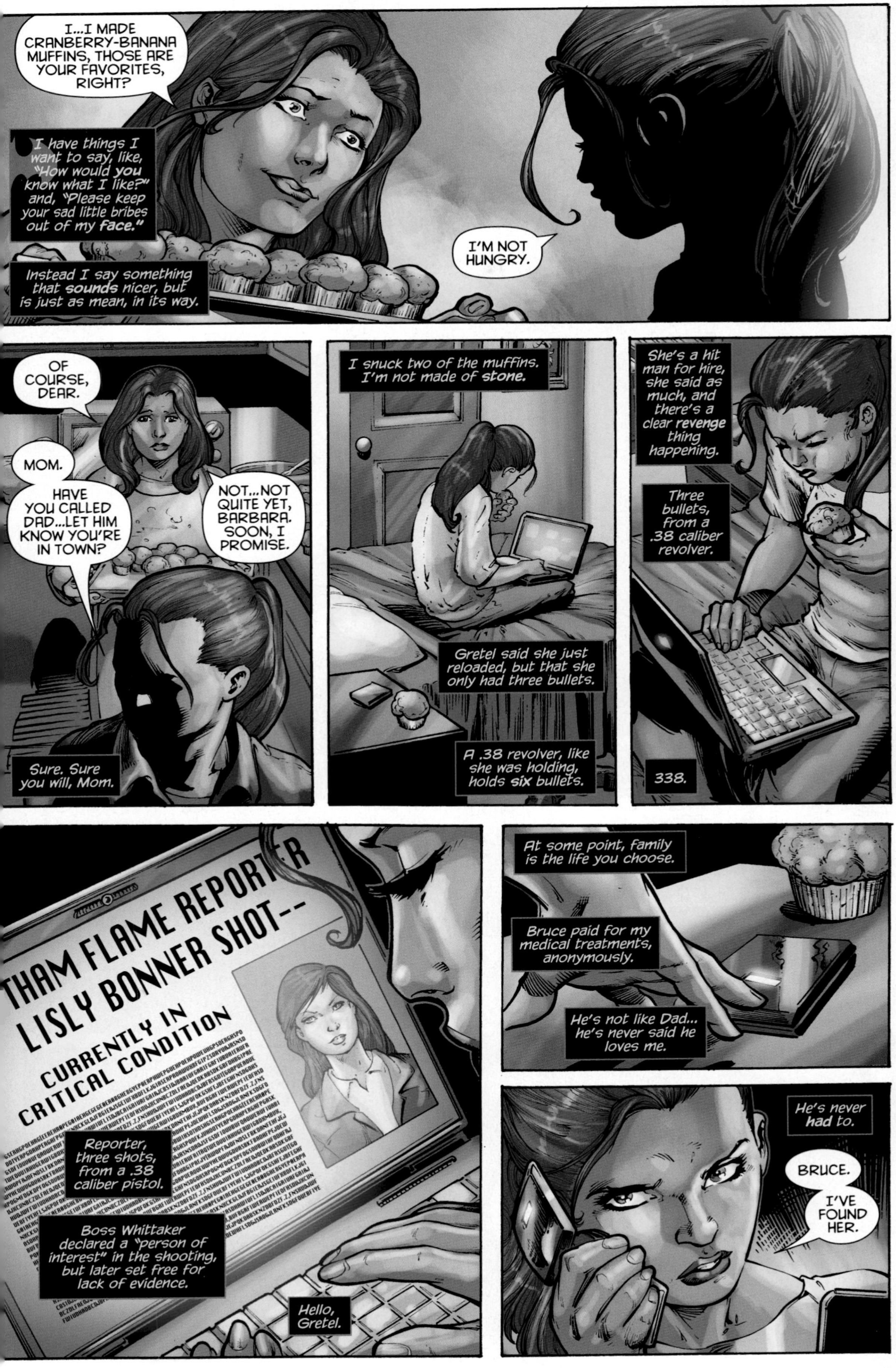
I...I MADE CRANBERRY-BANANA MUFFINS, THOSE ARE YOUR FAVORITES, RIGHT?
I have things I want to say, like, "How would you know what I like?" and, "Please keep your sad little bribes out of my face."
Instead I say something that sounds nicer, but is just as mean, in its way.
I'M NOT HUNGRY.
OF COURSE, DEAR.
MOM.
HAVE YOU CALLED DAD...LET HIM KNOW YOU'RE IN TOWN?
NOT...NOT QUITE YET, BARBARA. SOON, I PROMISE.
Sure. Sure you will, Mom.
I snuck two of the muffins. I'm not made of stone.
Gretel said she just reloaded, but that she only had three bullets.
A .38 revolver, like she was holding, holds six bullets.
She's a hit man for hire, she said as much, and there's a clear revenge thing happening.
Three bullets, from a .38 caliber revolver.
338.
THAM FLAME REPORTER
LISLY BONNER SHOT--
CURRENTLY IN CRITICAL CONDITION
Reporter, three shots, from a .38 caliber pistol.
Boss Whittaker declared a "person of interest" in the shooting, but later set free for lack of evidence.
Hello, Gretel.
At some point, family is the life you choose.
Bruce paid for my medical treatments, anonymously.
He's not like Dad... he's never said he loves me.
He's never had to.
BRUCE.
I'VE FOUND HER.

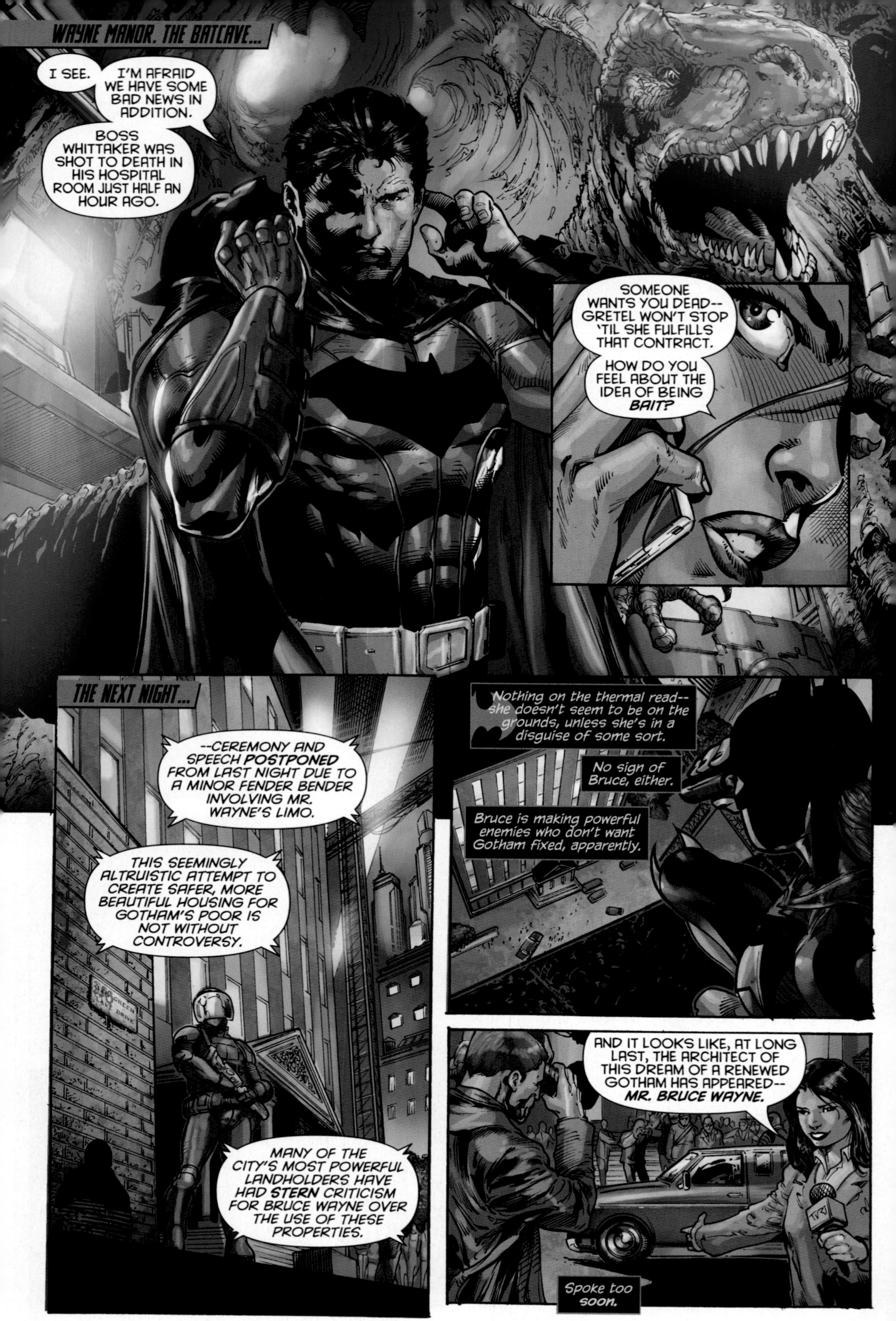
WAYNE MANOR. THE BATCAVE...
I SEE.
I'M AFRAID WE HAVE SOME BAD NEWS IN ADDITION.
BOSS WHITTAKER WAS SHOT TO DEATH IN HIS HOSPITAL ROOM JUST HALF AN HOUR AGO.
SOMEONE WANTS YOU DEAD-- GRETEL WON'T STOP 'TIL SHE FULFILLS THAT CONTRACT.
HOW DO YOU FEEL ABOUT THE IDEA OF BEING BAIT?
THE NEXT NIGHT...
--CEREMONY AND SPEECH POSTPONED FROM LAST NIGHT DUE TO A MINOR FENDER BENDER INVOLVING MR. WAYNE'S LIMO.
THIS SEEMINGLY ALTRUISTIC ATTEMPT TO CREATE SAFER, MORE BEAUTIFUL HOUSING FOR GOTHAM'S POOR IS NOT WITHOUT CONTROVERSY.
MANY OF THE CITY'S MOST POWERFUL LANDHOLDERS HAVE HAD STERN CRITICISM FOR BRUCE WAYNE OVER THE USE OF THESE PROPERTIES.
Nothing on the thermal read-- she doesn't seem to be on the grounds, unless she's in a disguise of some sort.
No sign of Bruce, either.
Bruce is making powerful enemies who don't want Gotham fixed, apparently.
AND IT LOOKS LIKE, AT LONG LAST, THE ARCHITECT OF THIS DREAM OF A RENEWED GOTHAM HAS APPEARED-- MR. BRUCE WAYNE.
Spoke too soon.

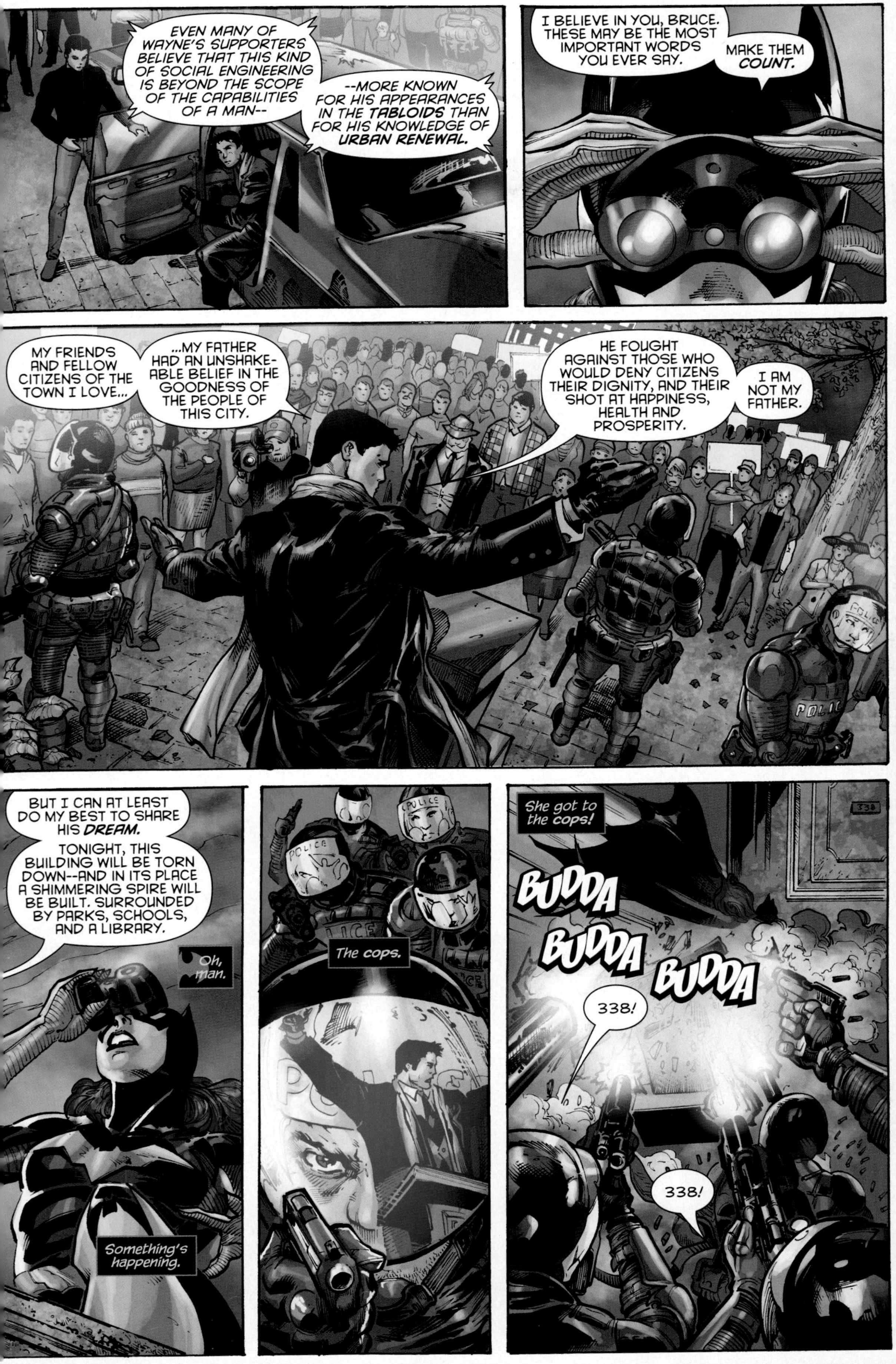
EVEN MANY OF WAYNE'S SUPPORTERS BELIEVE THAT THIS KIND OF SOCIAL ENGINEERING IS BEYOND THE SCOPE OF THE CAPABILITIES OF A MAN--
--MORE KNOWN FOR HIS APPEARANCES IN THE TABLOIDS THAN FOR HIS KNOWLEDGE OF URBAN RENEWAL.
I BELIEVE IN YOU, BRUCE. THESE MAY BE THE MOST IMPORTANT WORDS YOU EVER SAY.
MAKE THEM COUNT.
MY FRIENDS AND FELLOW CITIZENS OF THE TOWN I LOVE...
...MY FATHER HAD AN UNSHAKE-ABLE BELIEF IN THE GOODNESS OF THE PEOPLE OF THIS CITY.
HE FOUGHT AGAINST THOSE WHO WOULD DENY CITIZENS THEIR DIGNITY, AND THEIR SHOT AT HAPPINESS, HEALTH AND PROSPERITY.
I AM NOT MY FATHER.
POLIC
POLIC
BUT I CAN AT LEAST DO MY BEST TO SHARE HIS DREAM.
TONIGHT, THIS BUILDING WILL BE TORN DOWN--AND IN ITS PLACE A SHIMMERING SPIRE WILL BE BUILT. SURROUNDED BY PARKS, SCHOOLS, AND A LIBRARY.
Oh, man.
Something's happening.
POLICE
POLICE
The cops.
She got to the cops!
338
BUDDA
BUDDA
BUDDA
338!
338!

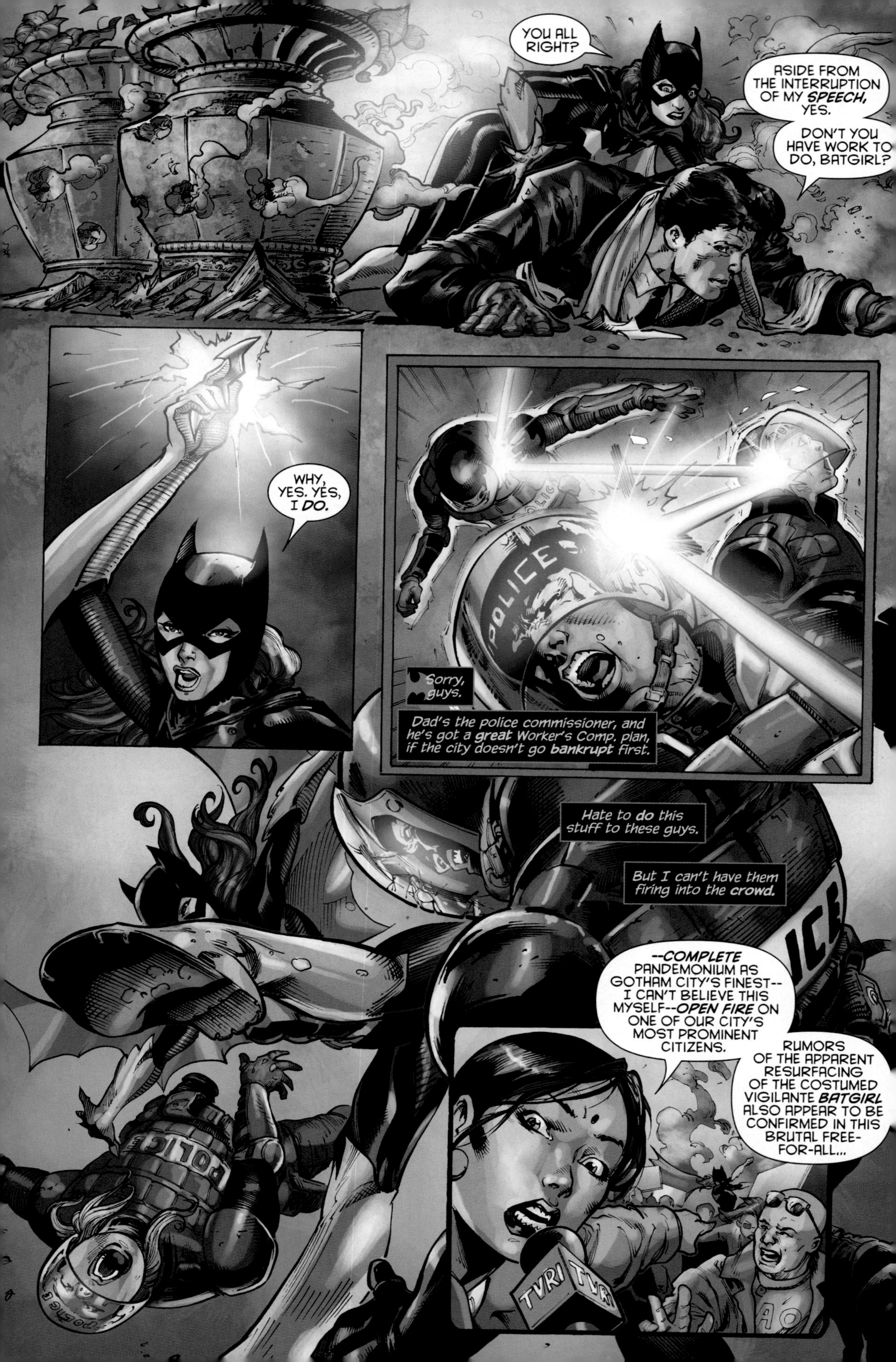
YOU ALL RIGHT?
ASIDE FROM THE INTERRUPTION OF MY *SPEECH,* YES.
DON'T YOU HAVE WORK TO DO, BATGIRL?
WHY, YES. YES, I *DO.*
Sorry, guys.
Dad's the police commissioner, and he's got a **great** Worker's Comp. plan, if the city doesn't go **bankrupt** first.
Hate to **do** this stuff to these guys.
But I can't have them firing into the **crowd.**
--COMPLETE PANDEMONIUM AS GOTHAM CITY'S FINEST-- I CAN'T BELIEVE THIS MYSELF--*OPEN FIRE* ON ONE OF OUR CITY'S MOST PROMINENT CITIZENS.
RUMORS OF THE APPARENT RESURFACING OF THE COSTUMED VIGILANTE *BATGIRL* ALSO APPEAR TO BE CONFIRMED IN THIS BRUTAL FREE-FOR-ALL...

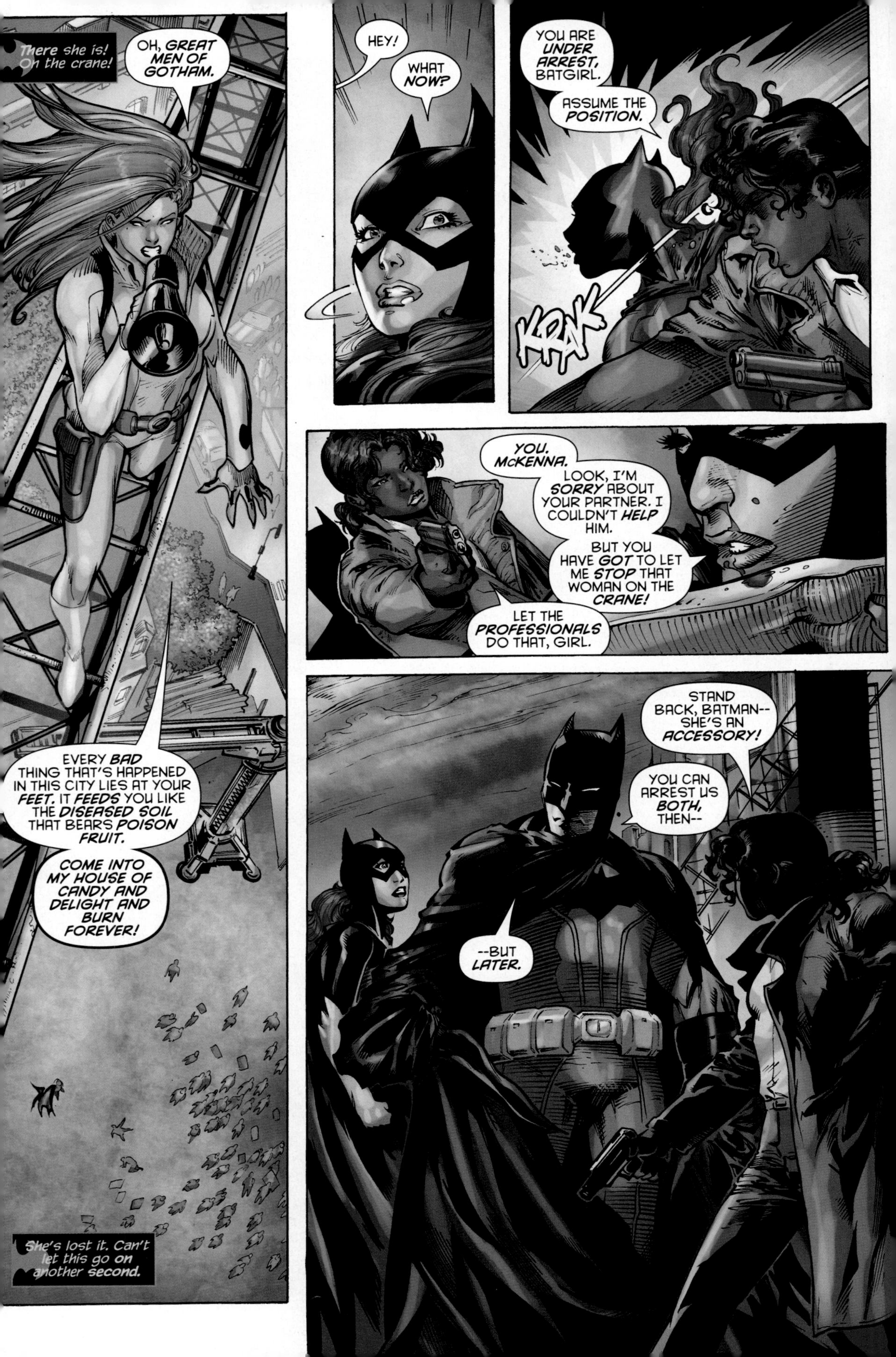
There she is! On the crane!
OH, GREAT MEN OF GOTHAM.
EVERY BAD THING THAT'S HAPPENED IN THIS CITY LIES AT YOUR FEET. IT FEEDS YOU LIKE THE DISEASED SOIL THAT BEARS POISON FRUIT.
COME INTO MY HOUSE OF CANDY AND DELIGHT AND BURN FOREVER!
She's lost it. Can't let this go on another second.
HEY!
WHAT NOW?
YOU ARE UNDER ARREST, BATGIRL.
ASSUME THE POSITION.
KRAK
YOU. McKENNA.
LOOK, I'M SORRY ABOUT YOUR PARTNER. I COULDN'T HELP HIM.
BUT YOU HAVE GOT TO LET ME STOP THAT WOMAN ON THE CRANE!
LET THE PROFESSIONALS DO THAT, GIRL.
STAND BACK, BATMAN-- SHE'S AN ACCESSORY!
YOU CAN ARREST US BOTH, THEN--
--BUT LATER.

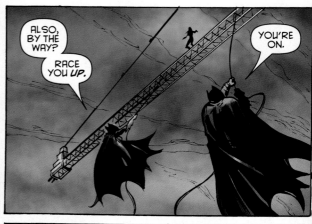

NICE *SAVE.* YOU DRESS MIGHTY *RAPIDLY,* I HAVE TO SAY.

IT'S ALL THE MORE IMPRESSIVE, SINCE I USUALLY HAVE *HELP.*

SHE'S... SHE'S BROKEN, BATMAN.

TRY TO BE KIND.

POOM

ALSO, BY THE WAY?

RACE YOU *UP.*

YOU'RE ON.

THEY'RE COMING FOR ME. OF COURSE THEY ARE COMING FOR ME.

THEY WERE NEVER GOING TO LET SOMEONE LIKE *ME* OUT THERE TO THREATEN THEIR UNASSAILABLE *POSITIONS.*

IF I DIE TONIGHT, LET IT BE *FIGHTING.*

GRETEL.

LISLY.

YOU DON'T HAVE TO DIE AT *ALL.*

LOOK, A BAD MAN TURNED YOUR LIFE INSIDE OUT.

I *KNOW* WHAT THAT'S ABOUT.

HE'S *DEAD.* HIS CRIME FAMILY, IT'S ALL GONE NOW. YOU SAW TO THAT.

LET THAT BE THE *END* OF THIS LIFE FOR YOU.

POWER DOES NOT GIVE *UP* POWER, YOU *KNOW* THAT!

THEY WIN BECAUSE THEY *ALWAYS* WIN.

Oh, no, Bruce, not yet. Give me ten more seconds!

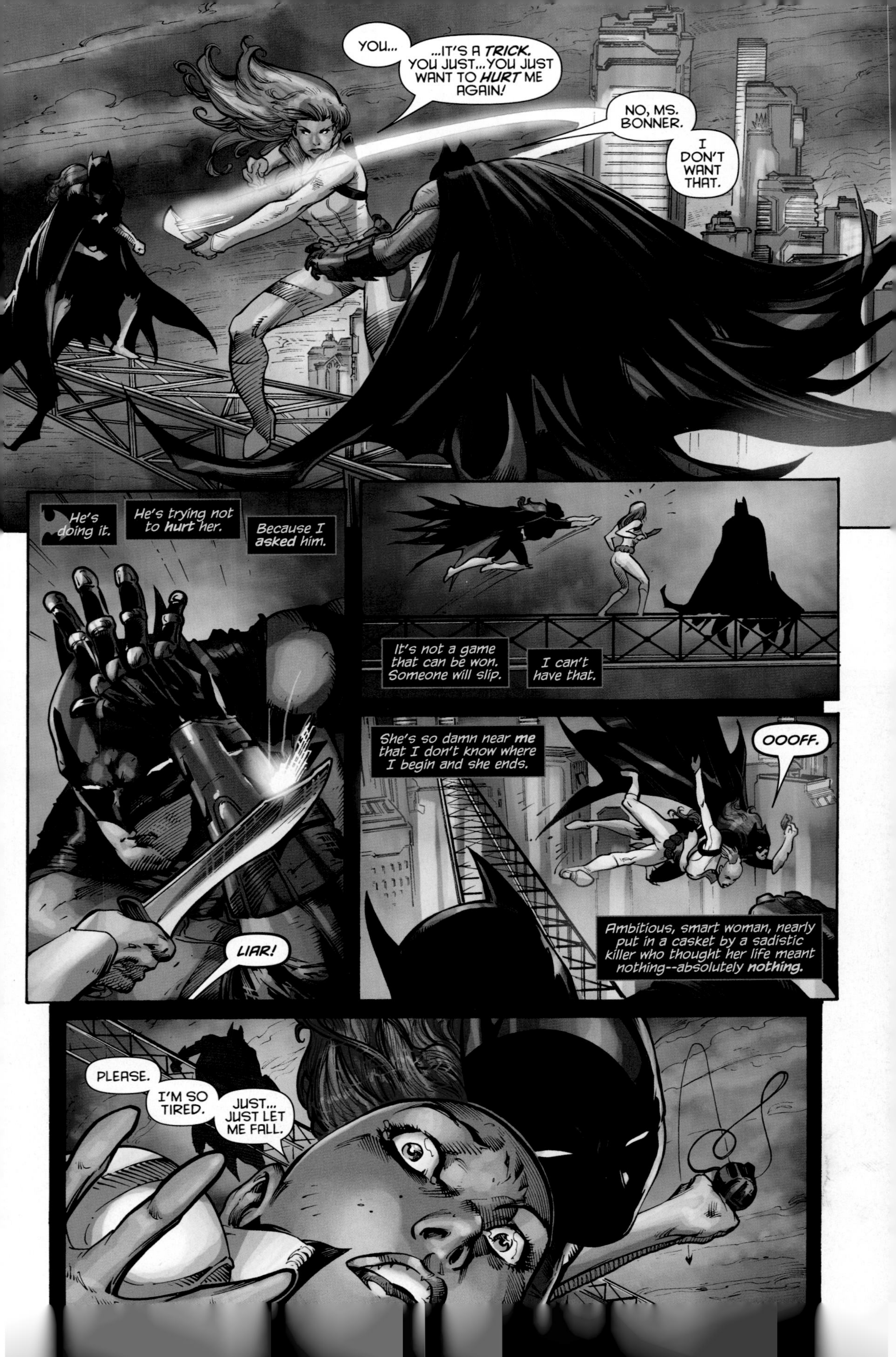

YOU...
...IT'S A TRICK. YOU JUST...YOU JUST WANT TO HURT ME AGAIN!
NO, MS. BONNER.
I DON'T WANT THAT.
He's doing it.
He's trying not to hurt her.
Because I asked him.
LIAR!
It's not a game that can be won. Someone will slip.
I can't have that.
She's so damn near me that I don't know where I begin and she ends.
OOOFF.
Ambitious, smart woman, nearly put in a casket by a sadistic killer who thought her life meant nothing--absolutely nothing.
PLEASE.
I'M SO TIRED.
JUST... JUST LET ME FALL.

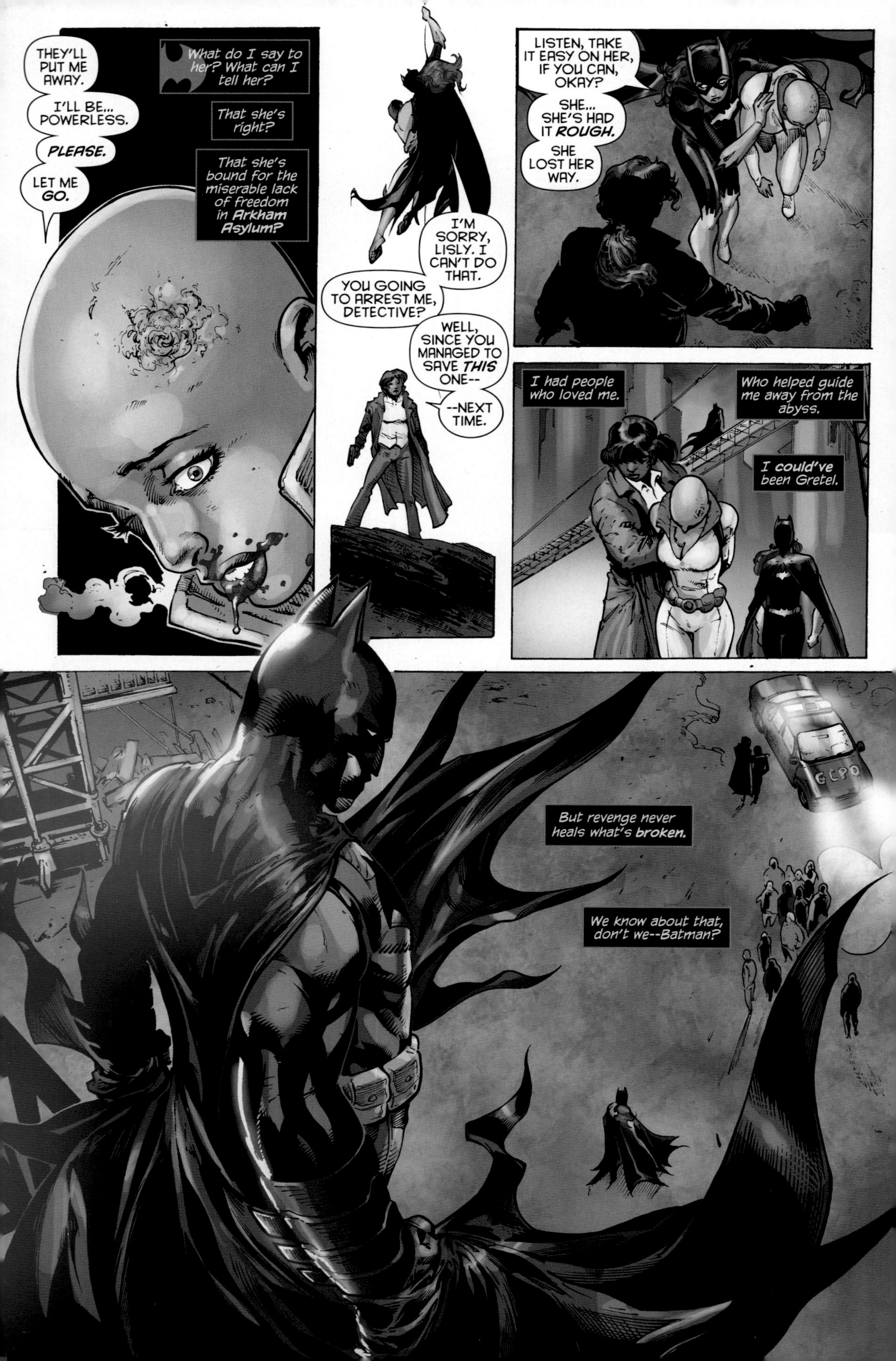

THEY'LL PUT ME AWAY.
What do I say to her? What can I tell her?
I'LL BE... POWERLESS.
That she's right?
PLEASE.
LET ME GO.
That she's bound for the miserable lack of freedom in Arkham Asylum?
I'M SORRY, LISLY. I CAN'T DO THAT.
YOU GOING TO ARREST ME, DETECTIVE?
WELL, SINCE YOU MANAGED TO SAVE THIS ONE--
--NEXT TIME.
LISTEN, TAKE IT EASY ON HER, IF YOU CAN, OKAY?
SHE... SHE'S HAD IT ROUGH.
SHE LOST HER WAY.
I had people who loved me.
Who helped guide me away from the abyss.
I could've been Gretel.
GCPD
But revenge never heals what's broken.
We know about that, don't we--Batman?

BATGIRL
CHARACTER DESIGN BY JIM LEE

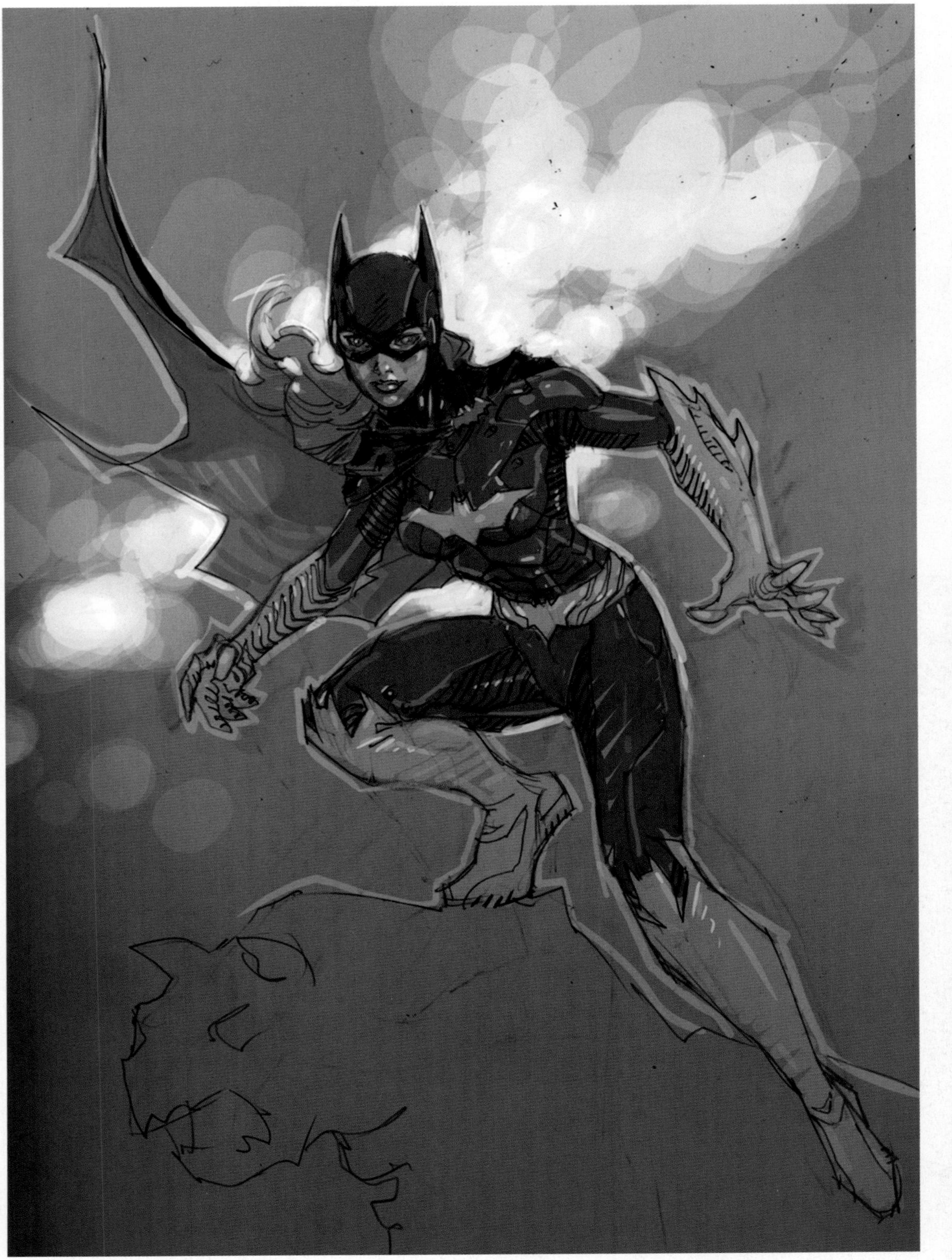

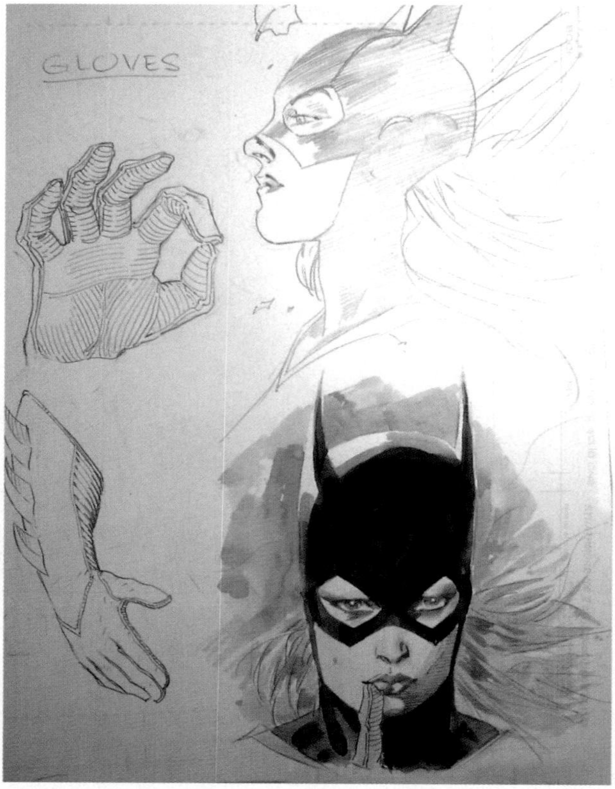
GLOVES

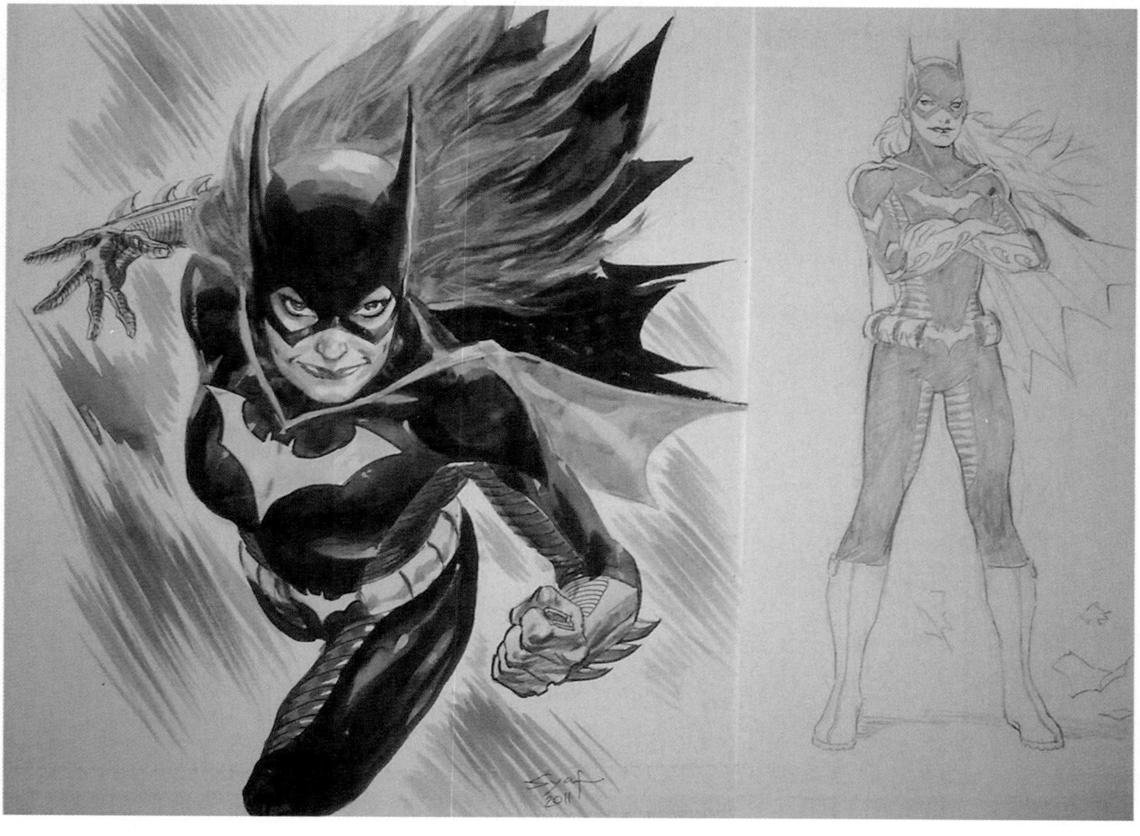

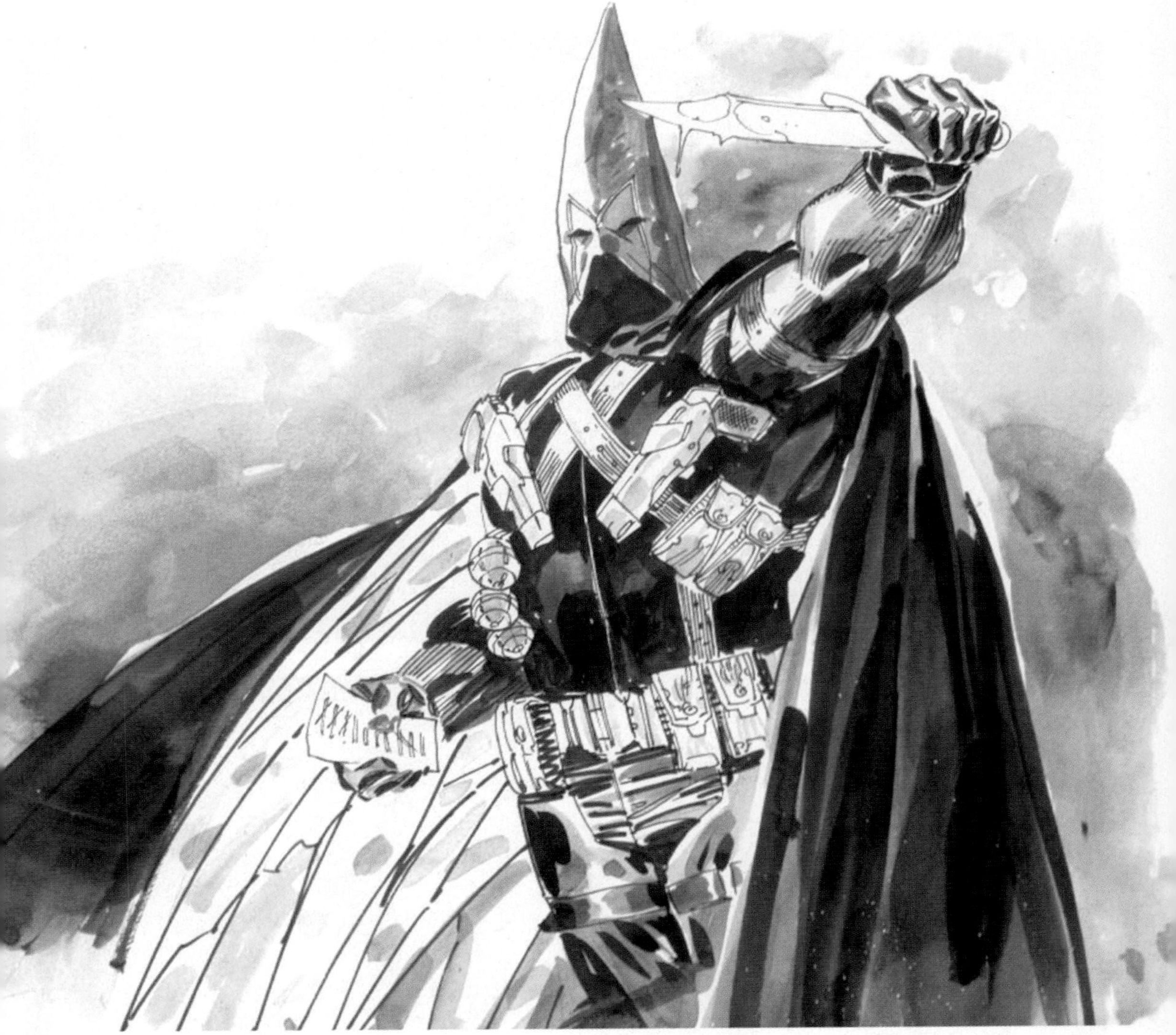

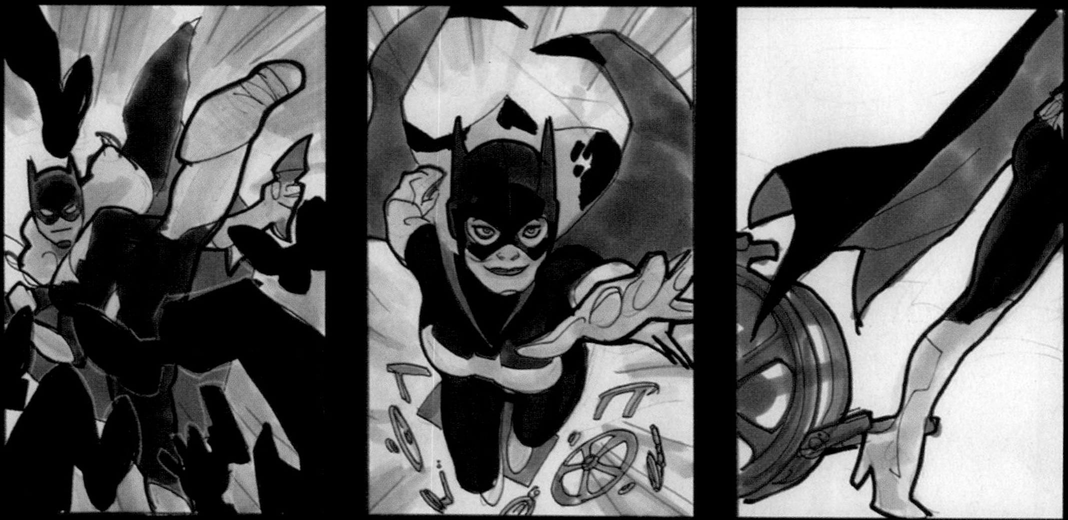

BATGIRL NO. 1 SKETCHES ADAM HUGHES

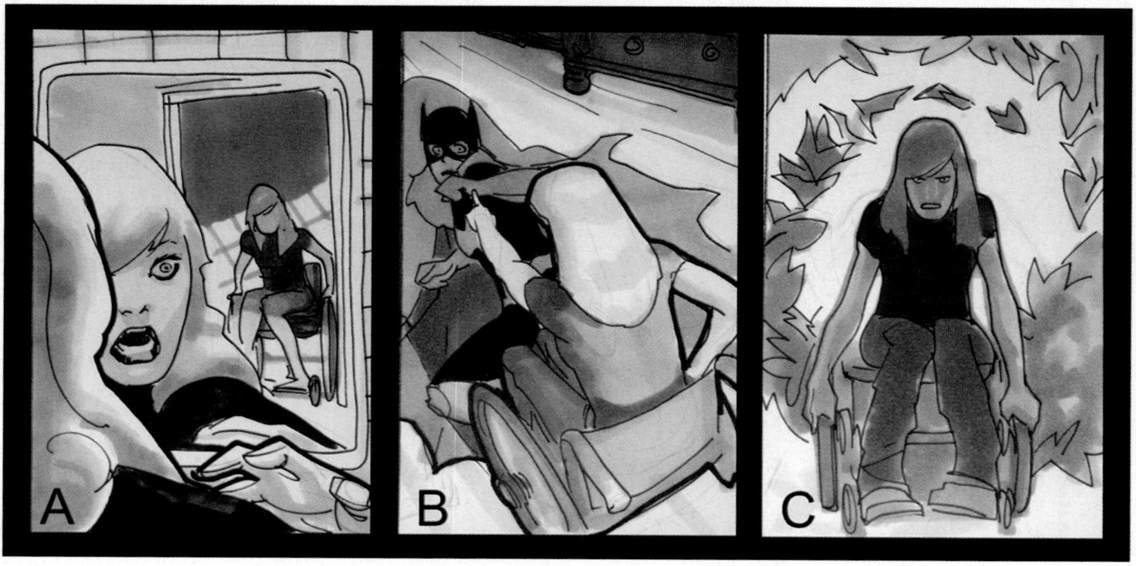
A
B
C

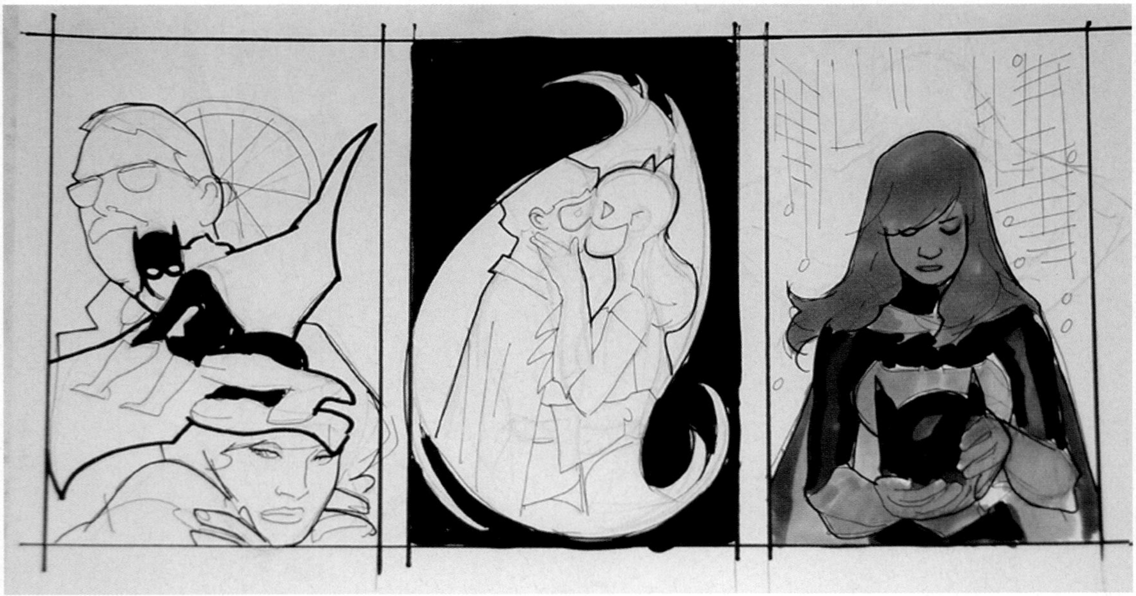

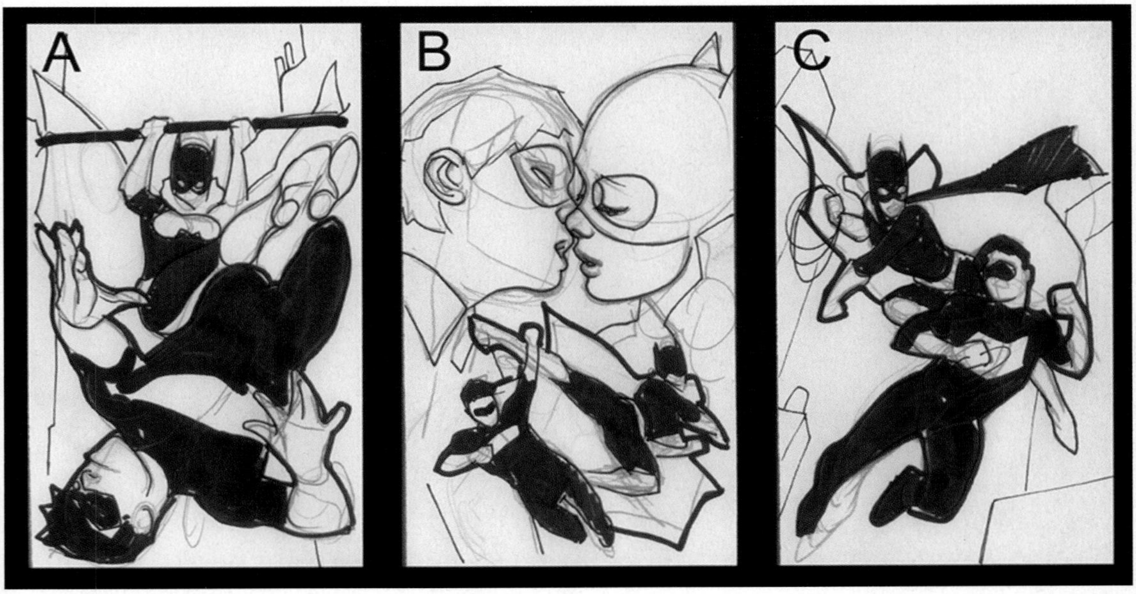
A
B
C

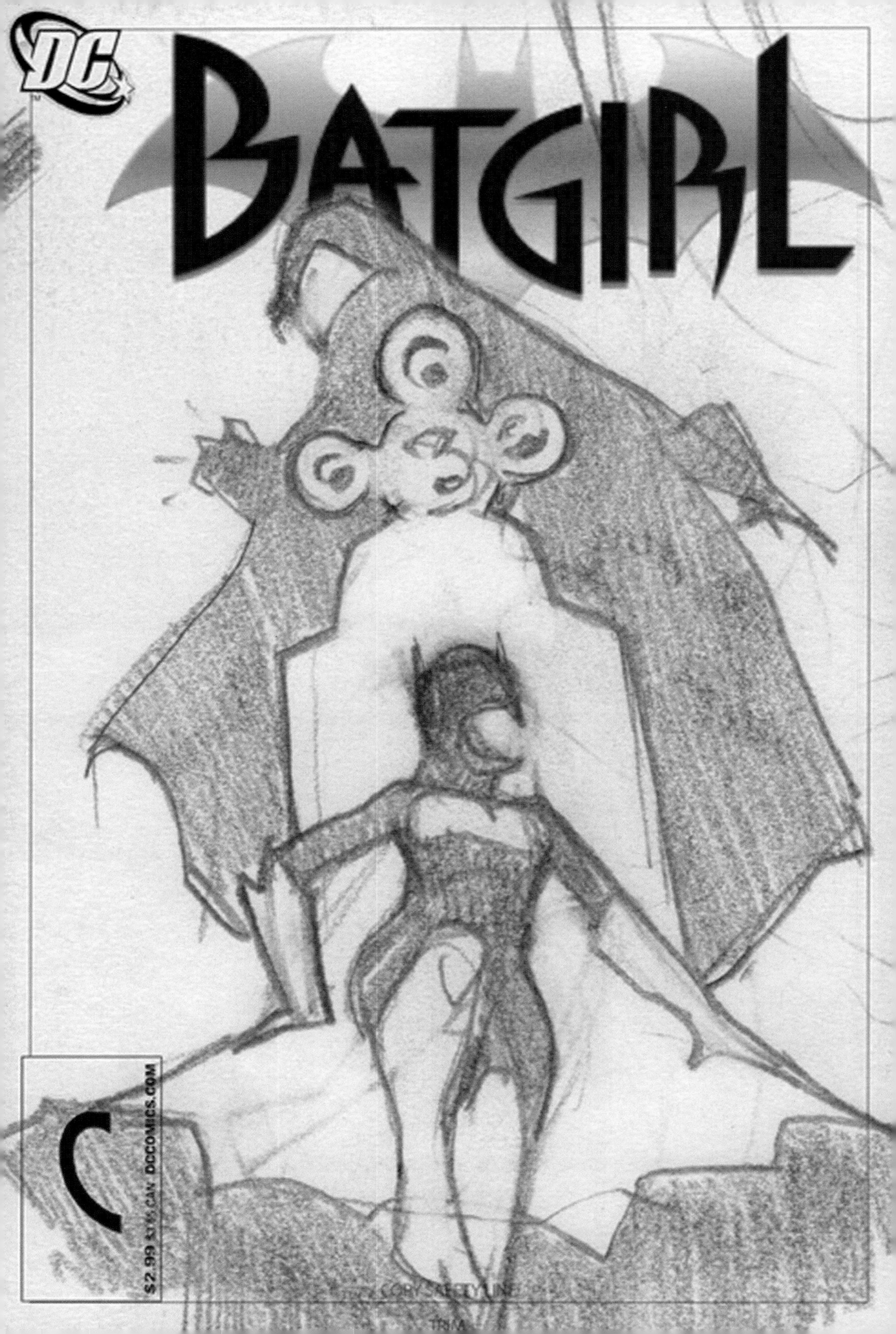

BATGIRL
$2.99
CAN
DCCOMICS.COM

BATGIRL
LAYOUTS BY ARDIAN SYAF

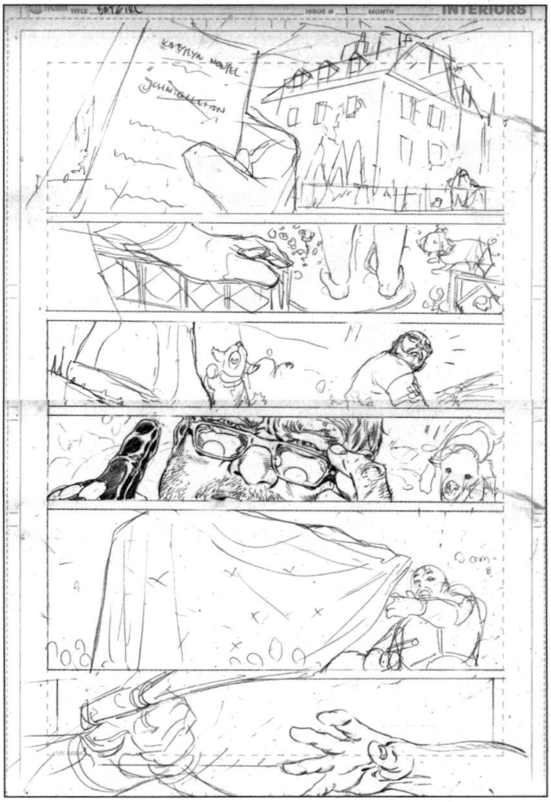
INTERIORS

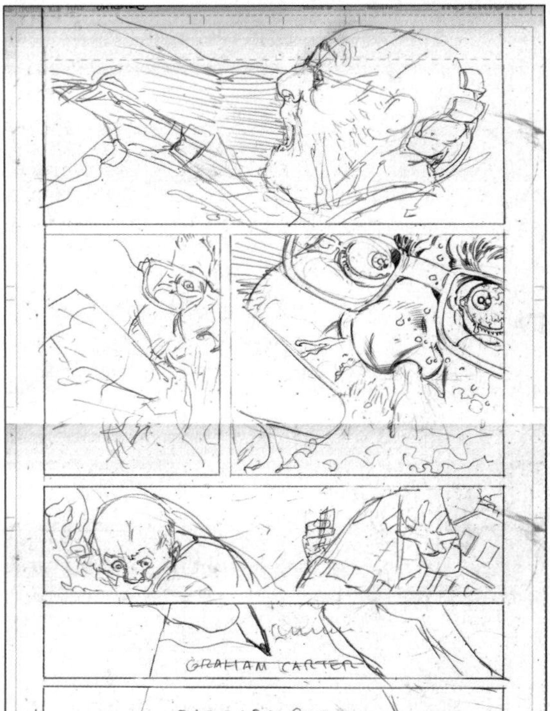
GRAHAM CARTER
BARBARA GORDON

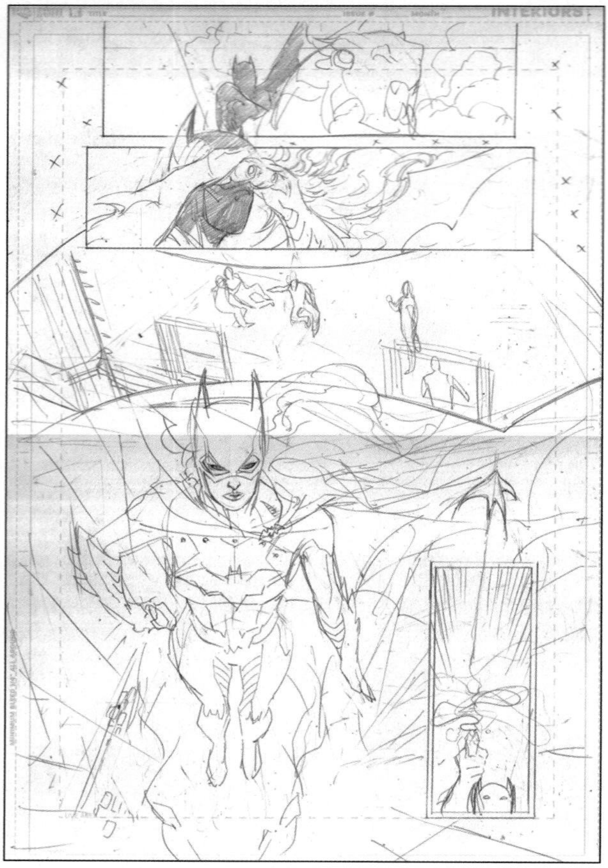
INTERIORS

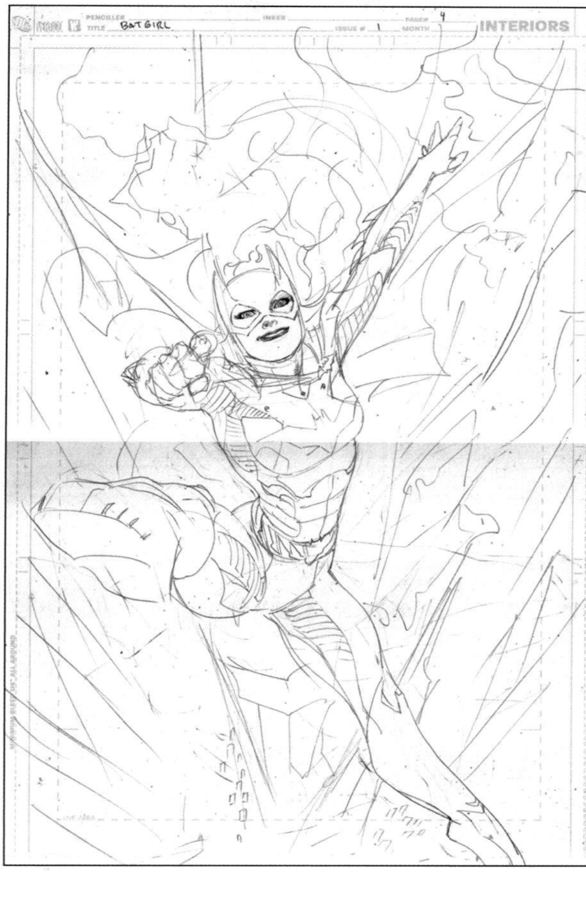
PENCILLER
INKER
PAGE# 4
TITLE BATGIRL
ISSUE # 1
MONTH
INTERIORS